Immigration Policy and Security

Immigration policy in the United States, Europe, and the Commonwealth went under the microscope after the terror attacks of 9/11 and the subsequent events in London, Madrid, and elsewhere. We have since seen major changes in the bureaucracies that regulate immigration—but have those institutional dynamics led to significant changes in the way borders are controlled, the numbers of immigrants allowed to enter, or national asylum policies? This book examines a broad range of issues and cases in order to better understand if, how, and why immigration policies and practices have changed in these countries in response to the threat of terrorism. In a thorough analysis of border policies, the authors also address how an intensification of immigration politics can have severe consequences for the social and economic circumstances of national minorities of immigrant origin.

Terri E. Givens is Vice Provost and Associate Professor of Government at the University of Texas at Austin.

Gary P. Freeman is Professor and Chair of the Department of Government at the University of Texas at Austin.

David L. Leal is Associate Professor of Government and Director of the Public Policy Institute at the University of Texas at Austin.

Immigration Policy and Security

U.S., European, and Commonwealth Perspectives

Edited by

Terri E. Givens
The University of Texas at Austin

Gary P. Freeman
The University of Texas at Austin

David L. Leal
The University of Texas at Austin

 Routledge
Taylor & Francis Group

NEW YORK AND LONDON

First published 2009
by Routledge
270 Madison Ave, New York, NY 10016

Simultaneously published in the UK
by Routledge
2 Park Square, Milton Park, Abingdon, Oxon OX14 4RN

*Routledge is an imprint of the Taylor & Francis Group,
an informa business*

© 2009 Taylor & Francis

Typeset in Galliard by RefineCatch Limited, Bungay, Suffolk
Printed and bound in the United States of America in acid-free
paper by
Edwards Brothers, Inc.

Library of Congress Cataloging in Publication Data
Immigration policy and security : U.S., European, and
Commonwealth perspectives / editors: Terri E. Givens, Gary P.
Freeman, David L. Leal.
    p. cm.
Includes bibliographical references and index.
ISBN 978–0–415–99082–0 (hardback : alk. paper)—
ISBN 978–0–415–99083–7 (pbk. : alk. paper)—
ISBN 978–0–203–89468–2 (ebook)
1. United States–Emigration and immigration–Government policy.
2. European Union countries–Emigration and immigration–
Government policy. 3. National security–United States–History–
21st century. 4. Security, International–History–21st century.
I. Givens, Terri E., 1964– II. Freeman, Gary P. III. Leal, David L.
JV6483.I5545 2008
325′.1–dc22
2007052728

ISBN 10: 0–415–99082–3 (hbk)
ISBN 10: 0–415–99083–1 (pbk)
ISBN 10: 0–203–89468–5 (ebk)

ISBN 13: 978–0–415–99082–0 (hbk)
ISBN 13: 978–0–415–99083–7 (pbk)
ISBN 13: 978–0–203–89468–2 (ebk)

Contents

List of Illustrations

Acknowledgments

The editors would like to acknowledge the financial and logistical support of the following units of the University of Texas at Austin, which made possible the conference that led to this edited volume: the Center for European Studies, Public Policy Institute, School of Law, Department of Government, and College of Liberal Arts. We also acknowledge the assistance of Public Policy Institute staff and graduate students, particularly Jill Strube, Taofang Huang, and Byung-Jae Lee.

David Leal thanks the College of Liberal Arts at the University of Texas at Austin for a Dean's Fellowship in the fall of 2007, which helped to ensure the timely completion of the manuscript.

Marc Rosenblum would like to acknowledge that research for his chapter was made possible by a Council of Foreign Relations International Affairs Fellowship. He thanks the Migration Policy Institute and Senator Edward Kennedy's Judiciary Committee Staff for hosting him during the fellowship.

Susan Brown and Frank Bean express thanks to Marshall Kaplan and Jeanne Batalova for comments on previous drafts and to Jody Agius, Mark Leach, and Rosaura Tafoya-Estrada for research assistance.

Adam Luedtke wishes to thank the following sources for research support: the Research Fellowship Program of the German Marshall Fund of the United States, as well as the Chris Piening Memorial Scholarship and the Chester Fritz Fellowship, both from the University of Washington.

Introduction
Terrorism and the Changing Politics of Immigration

Gary P. Freeman, Terri E. Givens,
and David L. Leal

The stunning events of September 11, 2001 and the successive terrorist attacks in London, Madrid, and elsewhere had manifold consequences for domestic and international politics—consequences that are still playing out in military conflicts and national security efforts around the globe. This volume addresses international migration, one aspect of national and global politics that was especially affected by the new concerns about terrorism.

All of the 9/11 hijackers entered the United States using various immigrant visas, some perfectly in order and others obtained fraudulently. Many commentators concluded that the fact that some terrorists held legal documents was more outrageous than the fact that others were able to secure such documents through deceit. Coupled with earlier events—particularly the attack on the Twin Towers in 1993, the foiled attempt of Ahmed Ressam to bring explosives into the United States from Canada to blow up Los Angeles International Airport at the Millennium, and the involvement of persons of recent immigrant origin in terrorist plots in Europe—the security of national borders and the effectiveness of national policies designed to foster the settlement of immigrants came under unusually close scrutiny across the Western democracies.

For many observers, the measures adopted by some states to shore up border controls and more aggressively police migrant populations were long overdue corrections to inexcusably lax enforcement policies that had left national populations vulnerable to the murderous inclinations of foreign enemies. For others, many if not all of the new policies were thought to be either unnecessary overreactions bred of panic or the fruit of deliberate attempts by anti-immigrant forces to exploit the new security context to enact restrictive measures that had previously lacked political support.

This volume brings perspective to the analysis of post-9/11 immigration politics through close examination of the linkages between national security concerns and recent immigration and asylum policies in the Western democracies. Most of the chapters were commissioned for delivery at the "Conference on Immigration Policy Since 9/11" held at the University of Texas at Austin in the spring of 2006. Four chapters evaluate United States policies, five examine Europe, and the last covers the Commonwealth democracies of Britain,

Canada, and Australia/New Zealand. The authors were invited to consider if and how the terrorist attacks of 9/11 and the subsequent Global War on Terror had modified the regional context of immigration policymaking. Was migration politics reframed, at least partially, as a security issue? What was the process by which this occurred and what were the consequences?

The broad comparative sweep of the case studies permits us to draw conclusions about the readiness of political actors to embrace security measures in the different regions and countries under review. The chapters permit pointed expositions of the differences between immigration/security linkages in the United States, for example, and those in the other traditional immigration countries of Canada, Australia, and New Zealand. Even starker differences emerge when the U.S. response to immigration and security is juxtaposed with that of the European states.

While the chapters deal largely with national governments, several investigate the role of multilateral institutions, especially the European Union. In addition, the authors treat, with varying degrees of comprehensiveness, the whole range of migrants: legal, unauthorized, students, tourists, and refugees. If our primary focus is on policies, the authors are nonetheless cognizant that an intensification of immigration politics can have severe consequences for the social and economic circumstances of national minorities of immigrant origin. There is the danger of guilt by association, a fate of particular relevance to the Muslim communities of the Western democracies. In the same way, ethnic groups associated with migration in the public mind—such as Latinos in the United States—suffered a good deal of what may be thought of as collateral damage in the wake of events for which there is no evidence their co-ethnics were involved. In addition, while much of the new concern for security was targeted at national borders, the authors give considerable attention to the success or failure of integration policies for immigrants and their descendants.

Although mass migration has intensified in all regions in the last several decades, it has affected world regions differently. The United States has greatly expanded legal entries since 1965, but it has also experienced massive unauthorized migration, which has been less important in Canada, Australia, or New Zealand. The traditional settler societies are experiencing migration at record levels, but they are accustomed to accommodating large numbers of newcomers even if the process is often ragged and marked by a certain level of tension.

European states, on the other hand, have mostly experienced mass migration only since the Second World War. Temporary labor migration programs in the 1960s and 1970s were the opening wedge, accompanied by substantial influxes of migrants from colonies or former colonies in the cases of Britain, France, the Netherlands, and Belgium. By the end of the 1980s, "guest worker" programs were shelved, entitled colonial migration was largely complete (although the countries of origin of migrants to various European states continued to reflect colonial ties), and family reunification had begun to decline. Current migration to Europe involves three key types: asylum seekers, unauthorized migrants, and highly skilled individuals who are being actively recruited. Because most legal routes into Europe for unskilled migrants have been closed off, asylum seeking and clandestine entry have expanded significantly.

How these varying contexts might have shaped the impact of 9/11 and the threat of terrorism more generally is not obvious. Although the United States, Britain, and Australia engaged in the War on Terror with more alacrity than almost any European government, they might be expected to shrink from extreme anti-immigration policies because of their strong traditions of openness to migration. Europe, on the other hand, had already yielded to the temptations of extremist parties that had scored successes with national electorates in France, Austria, and the Netherlands, and played well in local strongholds in many other European countries. Lacking a longstanding commitment to immigration, European states might be expected to react decisively to immigrant-related security threats.

The evidence in the chapters is mixed. The American response to terrorism imposed more costly measures on migrants than have been seen in the other settler societies or in most parts of Europe. The attack on the Twin Towers clearly derailed what would have almost certainly been a major expansion and liberalization of American immigration law that the Bush administration had promised President Vincente Fox of Mexico. As several of our contributors detail, the U.S. government took a number of extraordinary steps to deal with the perceived threat from porous borders—a much more aggressive response than was taken by Canada, Australia, or New Zealand. On the other hand, the political fallout from the linkage between acts of terror and immigrant communities has probably been more serious in the Netherlands than elsewhere. The rise of an anti-immigrant political party, the assassination of its leader in May 2002, and the murder of the film-maker Theo Van Gogh by a native-born Muslim militant in November 2004 caused Dutch officials to question the wisdom of their strong policy of multiculturalism as the best means to integrate immigrants. Many of the measures adopted by the other European states, on the other hand, were in part imposed by American initiatives, as Valsamis Mitsilegas demonstrates in his contribution.

One question that a number of the chapters address is the seriousness of the threat to national security that immigration actually poses. There is a mix of opinions on the matter. Those authors like Hampshire, Waslin, and Jupp, for example, who take the most thoroughly critical stance vis-à-vis security measures, imply, if they do not explicitly document, that dangers associated with migration are excessively hyped. It is obvious that the vast majority of migrants and their descendants living in the Western democracies are law-abiding, contributing residents of their new countries. By itself, however, this does not eliminate the possibility that some migrants pose a threat. At the margins, a combination of porous borders, populations of migrants living under the radar of the regulatory instrumentalities of the modern state, and the mixing of cultures that in some respects disagree fundamentally on such matters as the proper balance between religion and public life may pose substantial challenges for the forces of law and order. The issue from the point of view of government policy is to make a sensible assessment of the scale of the danger and to devise reasonable responses that do not infringe unacceptably on the liberties of immigrants and citizens alike. This volume provides critical data that permit the reader to assess the proportionality of state responses to threat.

Four of the chapters examine post-9/11 immigration policy in the United States. They all demonstrate that, while the rhetoric of immigration policy has been deeply affected by the attacks of 9/11 so that the immigration reform debate is now largely framed in the security context, the actual policy consequences are much more mixed.

Marc R. Rosenblum performs a useful service by setting post-9/11 immigration politics in the context of the history of immigration to the United States. He defines the national interest in immigration policy as entailing control of the borders and furtherance of economic and diplomatic purposes. A quick review indicates that U.S. policy has often failed to achieve these goals for reasons he attributes to particularistic political forces. Rosenblum reminds us that four important developments modified the trajectory of U.S. immigration politics even before 9/11: the collapse of the Soviet Union; the security concerns that emerged at least as early as the first World Trade Center bombing in 1993; the intensification of globalization and its regional effects in the Western hemisphere; and, finally, the increasing demand for both low- and high-skilled foreign labor from vital sectors of the American economy. In other words, the emphasis on reinforcing border control and attacking illegal immigration was well underway before the events of 2001. Rosenblum presents a close examination of unsuccessful efforts to craft a comprehensive immigration reform bill in 2005. He shows that the new security context has not overcome the embedded interests that defeated such initiatives in the past. He argues that the single-minded focus on controlling the border is misguided and reflects the short-term political interests of Congress. Immigration politics has been reshaped by 9/11, and has become meaner, but it is no more systematic or coherent than before.

Michele Waslin looks at immigration policy since 9/11 from the perspective of U.S. Latinos, for whom the stakes in the immigration debate are particularly high. In historical perspective, the United States is currently experiencing a fourth "great wave" of immigration, which is largely (but not exclusively) driven by migration from the Hispanic nations of Latin America and the Caribbean. Of the top twelve sending nations of immigrants who received legal permanent residence (LPR) status in 2005, five were in Latin America and the Caribbean—Mexico, Cuba, the Dominican Republic, Colombia, and El Salvador (U.S. Foreign Press Centers 2004). The reasons for admission varied considerably, however. The large majority of admissions from Cuba were for humanitarian reasons, most of those from the Dominican Republic were admitted under family reunification provisions, and half of those from El

Salvador were admitted via the Nicaraguan and Central American Relief Act (NACARA) of 1997. Latinos are therefore likely to be the population most affected by immigration reform, although the specific nature of the reform will differentially affect the multiple Latino national-origin groups.

Official migration data do not include undocumented immigration, which is also primarily from Latin America. Approximately 10.5 million unauthorized immigrants resided in the United States in 2005, up from 8.5 million in 2000 (U.S. Department of Homeland Security 2005). Of these, about 6 million were from Mexico. By contrast, the nations of El Salvador, Guatemala, India, and China together contributed 1.4 million unauthorized immigrants. Over the five-year period, the greatest annual average increase was from Mexico— about 260,000 individuals. Any reforms that address this issue will therefore primarily affect Mexicans and to a lesser degree other Latinos. Between a quarter to a third of Latinos,[1] because of their recent immigrant origins, would be directly affected by changes in immigration laws, enforcement activities, or eligibility for government services.[2]

Waslin's general thesis is that whatever the benefits in terms of enhanced security wrought by the policy changes enacted after 9/11, they had a disproportionately negative effect on the Latino community. She presents a detailed catalogue: the failure to extend the provision in the Immigration and Nationality Act known as 245(i) that had allowed unauthorized aliens to pay a fine rather than leave the country in order to adjust their status; the creation of the Department of Homeland Security into which the various pieces of the dismantled Immigration and Naturalization Service were inserted; new enforcement of the requirement that non-citizens report changes of address; an unprecedented involvement of state and local authorities in the enforcement of immigration laws; and restrictions on the acquisition and uses of various sorts of identification by non-citizens, including driver licenses and the *matrículas consulares* issued by Mexican consulates in the U.S. The consequences of these administrative and legislative steps, as well as the heightened tensions generated by the conflation of security with migration, has resulted, Waslin concludes, in "millions of Latino immigrants in the U.S. [remaining] unauthorized, fearful, and vulnerable to exploitation" (see p. 48).

Muslims are the other immigrant group that faced the prospect of being severely affected by post 9/11 policy changes. Although reliable figures are difficult to obtain, it is estimated that approximately 12 million Muslims are currently living in Western Europe. Of these, more than 4 million live in France, with the great majority being from the Maghreb, the African region north of the Sahara Desert and west of the Nile River (1,550,000 of Algerian origin, 1,000,000 of Moroccan origin, and 350,000 of Tunisian origin). More than 1.5 million Muslims live in the United Kingdom, with the substantial majority being of South Asian heritage. Current estimates put the Muslim population of Spain at 500,000, predominantly Moroccan. There are approximately 3.5 million Muslims in Germany; of these, 70 percent are of Turkish origin.[3] Estimates of the Muslim population in the United States range from one to nearly five million. Whatever the true numbers, it is obvious that Muslims constitute a smaller share of the population in the U.S. than in Europe.

Idean Salehyan investigates the effects on Muslims of changes in U.S. refugee and asylum policy in reaction to the threat of terrorism. He anticipated that Muslims would be targets of discriminatory asylum policies after 9/11. This is because the 9/11 hijackers had immigrated from the Muslim world; Muslim communities in the U.S. have not been as large, as longstanding, or as well-organized politically as Latinos; and U.S. asylum and refugee policies have often been manipulated in response to geopolitical events.

Surprisingly, his data provide scant support for the hypothesis. Salehyan shows that some early steps to single out Muslims or persons from Muslim countries for special scrutiny were condemned as racial profiling or discrimination (e.g. Operation Liberty Shield) and were discontinued. Turning to the actual number of refugees admitted in fiscal years 1999–2004, Salehyan finds contradictory evidence of discrimination against Muslims. Admissions from the Near East/South Asia (where the largest populations of Muslims reside) decreased more than other regions and have not rebounded from the general decline experienced by all regions immediately after 9/11. Taking into account not only admissions but also applications, however, indicates that for whatever reasons applications for asylum from Muslim countries have fallen almost as much as admissions. Exactly why is difficult to pinpoint, but it is not obvious that perceptions of U.S. hostility have deterred applications, and approval rates for some Muslim countries (Iran, Syria, and Pakistan) declined less than approval rates for all countries. Salehyan concludes that his data do not support the claim that U.S. asylum policy has taken an anti-Muslim turn.

Brown and Bean investigate the consequences of post-9/11 immigration policies for the science and engineering sector of the U.S. economy, especially as it is affected by the admission of foreign graduate students to American universities. They note that the applications, admissions, and enrollments of foreign graduate students in science and engineering declined notably after 2001. The authors argue that a substantial portion of this decline resulted from a tightening of visa review processes. They note "the irony that the imposition of 'hard' national security measures can erode 'soft' power and thus in turn the very security such measures were designed to enhance. In the post-9/11 U.S. case, the implementation of hard post-9/11 visa criteria for the admission of international science and technology students may have undermined, at least in the short term, the country's soft power" (see p. 67).

If the studies of the American case yield a mixed picture, the European experience is even more difficult to assess. James Hampshire and Christina Boswell, even conceding the rather different formulations of their research agendas, draw distinct conclusions about the securitization of British immigration policy. Put directly, Hampshire, influenced by the field of critical security studies, argues that a profound, but not complete, state-led securitization of immigration policy has developed in Britain. By this he means that immigration is represented in debate as a threat to British society and that this threat justifies exceptional policies in response. He observes that such policies have been adopted with respect to certain aspects of British immigration policy and have breached previously sacrosanct liberal norms.

For her part, Boswell argues on the basis of a review of events in Britain, Germany, and Spain that "despite some initial attempts to link terrorism and migration, political discourse on migration control . . . has remained surprisingly untouched by the anti-terrorism agenda" (see p. 93). She challenges one of the principal theoretical tenets of the securitization thesis, namely "that states and political elites have a fundamental interest in portraying migration as a security threat in order to legitimize more stringent control measures" (see p. 93). Whereas Hampshire treats both discourse and policy acts in Britain, Boswell focuses more or less exclusively on discourse, as her purpose is to interrogate the modes by which policies regarding border control and irregular migrants are legitimated. She concludes that "European governments were unwilling or unable to sustain linkages between migration control and terrorism because of conflicting political interests, as well as the difficulties of sustaining a coherent account of the causal linkages between the two" (see p. 102).

Immigration policy in Europe is shared between national governments and the institutions of the European Union, which have played an increasingly important role in recent years. The Tampere Council, meeting in 1999, adopted an ambitious program for the harmonization of European immigration and asylum policy. On the eve of 9/11, therefore, Europe appeared poised to move decisively in the direction of common policies, and those common policies seemed certain to be committed broadly to recognizing the rights of migrants and ensuring their full integration into European society. This agenda was seriously impeded by 9/11, as is detailed in several chapters focusing on the EU.

Adam Luedtke shows that Justice and Home Affairs dramatically transferred its attention from implementing the Tampere proposals to responding to the newly intensified security concerns. National delegates to Brussels involved in immigration negotiations tended to resist cooperation in favor of nationally preferred policies. As an example, Luedtke notes that three of the five successful directives on legal migration after 2001 permitted member states with generous legislation to lower their standards. With respect both to the Long-Term Residents Directive and the Family Reunification Directive, Luedtke documents how states with national policies below the EU's proposed standards were able to water down the directives or otherwise slip in loopholes that had the effect of weakening the Community's general stance. In short, Luedtke argues that the after-effects of 9/11 and subsequent concern about the links between migration and security produced a slackening of the pace toward common immigration and asylum policies. In addition, where those policies were nonetheless adopted, such concerns led to their being more restrictive than would have been foreseen from the optimistic viewpoint of 1999.

Valsamis Mitsilegas offers another view of the effect of 9/11 and security concerns on EU states. He begins with a detailed review of security measures taken by the U.S. government after 9/11, including the USA Patriot Act, most importantly, but also the establishment of the Department of Homeland Security and the implementation of a variety of security policies that involved or required the cooperation of third countries or served as models for similar policies adopted abroad. He observes that U.S. policies focused most seriously on issues of border security and information-sharing and involved gathering data not just on persons who might reasonably have been labeled members of suspect groups, but on the entire population. U.S. security fears, which he clearly finds exaggerated, played out in Europe in two ways. First, the U.S. imposed security measures on other countries as the price of continuing to do business in the U.S. (for example, the Passenger Name Data program affecting foreign air carriers serving the U.S.). Second, U.S. security initiatives, especially those involving identification documents, biometrics, and the development of large interoperable databases, led to the adoption of similar measures in Europe either via coercion or imitation. Mitsilegas goes so far as to argue that transatlantic immigration policy has shifted from a concentration on border controls to the "maximum surveillance of populations" (see p. 159).

Eiko R. Thielemann delves into the development of the EU refugee regime and how it has been affected by the recent outbreak of terrorist attacks in the U.S. and Europe. He notes that border security has been the driving force behind efforts to build more cooperation into refugee and asylum policies, but border security was not seen mostly in terms of the particular terrorist acts or threats of further attacks. Rather, the creation of the single market and the free movement regime adopted by the Schengen partners left individual member states vulnerable to the decisions taken by those states with external borders. More specifically, security fears derived from the possibility that failures by some states to manage borders effectively would result in certain member states having to assume the lion's share of the refugee burden within the Community. The very active efforts to design and implement a burden-sharing scheme in the case of refugees can be explained as a consequence of this configuration of non-terror-related security threats.

No countries have closer economic, cultural, and political ties with the United States than the four countries of the British Commonwealth, the focus of James Jupp's sweeping comparison. Jupp shows that terrorism was not particularly high on the political agendas of Britain, Canada, Australia, or New Zealand in the months leading up to September 2001. This changed after the Twin Towers fell, but Jupp demonstrates that the four governments responded with considerable variation in energy and comprehensiveness. He attributes this to their varying geopolitical locations, differences in their existing institutions for policing and guaranteeing security, and the wide variation in the size and nature of their Muslim populations. Britain had the most experience of terrorism due to the long conflict in Northern Ireland, but its initial focus on immigration control was curtailed once it became apparent that most Muslim terrorists were born in the U.K. The shared border with the United States left Canada no choice but to address border security aggressively. In Australia, the

Bali bombing raised the threat of Islamic violence against Australian citizens, but government responses tended to deal primarily with asylum seekers, an approach Jupp finds unjustified. New Zealand enjoyed some immunity against terrorist attacks due to its remoteness and freedom from American influence.

Jupp's conclusions about the diverse responses of the Commonwealth nations resonate with the message the chapters in this volume convey collectively. There has been no common response to the new security concerns. Immigration has everywhere become a higher-priority item on the public agenda and everywhere it has come to be linked to possibilities of terrorist attacks. The rhetoric of immigration politics has intensified as a result, although, as Boswell points out, this can be overstated. Actual policy developments are not so clear-cut. Immigration policies before 9/11 tended to be episodic, disjointed, inconsistent, and ad hoc, but the shock of 9/11 and other terrorist attacks was insufficient to produce coherence.

Two key questions need to be answered: (1) to what extent have terrorist attacks and the discovery of terrorist cells and plots inside European societies affected the attitudes toward and treatment of immigrant-origin populations already living in Europe, and (2) how will security fears shape policies regulating the entrance of new immigrants and asylum seekers over the next few years?

In the United States, there has been a mix of sensible reaction and unfortunate overreaction, and a comprehensive immigration reform plan involving a large guest-worker program and legalization has been delayed. The American authorities have increased efforts to control the border and imposed stricter regulatory measures on third parties and third countries. Nevertheless, the familiar interest groups that have historically shaped U.S. policy are still in place, which suggests that immigration policy decisions in the future will not necessarily be restrictive. Economic interests may override anxieties about terrorism. For instance, it seems a safe bet that the decline in foreign engineering and science students matriculating in the United States detailed by Brown and Bean will be temporary, as industrial and commercial interests reassert themselves. There is no reason to doubt that the United States will continue to see large numbers of legal and illegal immigrants for the foreseeable future. Efforts to identify and remove unauthorized immigrants have certainly been stepped up and will probably be accelerated even further, but it seems most unlikely that the unauthorized population will be substantially reduced by any means other than some form of blanket or piecemeal legalization.

Europe's response to the immigration/terrorism nexus was mixed, as well, and it is a challenge to sort out how much of the change was motivated by purely domestic considerations or was at least partially imposed due to American insistence. Progress towards a common EU immigration and asylum policy has clearly been set back. Whether it can get back on track is critical for the future of immigration policy in Europe. Given the evidence in these chapters of the striking differences in the national contexts in which security and migration are addressed, forging a consensus across the rapidly expanding

European Union seems farther from realization than ever. The hopes in some quarters that European states would adopt annual immigration quotas on the order of the settler societies may be dashed in the face of concern over the integration of foreign-origin residents. Ironically, although the European response to 9/11 and its aftermath has been more tempered than that of the United States, the long-run fallout from the association of Islamic extremism with immigrant-origin populations may be more substantial in Europe than America.

Notes

1 Depending on the size of the non-citizen undercount.
2 Latinos have good reason to be concerned about immigration reform during moments of national stress. During the Great Depression, state and local governments responded by "encouraging" an estimated 1 million Mexicans to return to Mexico—although some of those who were returned were citizens (Balderrama and Rodríguez 1995). In the McCarthy Era, the INS launched Operation Wetback in 1954, a series of immigration sweeps in the southwest that forced between 1 and 2 million Mexicans out of the United States (Calavita 1992), although some were U.S. citizens.
3 See country profiles at the Euro-Islam website: http://www.euro-islam.info/.

References

Balderrama, Francisco E., and Raymond Rodríguez. 1995. *Decade of Betrayal: Mexican Repatriation in the 1930s*. Albuquerque: University of New Mexico Press.
Calavita, Kitty. 1992. *Inside the State: The Bracero Program, Immigration and the INS*. New York: Routledge.
U.S. Department of Homeland Security. 2005. "Estimates of the Unauthorized Immigrant Population Residing in the United States," http://www.dhs.gov/xlibrary/assets/statistics/publications/ILL_PE_2005.pdf.
U.S. Foreign Press Centers. 2004. "CRS Report for Congress: U.S. Immigration Policy on Permanent Admissions," http://fpc.state.gov/documents/organization/31352.pdf.

Part I
United States

1 Immigration and U.S. National Interests

Historical Cases and the Contemporary Debate

Marc R. Rosenblum

Introduction

In the half-decade since nineteen foreign-born men executed the dramatic and deadly terror attacks of September 11, 2001, U.S. immigration policy mainly has been debated in terms of national security and controlling the U.S.–Mexican border. While the House and Senate took broadly different approaches to immigration reform during the 109th Congress, both chambers agreed on the need to increase border enforcement, with the House voting to add 700 miles of new U.S.–Mexico border fencing, and the Senate voting to add 370 miles of fencing and to construct a high-tech "virtual fence" along longer stretches of the border. President Bush's May 2006 call to place National Guard troops on the border was also embraced by all sides in the debate, and an amendment endorsing their deployment was passed by unanimous consent on the Senate floor. Ultimately, when House and Senate members were unable to agree on anything else as the 109th Congress drew to a close, they still managed to pass the Secure Fence Act, authorizing 700 miles of fencing and other border infrastructure.

Yet a single-minded focus on the U.S.–Mexican border is a misguided approach to immigration policymaking. In short, migration control requires policies that extend beyond the border, both within the United States and abroad. More importantly, migration control is only one aspect of the national interest in U.S. immigration policy. The post-9/11 focus on "getting control of the border" distracts many policymakers from the broader set of costs and benefits associated with immigration.

This chapter explores the relationship between immigration and the national interest. The following section defines the U.S. national interest in immigration policy in terms of U.S. security, prosperity, and diplomacy. These encompassing interests often conflict with particularistic group pressures, so that immigration policy does not reliably reflect the national interest—a pattern confirmed by a historical review of U.S. immigration policy in the next section. The remainder of the chapter explores immigration and the national interest in the contemporary period: how has the national interest in immigration policy been shaped by the end of the Cold War and the 9/11 attacks, and why did Congress fail to pass comprehensive immigration reform consistent with these goals during the 2005–6 and 2007 debates? I conclude by evaluating future prospects for reform.

Immigration and the National Interest

What is the U.S. national interest in migration and immigration policy? Immigration affects vital U.S. interests in three distinct areas. First, immigration control—maintaining authority over a state's territory—is a basic element of national sovereignty. Yet immigration only threatens security in three circumstances. In the most extreme case, immigration may represent a form of low-intensity conquest, changing the demographic facts on the ground and potentially contributing to a broader assault on a host state's territory. Israel's occupation of the West Bank has relied on immigrant settlements in the disputed region, for example, as did Morocco's 1975 occupation of the Spanish Sahara (Teitelbaum 1984).

Immigration may also threaten security when the pace or specific circumstances of immigration destabilize or weaken the host state. Spillover conflicts in the former Yugoslavia and the African Great Lakes region are important examples. A final security issue associated with immigration comes in the form of intentional threats by individual migrants or groups of migrants. Examples include imported revolutionary movements, such as the Cuba-led guerrilla campaigns in Latin America during the 1960s and 1970s, and "fifth-column" threats arising from first- or second-generation immigrants operating within host states, including the Spanish and British railway bombings in 2004 and 2005. Thus, while most migratory flows are not threatening to security, migration control becomes a legitimate security concern when unwanted immigration overlaps with or reinforces other security threats.

A second set of national interest considerations concerns the effect of migration on economic growth and prosperity. Any new labor inflow increases returns to capital investments, and liberal migration policies thus tend to promote growth, although they also exacerbate inequality (i.e., by shifting resources from owners of labor to owners of land and capital). Here, too, context matters. On the one hand, the overall economic benefits of immigration are a function of the scarcity of native labor, and thus the dependence of the host state on immigrant labor. In extreme cases, where immigration is the only possible source of needed economic inputs, immigration becomes a matter of basic economic security, an eventuality potentially looming for many industrialized states with aging populations and shrinking labor forces (McDonald and Kippen 2001).

On the other hand, the distributive effects of immigration are also sensitive to the skills of immigrants and natives. Where migrants possess similar skills as natives (i.e., migrants are "substitutes"), migration has a greater downward effect on wages. Where skill sets are complementary, as is typically the case with South–North flows, immigration has little or no depressive wage effect

(Ottaviano and Peri 2005). Distributive effects also depend on migrants' legal status: undocumented immigrants are more likely to be exploited and drive down wages, and they are less likely to pay their share of taxes.

Finally, while few question the right of sovereign states to set rules for entry, the subjects of immigration policy are inevitably the citizens of other states. Indeed, in many cases the stakes are highest for these countries of origin in two specific areas: economically, because these states have more at stake in gaining access to targeted labor markets, and socially, because immigration enforcement may involve the use of force against sending-state citizens. For these reasons, a third core interest in immigration policy is diplomatic.

In this case, it is important to distinguish between humanitarian (i.e., refugee and asylum) and non-humanitarian (i.e., family- and labor-based) immigration. With respect to the former, good diplomatic relations tend to discourage humanitarian admissions because the acknowledgment that individuals have legitimate humanitarian claims implicitly defines the country of origin as unable or unwilling to protect the human rights of its citizens. Conversely, accepting refugees and asylum applicants from a hostile regime may be an intentional diplomatic slap in the face, as well as an opportunity to import valuable human capital and country-specific knowledge about an adversary (Loescher and Scanlan 1986; Teitelbaum and Weiner 1995).[1] Non-humanitarian migration exhibits the opposite dynamic: diplomatic relations are enhanced by the family, commercial, and social linkages created by migration flows, but may be undermined by overly aggressive migration control efforts (Mitchell 1992; Rosenblum 2004a).

Thus, the United States has a national interest in controlling undocumented immigration, especially in the rare cases in which the specific conditions of undocumented migration threaten U.S. security. Immigration policy should also ensure that the number and type of immigrants entering the country promote economic growth without depressing wages. A final core interest in migration policy is the harmonization of migration and U.S. foreign policy goals—promoting legal migration from friendly regimes while remaining sensitive to the diplomatic costs and benefits of humanitarian admissions and migration enforcement strategies.

Yet even a cursory review of historical trends reveals that U.S. policy outcomes often fail to advance these goals. Rather, efforts to bend immigration policy to the national interest compete with particularistic policy demands originating at the party, sub-national (local and state), and sector- or class-specific levels. Moreover, economic, security, and diplomatic considerations may produce ambiguous policy demands as a function of the broader context in which policymaking occurs. Conversely, because immigrants congregate in geographically concentrated communities, and because interest groups directly impacted by the social and economic costs and benefits of immigration have intensely held preferences, particularistic group demands often overwhelm broader policy concerns.[2]

In addition, the national interest in migration policy also competes with normative and ideational policy demands centered on national identity and other cultural concerns. Whether or not "societal security" (Rudolph 2006) and cultural homogeneity (Huntington 2004) are legitimate policy goals, new migration inflows inevitably raise cultural anxiety within dominant ethnic groups. As a result, immigration has provoked populist backlashes within a wide range of host states during the last two decades (Kessler and Freeman 2005; Givens 2005; Reimers 1998).

Historical Review

The early American experience highlights the relationship among immigration, security, and prosperity. European settlers and their descendants clashed with Native Americans over scarce resources, and the colonists triumphed not simply through their superior force of arms, but also thanks to reinforcements in the form of additional migratory flows. Labor scarcity in the New World also placed an economic premium on additional migration—a fact that caused most settler states to promote immigration during the nineteenth century (Hatton & Williamson 1998). For these reasons, even though the earliest European Americans were xenophobic about "new" immigrants from Germany and Ireland (Fuchs 1990), the United States not only maintained a wide open federal immigration regime, but also organized a de facto immigrant integration system through the Homestead Act of 1862 and other policies to resettle immigrants in the U.S. interior.[3]

The closure of the American frontier in 1890, the emergence of labor-saving technology during the Industrial Revolution, and the economic disruption of World War One diminished the economic benefits of an easy labor policy. At the same time, the 1901 assassination of William McKinley by a second-generation Polish immigrant, along with foreign-led opposition to the U.S. entry into World War One, raised doubts about the loyalty of new immigrants and fears that the United States would fall victim to the violence erupting throughout Europe. Thus, while falling wages and cultural anxiety about the new immigrant demographics contributed to a wave of restrictionist legislation around the turn of the last century, the shifting national interest in immigration was also influential.[4] Similarly, even as Congress overrode presidential vetoes to pass restrictionist legislation during the 1910s, diplomatic considerations remained a check on the trend as the Coolidge and Hoover administrations blocked efforts to extend the National Origins system to the Western hemisphere in the name of preserving friendly regional relations.

Migration control has been especially likely to be defined as a national security priority during periods of international conflict. Woodrow Wilson responded to immigrant-led anti-war protests during World War One by supporting the Espionage and Sedition Acts of 1917 and 1919, which targeted foreign-language publications for their criticism of U.S. policy. The newly formed Federal Bureau of Investigation arrested and deported hundreds of foreign-born communists during the Palmer Raids of 1919–21. Attention shifted to the threat posed by Japanese Americans during World War Two, as over 120,000 first-, second-, and even third-generation immigrants were forcibly interned beginning in 1942. Communists were again targeted during the Cold War, as the 1950 Internal Security Act made aliens deportable on the basis of their membership in the Communist Party or advocacy of communist or anarchist ideology. Fears of communist infiltration across the U.S.–Mexican border also contributed to the Eisenhower administration's decision to draw up (but not implement) plans to place U.S. Army troops along the border in 1953.[5]

Yet wars also raise concerns about economic security, and wartime shortages increase the priority placed on immigrant workers (E. Meyers 2004). The Department of Labor responded to agricultural shortages during World War One by suspending the new head tax and literacy requirement for agricultural workers and establishing a special visa for Mexican "guest workers." Similar concerns compelled the United States to seek additional workers during World War Two. In this case, the United States also sought to use migration policy as a tool of diplomacy, locking in Mexico's support for the Allied war effort. As a result, the original Bracero Treaty was the most pro-immigrant contract labor agreement in U.S. history: Mexico assisted in the recruitment, screening, and oversight of contract workers, while the United States paid their transportation costs and guaranteed a minimum wage and basic benefits—terms which far exceeded the working conditions of U.S. citizens at the time. Although the treaty was renegotiated to the advantage of U.S. growers in 1947, the Korean War sparked new fears of labor shortages, and Mexico demanded additional concessions in 1951 before the more exploitative version of the program was established beginning in 1954 (Craig 1971; Rosenblum 2003).

The years around World War Two were also characterized by conflict as anti-immigration members of Congress resisted presidential efforts to enhance America's international standing through immigrant admissions. Congress refused Roosevelt's request to permit extra Jewish immigration from Hitler-era Germany, grudgingly supported Truman's 1948 Displaced Persons Act, and then passed the anti-humanitarian 1952 Immigration and Nationality Act (INA) over Truman's veto. Presidents were thus forced to work outside the legislative process, with Roosevelt establishing the War Refugee Board in 1944 to distribute cash to refugees, and Eisenhower exploiting a loophole in the INA to "parole" 15,000 refugees into the United States over congressional objections in the wake of the 1956 soviet invasion of Hungary (Tichenor 2002). It was only after Eisenhower established this precedent that Congress accepted humanitarian admissions as a tool of foreign policy, first through the passage of the Refugee-Escapee Act of 1957, and then by establishing a standing refugee quota with the passage of the 1965 amendments to the INA. The 1965 amendments also replaced the National Origins system with a flat per-country quota, a change largely inspired by the desire to shore up America's declining image in the developing world (Shanks 2001).

Three contextual changes beginning in the 1960s redefined the national interest in immigration. First, with the termination of the Bracero Program in 1964 and the exhaustion of Latin-American import substitution during the 1970s, these years saw the beginning of a secular increase in undocumented immigration to the United States which has continued into the present period. Second, the Nixon administration launched Operation Intercept in 1969, initiating a "war on drugs" which also continues to this day. Third, in the aftermath of the Cuban Revolution, hemispheric migration relations took on greater strategic importance within the context of the Cold War.

One result was that immigration policy increasingly came to be defined in terms of border security. Thus, along with the creation of the Drug Enforcement Administration (DEA) in 1973, the first decade of the war on drugs saw spending on immigration enforcement triple during the 1970s, with the bulk of the effort concentrated at the U.S.–Mexican border. This trend was held in check by the Carter administration, as the president resisted congressional calls for a border fence in an effort to preserve friendly U.S.–Mexican relations. Border militarization intensified once more during the 1980s—enforcement spending tripled again—as the Reagan administration approached the "war on drugs" with new vigor and warned of a wave of communist Central American "feet people" poised to invade the United States through Mexico (Dunn 1996; Schoultz 1992).

National interest considerations also led to politicized enforcement of immigration policy throughout this period in predictable ways. Nicaraguans and Cubans fleeing communist governments enjoyed far more favorable treatment than Salvadorans, Guatemalans, and Haitians subject to similar persecution at the hands of U.S.-friendly regimes (Loescher and Scanlan 1986; Schoultz 1992; Stepick 1992; Teitelbaum and Weiner 1995). Rosenblum and Salehyan (2004) also show that biased enforcement extended beyond these well-documented cases, including during the 1990s.[6]

At the same time, the United States unofficially facilitated non-humanitarian migration from friendly regimes. In 1961, for example, following the fall of the Trujillo regime in the Dominican Republic, the United States opened two new consulate buildings with expanded staffing to facilitate Dominican visa issuance. As a result, legal permanent immigration from the Dominican Republic increased by a factor of 20 between 1960 and 1963, stabilizing the Dominican economy and strengthening bilateral relations (Mitchell 1992). Similarly, even while Salvadorans were routinely denied asylum during the 1980s, U.S. officials responded to a 1987 appeal from Salvadoran President Napoleon Duarte by scaling back enforcement against the same individuals to ease the burden on the friendly Salvadoran government (Rosenblum 2004b; Schoultz 1992).

Immigration and the National Interest Since 1990

Four significant developments since 1990 have intensified the relationship between immigration and the national interest. First, the collapse of the Soviet empire and dissolution of the Soviet Union ended five decades of relative predictability and stability within the global system, allowing the re-emergence of long-suppressed ethnic conflicts and producing a number of new refugee flows. Indeed, as conflicts in Haiti, Rwanda, the former Yugoslavia, Sudan, Chechnya, and elsewhere illustrate, migration and refugee flows have become one of the most significant causes of armed conflict in the post-Cold War period (Helton 2002; Salehyan and Gleditsch 2006).

Second, even before the 9/11 attack, the 1993 World Trade Center bombing under the direction of the "Blind Sheik," Mullah Omar, heightened awareness of terrorist immigrants as a new type of national security threat. Six years later, the immediacy of this threat was reinforced when the Border Patrol apprehended the "millennium bomber" at the U.S.–Canadian border. Thus, by the time immigrants executed the 2001 attacks, the link between immigration and the threat of terrorism was well established (D. W. Meyers 2005).

Third, economic integration within the Western Hemisphere and economic globalization more generally have transformed the politics and economics of regional immigration. While the implications of Latin-American structural adjustment and regional economic integration are still being debated, one short-term consequence has been an increase in emigration pressures, as well as new opportunities for undocumented flows (Massey et al. 1998). Stronger economic links and the development of regional institutions like the North American and Central American Free Trade Agreements have also raised the diplomatic stakes of immigration policymaking; and Mexico and other countries of origin are increasingly insistent that migration policy should be the subject of bilateral and regional negotiations, rather than unilateral U.S. action.[7]

Finally, demographic and economic shifts within the United States place a new priority on labor-based migration to sustain growth. The last three decades have seen foreign-born workers grow from eight to fourteen percent of the U.S. workforce, and foreign-born workers have been responsible for a majority of new jobs created since 2000 (Sum et al. 2004). Immigrants will play an even larger role in future growth because migrants are now the only source of expansion in the U.S. prime-age workforce and because the low- and high-skilled jobs most dependent on immigrant workers are also projected to grow the fastest (Aspen Institute 2005; Lowell et al. 2006).

On the one hand, these contextual changes highlighted the need for improved migration control, and the pace of increased enforcement at the U.S.–Mexican border accelerated yet again during the 1990s. A turning point occurred in 1993, when the Border Patrol's El Paso Sector initiated Operation Blockade to repair border fences and place 400 agents on round-the-clock line-watch duty to discourage would-be crossers. This strategy of "prevention through deterrence" was formalized in the Border Patrol's 1994 strategic plan, and plans were made to extend these methods to other high-traffic areas and eventually to all U.S. land and sea borders. The 2005 Secure Border Initiative updated the 1994 plan with additional investment in infrastructure, technology, and personnel.

Interior immigration enforcement has also intensified and become increasingly linked to U.S. security and the war on terror (see Chapter 2 of this volume). The 1996 Illegal Immigration Reform and Immigrant Responsibility Act (IIRIRA) created a new enforcement tool, *expedited removal*, which allows the immediate detention and deportation of aliens not claiming political asylum without a hearing or other judicial review. In 1999, the Supreme Court's *Reno v. American-Arab Commission* decision upheld a Clinton administration policy of targeting legal immigrants for deportation simply on the basis of their rhetorical support for terrorist organizations. Most recently, the 2005 U.S. Patriot Act expanded the Attorney General's power to indefinitely detain or deport non-citizens if the administration has "reasonable grounds to believe" they endanger U.S. national security.

On the other hand, the new focus on border and interior enforcement conflicts with the diplomatic and economic demands on immigration policymakers. In an era of rapid economic innovation, business leaders, economists, and security experts all agree that America's competitiveness depends on its ability to recruit the world's "best and brightest" workers in an increasingly competitive global environment.[8] Congress responded in 1998 and 2000 with a pair of bills to temporarily raise the H-1B high-skilled non-immigrant visa cap, and by 2003 foreign students represented almost 40 percent of science Ph.D.s and almost 60 percent of engineering doctorates (National Science Foundation 2004).

President Clinton also responded to diplomatic pressure from Mexico and Central America by taking steps to mitigate the effects of increased border and interior enforcement. In 1995, for example, Immigration and Naturalization Service and State Department officials worked with their Mexican counterparts on the U.S.–Mexican Binational Commission to establish a series of border-level institutions to strengthen communication among Mexican and U.S. enforcement agents and local politicians and to protect the human rights of immigrants interdicted at the border. In addition, in 1997, when Congress offered amnesty to 100,000 Nicaraguans through the Nicaraguan Adjustment and Central American Relief Act (NACARA), but required a quarter-million Guatemalans and Salvadorans to apply for relief on a case-by-case basis, the Clinton administration responded to Salvadoran and Guatemalan pressure by passing regulations—over congressional objections—to reverse the normal burden of proof in these hearings (Rosenblum 2004b).

The 2005–06 Immigration Debate

By 2005, politicians and groups from all sides of the issue could agree that U.S. immigration policies failed to advance the national interest as defined above. Undocumented immigration continued to increase after a brief decline following the 9/11 attacks, and security experts worried that the illegal immigration infrastructure within the United States weakened U.S. counterterrorism efforts. Yet failed enforcement did not imply that other interests were being satisfied: employers still lacked ready access to strategically important high- and low-skilled immigrant workers, and Mexico and other countries of origin remained frustrated by the Bush administration's failure to advance a comprehensive reform agenda after emphasizing this goal during his re-election campaign.

The White House, House of Representatives, and Senate each staked out competing approaches in 2005. In his State-of-the-Union addresses, President Bush reiterated his support for a guest-worker program, calling on Congress to pass "an immigration policy that permits temporary guest workers to fill jobs Americans will not take, that rejects amnesty, that tells us who is entering and leaving our country, and that closes the border to drug dealers and terrorists" (White House 2005b). The administration repeatedly identified immigration reform (along with tax cuts and Social Security reform), as a top legislative goal in subsequent months. The president also called on Congress to pass an expanded temporary worker program, while pledging that his administration would streamline removal proceedings, place more personnel and equipment at the U.S.–Mexican border, and improve worksite enforcement (White House 2005a).

In the Senate, three different bills were filed during 2005 that shared a common three-part framework: enhanced enforcement at the U.S. border and worksites; new employment visas for "future flow" immigrants; and a program to legalize existing undocumented immigrants.[9] The bills differed in significant ways, however. The Cornyn-Kyl bill was the most restrictive of the three, offering strictly temporary visas to future workers and to existing undocumented immigrants, but providing no new opportunity for either group to adjust to legal permanent status or eventual citizenship. In contrast, the McCain-Kennedy and Hagel proposals emphasized an eventual "path to citizenship" for guest workers as well as for existing undocumented immigrants who paid penalties and back taxes and maintained a clean record and steady employment in the future.[10] The Hagel and McCain-Kennedy bills also increased the number of permanent visas available to future immigrants— Hagel focused on high-skilled workers, while McCain-Kennedy expanded low-skilled employment- and family-based flows. Judiciary Committee members Cornyn, Kyl, and Kennedy held seven hearings on the competing proposals between March and June of 2005.

The Senate's work was sidelined in the fall as the Judiciary Committee turned its attention to filling two Supreme Court vacancies, and the House stepped into the void by passing James Sensenbrenner's H.R.4437.[11] In contrast with the Senate's multiple hearings and extended debate (see below), the House moved quickly: the bill was introduced on December 6, marked up and passed by the Judiciary Committee two days later on a party-line vote, and debated by the full House for just over a day before passing (239–182) on a mostly party-line vote December 16. Also in contrast with the Senate bills, H.R.4437 restricted its attention to border and interior enforcement without creating new immigration benefits; and it included controversial provisions to restrict immigrants' access to courts, to expand the definition of immigrant smuggling to include acts of humanitarian assistance, and to turn civil immigration violations into felony criminal offenses.

Passage of H.R.4437 was a wake-up call to supporters of the Senate's more comprehensive approach, especially after the White House issued a strong statement of support for the Sensenbrenner bill during the House debate (White House 2005c). Thus, after completing its work on Supreme Court nominations in late January, the Senate Judiciary Committee began marking up an immigration bill in February. Committee Chairman Arlen Specter (R-PA) drafted a Chairman's Mark as the starting point, borrowing employment-based visa language from the Hagel bill, enforcement provisions from both the Cornyn-Kyl bill and H.R.4437, and some of the guest-worker program details from the McCain-Kennedy proposal, although without the latter's reliable path to citizenship. The Chairman's Mark adopted a middle position on undocumented immigrants, proposing that they be eligible to remain indefinitely within the United States (in contrast with Cornyn-Kyl), but that they be denied the right to become U.S. citizens (in contrast with McCain-Kennedy).

Progress in the Judiciary Committee quickly stalled, as members were unable to resolve differences over interior enforcement provisions without first reaching an agreement on the politically charged issues of legalization and temporary workers.[12] Seven out of eight Democrats on the Committee and three out of ten Republicans—i.e., a majority of the Committee—supported the McCain-Kennedy approach to these issues. In a break with Senate tradition, however, Specter threatened to block any Committee bill which lacked support from "a majority of the majority" on the Committee.[13] Intense staff-level meetings were held including Specter, Cornyn, Kyl, Kennedy, Durbin (D-IL), and Leahy (D-VT), but differences could not be resolved over which undocumented immigrants and guest workers should qualify for citizenship.[14]

Two events in mid-March marked a turning point in the Committee debate and shifted the focus away from the back-room negotiations. First, on March 16, Majority Leader Bill Frist (R-TN) imposed a deadline on the Judiciary Committee by offering a bill of his own, which included all of the enforcement provisions in the Chairman's Mark but none of the new immigration benefits. Frist placed his bill on the calendar for March 28 and pledged to begin floor debate at that time if a Judiciary bill had not been reported. With a recess scheduled the week of March 20, Frist's deadline seemed an impossible hurdle to overcome, and a direct affront to Senator Specter and the rest of the Committee. Second, in the week leading up to Frist's deadline, a million supporters of comprehensive immigration reform rallied around the country, including over half a million in downtown Los Angeles. The massive show of support— and of opposition to the House's enforcement-only bill—caused a perceptible shift in the debate when the committee reconvened, with California's Senator Feinstein speaking eloquently (and for the first time) in favor of legalization for undocumented immigrants.

Senator Specter scheduled a marathon mark-up session for March 27, pledging to keep the Committee in session until a bill was complete. Senator Brownback organized a last-ditch effort to forge a compromise between supporters of the McCain-Kennedy bill and the Republican swing voters, but Senator Graham and Committee Democrats forced votes on a pair of amendments to replace Specter's temporary worker and legalization provisions with language from the McCain-Kennedy bill. In dramatic fashion, both votes passed on identical 11–7 majorities (all eight Democrats plus the three supportive Republicans). Finally, after six days of mark-up and many months of work, Senator Specter backed down from his "majority of the majority" threat and joined the committee majority in the 12–6 vote on final passage in support of his amended bill.

The full Senate took up immigration reform two days later. Opponents of the committee bill introduced a series of amendments highlighting the bill's support for "amnesty" over tough enforcement. Senators Kyl and Cornyn, for example, offered an amendment denying legalization to undocumented immigrants with criminal records—a class already excluded under the Committee's bill—and which used ambiguous language that also appeared to deny legalization to hundreds of thousands of potential beneficiaries of the Committee bill. Johnny Isakson (R-GA) offered an amendment to delay implementation of the legalization and guest-worker provisions until the border could be certified as "sealed and secured," a standard reformers believed could never be met.

Supporters of comprehensive reform argued that passage of either amendment would render the bill unworthy of passage, but Democrats feared that voting against the amendments would make them vulnerable to attack ads in the coming campaign. In a break with some reform advocates, Democratic leaders avoided the issue by exploiting a procedural loophole to prevent votes on either controversial amendment.[15] Floor debate continued for another week, but discussion of immigration reform gave way to a partisan battle over process. Democrats attempted to salvage the bill by filing for cloture—a move which would limit additional poison pills and force a vote on final passage—but the cloture vote fell on a mainly party-line vote, and the Senate adjourned for recess without taking any substantive votes on the bill.[16]

Even as progress was derailed on the Senate floor, however, behind-the-scenes negotiations sought to broaden Republican support for the Judiciary Committee bill. With support from the White House and Senator Frist, Republican Senators Chuck Hagel (NE), Mel Martinez (FL), McCain, and Graham sought a compromise with Democrats Kennedy, Barack Obama (IL), and Ken Salazar (CO) on a legalization program that would cover enough undocumented immigrants to satisfy Democrats while allowing Republicans to avoid offering a broad "amnesty." In a late-night compromise, a two-track system was designed whereby aliens in the country for at least five years would be eligible for the McCain-Kennedy legalization procedure, but aliens with between two and five years of U.S. residence would be required to exit the

United States, re-enter as guest workers, and apply for green cards from an expanded pool of employment-based visas.[17] Democrats who opposed expanding the temporary worker program (already a source of contention with labor unions) were assuaged by offsetting cuts to the future flow of the temporary worker program and by improved wage protections.

This "Hagel-Martinez" compromise brought together a core group of bipartisan members who pledged to place their common interest in comprehensive immigration reform ahead of partisan loyalties, and to work together to defeat future "poison pill" amendments.[18] With the support of most Democrats and several additional Republicans, the coalition fought off five such amendments: a revised Isakson amendment to delay legalization benefits until selected border enforcement provisions are "fully operational"; a Kyl amendment to deny guest workers the ability to adjust to legal permanent status; an Ensign (R-NV) amendment to deny newly legal immigrants credit for their previously accrued Social Security benefits; a Chambliss (R-GA) amendment to weaken wage protections for agricultural guest workers; and a Cornyn amendment to weaken the confidentiality protections afforded to aliens' legalization applications. The coalition also suffered a handful of defeats from the left (a pair of Bingaman [D-NM] amendments to further reduce the size of the temporary worker program and to impose an absolute cap on legal permanent visas), and from the right (a Sessions amendment to expand border fencing, a revised version of the earlier Kly-Cornyn amendment to exclude criminal immigrants from the earned legalization program, an Ensign amendment to deny newly legal immigrants access to the Earned Income Tax Credit, and an Inhofe [R-AK] amendment declaring English the official language of the United States). With these changes, the amended bill easily survived a cloture vote (73–25) on May 24, and passed the following day by a still-comfortable vote of 62–36.[19]

The Senate and House bills differed in fundamental ways, as illustrated by the process each had gone through (just two days of debate by the House Judiciary Committee and full chamber versus twenty-one total days of debate in the Senate) and the scope of the competing proposals (the House bill ran to 256 pages, compared to 795 for the Senate bill). More fundamentally, while the bills included broadly similar enforcement provisions—increasing border infrastructure and personnel, strengthening document security, and requiring employers to participate in an electronic employment eligibility verification system to eliminate the jobs magnet—only the Senate bill reflected the broader national-interest perspective described above by including provisions to ensure that the U.S. economy has access to essential high- and low-skilled immigrant workers. And, while the Senate stopped well short of placing diplomatic considerations at the center of its debate, its bill required consultation with Mexican officials on the placement of border fencing and with Mexican and other sending-state officials on joint enforcement strategies. More importantly, the Senate avoided the most aggressive enforcement provisions found in the House bill—making all undocumented immigrants felons under U.S.

law, expanding border fencing—which would be especially damaging to U.S.–regional relations.

In December 2005, the House bill passed with White House support, representing a low point for advocates of the Senate's broader national-interest approach to immigration reform. During the spring and summer of 2006, however, all the pieces seemed to fall into place for the Senate's comprehensive bill to succeed. Public opinion polls reported unprecedented interest in the issue and a remarkably broad consensus in favor of the Senate bill.[20] In addition, over three million comprehensive reform advocates took to the streets to denounce the House's enforcement-only approach and to show their support for the Senate bill. Broad-based support was reinforced by a powerful left–right coalition of interest groups that coordinated their lobbying activities and worked closely with the expanded McCain-Kennedy coalition throughout the debate.[21] With each unexpected victory—the passage of the McCain-Kennedy temporary worker and legalization programs out of the Judiciary Committee; the return of immigration reform to the Senate floor following the Hagel-Martinez compromise; the Senate's passage of a comprehensive reform bill—the bill seemed to gain momentum.

Yet any sense of inevitability—or even probability—evaporated within days of the Senate vote for final passage when House leaders announced plans to hold hearings designed "to increase the negatives [of the Senate bill] while accentuating the positives of the House bill" rather than appointing conferees to work out a House–Senate compromise (CNN 2006).[22] Editorial pages were universally critical of House Republicans for using field hearings to run out the clock on the reform effort, but the strategy worked. Pro-comprehensive reform demonstrations that once hoped to draw hundreds of thousands of marchers in early September drew fewer than 25,000. When Congress reconvened after Labor Day, Bush's low approval ratings further solidified hard-liners' opposition to the Senate bill; and many supporters of comprehensive reform preferred to delay action on immigration in the hope that the issue would receive a more favorable vote under a Democratic Congress in 2007. With the midterm election looming, leaders felt compelled to "do something" in response to popular demands and settled for passage of the Secure Fence Act of 2006, a bill consisting of the border-area infrastructure language from the earlier House bill.

The 2007 Immigration Debate

Immigration did not play out as an issue in the 2006 midterm elections as Republicans had predicted. In most cases, immigration policy simply was not a cleavage issue in an election year dominated by the Mark Foley email scandal and continuing bad news from the Iraq War. And in the handful of races where immigration was a prominent campaign issue, comprehensive reform supporters defeated hard-liners in 12 out of 15 races (Dorval and LaRue 2006). Moreover, exit polls found that a solid majority of voters (57 percent versus

38 percent) favored legalization for most undocumented immigrants rather than deportation (Kondracke 2006).

Thus, supporters of the 2006 Senate-passed language were optimistic that a Democratic-controlled Congress—in a non-election year and with a supportive president—would move quickly to pass even stronger legislation in 2007. Yet reform efforts floundered from the start of the new Congress, as negotiations between Senators Kennedy and McCain broke down over how to define wage levels in a new temporary worker program, leaving the Senate without a bipartisan bill that could be taken directly to the floor.[23] As in 2005, the Judiciary Committee also failed to take up an immigration bill, in this case devoting its attention instead to the scandal surrounding the dismissal of several U.S. Attorneys.

President Bush revived reformers' hopes in March by initiating a new round of bipartisan negotiations, bringing together three Democrats (Kennedy, Salazar, and Robert Menendez) and ten Republicans, led by Jon Kyl, the leading opponent of the 2006 reform effort. Cabinet secretaries Michael Chertoff (Department of Homeland Security) and Carlos Gutierrez (Department of Commerce) also joined the talks, with Chertoff in particular devoting extraordinary personal attention to the reform effort. Negotiations received an important boost in May, when Senators McCain, Graham, Specter, and Martinez circulated a "Dear Colleague" letter pledging to filibuster any bill that did not emerge out of the bipartisan talks. This put Republican negotiators in a strong bargaining position, and the resulting legislative proposal called for a more employer-friendly temporary worker program, a radical new points-based green card system which shifted visas from family members to high-skilled workers, and tougher worksite enforcement rules; but in what backers celebrated as a "grand compromise," it also included more generous legalization provisions for undocumented immigrants than had passed the previous year. In response to a key complaint about the 2006 bill, the 2007 deal also included "enforcement triggers," ensuring that the earned legalization and temporary worker programs would not go into effect until border security and worksite enforcement benchmarks were met.

The compromise was offered on the Senate floor in May 2007 as the Secure Borders, Economic Opportunity, and Immigration Reform Act of 2007. In a process reminiscent of the May 2006 debate, the bill was the subject of nine full days of intense debate over a three-week period. Over 300 amendments were filed and 31 voted on, resulting in several significant changes from the left (imposing a five-year sunset on the temporary worker program and cutting its size in half) and from the right (imposing additional enforcement triggers, increasing the penalties in the legalization program, outlawing bilingual ballots and other government documents, and stripping important legal protections during the legalization process). As before, members formed a bipartisan coalition which held together to defeat additional amendments, including language which would have eliminated the temporary worker program, expanded state and local enforcement of immigration laws, eliminated the legalization program, excluded new classes of criminal immigrants, imposed a sunset on the new point system, and created additional visas for certain family members. And also reminiscent of 2006, when Democrats filed cloture, key Republican supporters of the bill joined hard-liners and liberal Democrats to defeat the measure, apparently ending the reform effort.

A final parallel to the 2006 process unfolded in the following weeks, as Senators Kennedy and Kyl returned to the negotiating table in an effort to bring the bill back from the dead. Working with Democratic and Republican leadership—but without some of the original members of the grand comprom-ise coalition—reformers reached a deal on a list of 13 additional amendments to be considered from each side of the aisle. But Republican hard-liners dom-inated the subsequent floor debate, and focused sustained attention on the extraordinary procedural tricks being employed to block additional amend-ments.[24] Despite a flurry of calls from President Bush and Secretaries Chertoff and Gutierrez, the Senate's Republican leadership exerted minimal pressure on ambivalent members, and a final cloture vote failed by a resounding 46–53 margin, with 15 Democrats joining 38 Republicans to kill the bill.

Analysis

Why were supporters of comprehensive reform stymied; and why did the 2007 reform effort fail so spectacularly despite the broad array of key actors support-ing the bill? In part, reform efforts ran into a truism about immigration politics: that they are characterized by cross-cutting cleavages that confound stable partisan coalitions (Hoskin 1991; Gimple and Edwards 1999; Tichenor 2002). Democrats were divided between the desire to appeal to Latino voters, who favored generous comprehensive reform, and the desire to appear tough on national security. Some Democrats also objected to the bill's temporary worker provisions, traditionally opposed by labor unions.[25] Republicans were even more divided. On one hand, the President had made support for com-prehensive immigration reform a central theme of his second term; national party leaders saw pro-immigrant reforms as a unique opportunity to solidify Bush's tentative gains with Latino voters; and traditional Republican business and mainline religious groups were strong backers of comprehensive reform. On the other hand, grassroots social conservative groups like the Eagle Forum, anti-immigration advocates like the Federation for American Immigration Reform (FAIR) and Numbers USA, and evangelical groups like the Christian Coalition all brought significant restrictionist pressure to bear on Republican members, including through a successful summer 2006 campaign to mail bricks (for building a border fence) to members of Congress.

With the parties internally divided in this way, electoral considerations became an obstacle to reform in both years. In 2006, Democratic leaders believed that the Republican majority would be blamed if Congress failed to pass immigration reform, reinforcing the Democratic campaign theme of a "do-nothing" Congress. Republicans recognized that national polls supported action on immigration policy, but many House members (most of whom represented conservative districts) and southern senators strongly opposed any form of "amnesty"—a term which hard-liners defined to include almost any policy short of mass deportation.[26]

Ironically, electoral politics were an even more important factor in 2007 when the early start to the presidential campaign essentially demobilized John McCain, Lindsay Graham, Mel Martinez, and Sam Brownback, all of whom had been active supporters of the 2006 bill.[27] In addition, if the House's 2005 bill had been a wake-up call to pro-reform groups, the Senate's 2006 bill was a five-alarm fire for grassroots opponents of liberalizing reforms. By 2007, right-wing media outlets had taken ownership of the immigration debate, and the anti-immigration group Numbers USA had developed a far-reaching and highly sophisticated grassroots lobbying network. Numerous Senate staffers, including several with years of Capitol Hill experience, described the opposition to the 2007 bill as the most intense and one-sided pressure their offices had ever received on an issue.

Immigration reform was also undermined by President Bush's ineffective leadership on the issue. In 2006, while the President gave an important prime-time address from the Oval Office on May 15 that helped restart the Senate debate, the White House generally sent mixed messages throughout the year: endorsing the House's enforcement-only bill in December, failing ever to formally endorse the Senate's compromise legislation, and even lobbying against the McCain-Kennedy coalition on several key amendments. Supporters of comprehensive reform were repeatedly disappointed by the President's failure to deliver higher-profile and more consistent support for the Senate bill.

President Bush directed new energy to the immigration reform effort after House Republicans announced their opposition to convening a conference committee, lobbying House leaders and rank-and-file members to reverse that decision. The President and Secretaries Chertoff and Gutierrez were even more heavily invested in day-to-day negotiations and both public and behind-the-scenes lobbying work in 2007, but by the summer of 2006—and even more so the following year—the President's low approval ratings limited his effectiveness (Gaouette 2006).[28]

A fourth factor contributing to the defeat of comprehensive reform is the lengthy U.S. policymaking process, which creates multiple opportunities for groups to mobilize opposition to any reform effort. Outside pressure initially worked to reformers' advantage in 2006, as massive spring street protests against the House's enforcement-only bill emboldened swing voters in the Senate Judiciary Committee's passage of its surprisingly pro-immigrant bill to the Senate floor. But the media blamed Democrats for the April 2006 procedural deadlock on the Senate floor, and popular support eroded over the course of the May debate as each legislative compromise peeled off supporters from the left–right coalition.[29] Senators and Senate staff emerged exhausted from the second round of floor debate on May 26, and were unprepared to fend off attacks on the bill by House leaders, or to respond to procedural problems that put the bill in a holding pattern.[30] Two weeks later, when Republican Brian Bilbray won a special election for a House seat in San Diego, hard-liners and many in the media framed his victory as a vindication of their combative stance, and members of both parties became convinced that pro-immigration votes would be costly in the 2006 election.

Similarly, in 2007, with grassroots opposition to reform efforts running high, each additional day of floor debate placed more pressure on moderates in both parties to withdraw their support from the bill.[31] Thus, opponents relied heavily on delay tactics, and pressed relentlessly for votes on additional amendments. A crucial turning point came during the first-floor debate when reformers agreed to extend the debate into a third week following a previously scheduled recess. Back home in their districts, many senators came under intense pressure to withdraw their support from the bill—including key members of the grand compromise coalition like Senators Chambliss, Isakson, and Graham. Reform advocates naturally sought procedural mechanisms to freeze out competing amendments and streamline the debate—the June 2007 "clay pigeon" being the most extreme example—but the anti-democratic nature of these maneuvers became an important story line of their own, and an additional rallying point for opponents of the bill.

Finally, with respect to the contrasting outcomes in 2006 and 2007, it bears emphasis that the Senate's passage of S.2611 in 2006 was, in some ways, a smaller victory than it seemed: many Republican senators voted for the bill despite some reservations about it because they knew the Republican-controlled House would have demanded significant changes in a conference committee prior to the bill becoming law. Conversely, the defeat in 2007 appeared more lopsided than was actually the case. Staffers from both parties could name a dozen Republican senators who would have voted for cloture if their votes had been decisive, but once it became clear that cloture would fail it became a "free vote" and members felt no pressure from party leadership to vote against constituent demands.[32]

Conclusion

Immigration is indisputably a "domestic" policy issue: the Supreme Court has affirmed Congress "plenary power" to make immigration law; within Congress immigration policy has fallen to Judiciary Committees rather than Foreign Affairs and Foreign Relations; and Justice and Homeland Security, rather than the State Department, have taken primary responsibility for immigration policymaking and enforcement within the executive branch. Yet few domestic issues have more significant implications than immigration policy for U.S. security, prosperity, and diplomatic relations.

For this reason, even as many members of Congress have viewed immigration policy through the lens of competing interest group and popular demands, efforts to ensure that immigration policy is consistent with the national interest have also been a recurring theme. Presidents and their congressional allies blocked restrictionist bills and negotiated country-specific immigration relief provisions during the first half of the twentieth century in the name of diplomacy and economic security. National interest considerations were especially influential when diplomacy and prosperity overlapped with security concerns, as in the generous pro-Mexico provisions of the wartime Bracero Program, and the development of anti-communist humanitarian relief policies and the elimination of the National Origins quota system at the height of the Cold War.

The national interest implications of immigration policy are particularly significant in the current period: the end of the Cold War has produced a surge in regional and intra-state conflicts, producing new refugee flows; economic integration has created new emigration pressures within the Caribbean Basin while also raising the costs of enforcement; the terror attacks of 1993 and 2001 highlighted U.S. vulnerability to asymmetric threats within the United States; and demographic changes at home make the United States particularly dependent on immigrant labor for sustained economic growth.

Both the House and the Senate responded to these new pressures in 2005–07 by drafting legislation to strengthen border and worksite enforcement, proposals which were broadly consistent with narrow U.S. security goals and also popular with voters. Beyond the border, however, the House bill was insensitive to the economic implications of immigration policy, failing to join the Senate by expanding legal access for high-skilled and low-skilled immigrant workers making essential contributions to the U.S. economy. The Senate bills were also somewhat more sensitive to the diplomatic implications of U.S. immigration policy: meeting Mexican demands for a temporary worker program, downplaying border fencing, and calling for more bilateral and regional cooperation on enforcement. The House bill's reliance on extensive border fencing and its criminalization of undocumented immigrants played directly into Latin American stereotypes of U.S. unilateralism (Hakim 2006). Most significantly, current and former Department of Homeland Security (DHS) officials and other key players were virtually unanimous that the Senate's more comprehensive approach created the conditions for enforcement to succeed, while the House bill wasted resources by expanding efforts at the already heavily fortified border (e.g., Coalition for Immigration Security 2006; Baker 2006).

Ultimately, the failure of reform efforts in 2006–07 reflects the inherent political difficulty of immigration policy reform as well as more fundamental challenges associated with the complexity of these policy questions. Politically, immigration reform is difficult because Congress only considers major reform bills once the system is sufficiently "broken" to demand its attention—as is the case in the post-9/11 period. Yet major immigration failures tend to make the issue highly politically salient as well, dramatically raising the partisan and interest group stakes of the debate, and making it far more difficult for members to place national interest considerations above their particularistic electoral concerns.

More fundamentally, reform efforts failed in 2006–07 because members of Congress—and the Americans they represent—disagree on a basic level about the goals of U.S. immigration policy. This chapter emphasizes America's economic, security, and diplomatic interests in immigration policy. Yet questions about the economy and U.S. international relations (security and diplomacy) only represent two dimensions out of what is actually a three-dimensional policy debate, also encompassing ideational and cultural concerns, as noted above. To a large extent, opposing sides in 2006 and 2007 talked past each other: advocates for comprehensive reform emphasized the economic and security benefits of legalizing current undocumented immigrants and facilitating future legal flows, and opponents of the Senate bills raised concerns about the *fairness* of a legalization program, and opposed expanding legal migration on cultural and ideational grounds.

What are the prospects for reform in the future? The contemporary era resembles the post-World War One and post-World War Two periods when system-reorienting shocks to U.S. international and economic interests caused Americans to re-examine immigration policy from the ground up. In both of those periods, the debate coincided with equally significant cultural/values shifts, toward greater restrictions in the former period and greater openness in the latter. Thus, the three dimensions of the immigration debate lined up in coherent ways, resulting in policy regime changes in 1917–24 and in 1957–65. In contrast, policy pressures were cross-cutting in the 1980s and 1990s, with economic interests demanding increased flows, but security and ideational concerns focused on border security, resulting in inchoate migration policy during the last two decades. These incoherent policies and consequent demand for reform remain in place, and the issue will likely return to the agenda shortly after the 2008 presidential election. But major reform—in either direction—will remain elusive until Americans reconcile their conflicting views regarding immigration and U.S. interests.

Notes

1 These diplomatic considerations may conflict with a nation's compliance with the humanitarian intent of national and international laws protecting vulnerable populations (Rosenblum and Salehyan 2004).
2 See Money (1999) on geographic determinants of interest group pressure and Freeman (1995) on economic determinants. See Rosenblum (2004b) on the tension between domestic interest group demands and the national interest in migration policy.
3 The contrast between the United States and Mexico is instructive: while both facilitated European migration, Mexico worried about Anglo migration from the United States to the northern Mexican territory of Texas, and sought to restrict such flows in an 1821 agreement with the settler Stephen F. Austin. Nonetheless, undocumented Anglo immigration to Texas continued—changing the demographic facts on the ground—and the United States eventually supported the "Texians'" claim to independence, leading to the U.S.–Mexican War (1846–8) in which the United States claimed one third of Mexico.

4 Chinese migrants were declared inadmissable in 1882; persons "likely to become a public charge," anarchists, and various other undesirable individuals were made ineligible for admission between 1891 and 1903; a literacy requirement and head tax were added in 1917; and the so-called National Origins system was created between 1921 and 1924.

5 A 1951 *New York Times* investigation warned of a security breach so wide that "Joseph Stalin might adopt a perfunctory disguise and walk into the country" at any point along the border (Hill 1951).

6 Controversies over security also translated into immigration disputes, as congressional Democrats sought relief for Salvadoran refugees in part to protest U.S. support for the repressive government there, finally securing Extended Voluntary Departure relief for Salvadorans as part of the 1990 Immigration Act over President Bush's objections.

7 One in ten Mexicans and Dominicans now live in the United States, as do almost one in five Salvadorans. Migrant remittances have become among the largest and most reliable forms of foreign exchange for these states: US\$ 20 billion in Mexico's case and an average of US\$ 2.2 billion for the five migrant-sending states in Central America (IADB 2006). The politicization of U.S. immigration policy within Mexico and other countries of origin has intensified since the 1990s, a point driven home by the Mexican Congress's unanimous passage in 2006 of a resolution calling for shared responsibility for migration enforcement (Rosenblum 2007; Hernández et al. 2005).

8 One study found that immigrants founded one third of all Silicon Valley startups during the 1990s (Saxenian 2001); also see Greenspan (1999), Wadhwa et al. (2007).

9 Senators John McCain (R-AZ) and Edward Kennedy (D-MA) introduced S.1033, the Secure America and Orderly Immigration Act, in March; Senators John Cornyn (R-TX) and Jon Kyl (R-AZ) introduced S. 1438, the Comprehensive Enforcement and Immigration Reform Act, in July; and Senator Chuck Hagel (R-NE) introduced a package of four separate bills, S.1916–S.1919, in October.

10 The McCain-Kennedy bill offered "earned legalization" to immigrants who had been in the United States for at least two years, while Hagel's offer required five years of residency.

11 The Border Protection, Antiterrorism, and Illegal Immigration Control Act of 2005.

12 Especially controversial were provisions in the Chairman's Mark to expand the definition of immigrant smuggling, and to criminalize the act of overstaying an immigrant visa. Resolving the latter required that the Committee first take a position on whether such immigrants would be otherwise eligible for legalization. Ultimately, a broad humanitarian exception was added to the anti-smuggling language; and visa overstays were not deemed criminal offenses.

13 Diane Feinstein (CA) was the only Democrat on the Committee who opposed the McCain-Kennedy guest-worker and legalization language. Among Republicans, Lindsay Graham (SC) and Sam Brownback (KS) were original McCain-Kennedy co-sponsors, and Mike DeWine (OH) was a strong supporter. The Committee also included two of the Senate's most ardent opponents of comprehensive immigration reform, Jeff Sessions (R-AL) and Tom Coburn (R-OK); and Charles Grassley (R-IA) and Orrin Hatch (R-UT) were considered safe votes against comprehensive reform. Thus, a "majority or the majority" rule made Specter, Cornyn, and Kyl the crucial swing voters, though Specter's staff also indicated that he would support a bill as long as one of these two—most likely the more moderate Cornyn—could also be brought along.

14 Republicans in these negotiations accepted the idea that *some* undocumented immigrants deserved a chance at legal status, but proposed restricting the offer to the most extreme humanitarian cases (e.g., a grandmother who had lived in the United States for decades and was raising U.S.-citizen grandchildren) and to "indispensable" workers with specialized job skills; and they wanted legalization cases adjudicated on an individual basis. Democrats insisted that the vast majority of undocumented immigrants should be covered and that legalization should be offered on a categorical basis.

15 Despite the Judiciary Committee's frenetic work to beat his deadline, Frist chose to offer his own enforcement-only bill first, and debate over the Specter bill technically concerned an amendment to the underlying Frist bill. As a result, when Republicans opted to set aside the pending Specter "amendment" to consider additional amendments (i.e., Cornyn-Kyl and Isakson), votes on the latter amendments could only be scheduled by unanimous consent, giving Democrats a veto over which votes could be taken.

16 Six Democrats crossed party lines to vote against cloture. Even solid Republican supporters of comprehensive reform like John McCain and Lindsay Graham voted against cloture based on their conviction that Democrats were violating Senate norms by blocking votes on the disputed amendments.

17 These "touch-base returns" provided political cover against the charge of amnesty because immigrants would re-enter in legal status before getting on a path to citizenship. As in the Judiciary Committee and McCain-Kennedy bills, aliens in the country for less than two years were denied legalization.

18 The core group included Republican Senators Brownback, DeWine, Graham, Hagel, Martinez, McCain, and Specter, and Democratic Senators Durbin, Kennedy, Lieberman (CT), Menendez (NJ), Obama, and Salazar. The group met almost daily during the second-floor debate to map out legislative strategy and to reaffirm their support for the compromise bill.

19 Four out of 43 Democrats crossed party lines to oppose the bill, and 23 out of 55 Republicans supported it, while two Democrats were absent.

20 A July Tarrance Group poll found that 11 percent of respondents identified candidates' positions on illegal immigration as the most important issue determining their vote in the fall. Other surveys produced similar results, consistently placing immigration as a top three issue, along with "the economy" and the war in Iraq. Three-quarters of respondents to a Gallup-*USA Today* poll in April believed it was important that the government take steps this year to address undocumented immigrants living in the United States. Three separate polls conducted by CNN in April and May and by CBS in May found between 75 and 79 percent of respondents supporting the Senate's legalization provisions. Even strong majorities of Republican voters favored the Senate plan—75 percent in a June Tarrance Group poll—while only 47 percent supported the House's enforcement-only approach.

21 Key interest groups supporting the comprehensive Senate bill included the U.S. Chamber of Commerce, the Essential Workers Immigration Coalition (EWIC, itself a coalition of pro-immigration business groups), the U.S. Conference of Catholic Bishops, the National Council of La Raza, the National Immigration Forum, the American Immigration Lawyers' Association, and the National Immigration Law Center.

22 The White House supported backroom by Representative Mike Pence (R-IN) and Senator Kay Bailey Huchison (R-TX) to circumvent the conference process. The Pence plan would have eliminated the Senate's complex three-tier structure and instead required all undocumented immigrants to leave the country and apply for re-entry through privately managed "Ellis Island Centers." Returning immigrants would be allowed to work for up to 14 years,

and then apply for legal permanent visas and eventual citizenship through existing mechanisms. Sponsors of the Senate bill rejected the proposal as unfair (and unworkable) for existing undocumented immigrants, and both House and Senate sponsors saw the private Ellis Island Centers as unworkable.

23 Representatives Luis Gutierrez (D-IL) and Jeff Flake (R-AZ) were also involved in the negotiations in early 2007, and their "Security through Regularized Immigration and a Vibrant Economy (STRIVE) Act of 2007" (H.R. 1645) reflected the McCain-Kennedy compromise position, but House leaders chose to postpone debate until after the Senate passed a bill.

24 As part of the leadership deal to hold votes on the pre-determined list of amendments and no others, Senator Reid employed an obscure "clay pigeon" procedure, breaking a single massive amendment into 26 separate "divisions," each receiving an independent vote.

25 Labor unions were also divided: the AFL-CIO opposed the Senate bill because of its temporary worker program, but the Service Employees International Union and UNITE-HERE were strong supporters.

26 Even supporters of reform conceded, in the words of one staffer, that "the emotion and energy were all on the other side."

27 McCain and Brownback were both running for president; Graham was "in cycle," or up for re-election, in 2008; and Martinez was named chairman of the Republican National Committee. Only McCain remained an outspoken supporter of comprehensive immigration reform—and Brownback dramatically reversed his position on the issue—but McCain's effectiveness in the debate was limited because his campaign schedule resulted in extended absences from Washington.

28 In the words of a Democratic Senate staffer, "President Bush was losing his political stroke . . . When Bush made direct calls as often as not it seemed to turn some Republicans the other way." A Republican staffer involved in the effort to defeat the bill was even more blunt when asked about White House pressure: "F— Karl Rove! We hate that guy . . . The Bush administration had zero credibility with the five of us" (referring to Senators Coburn, Cornyn, DeMint, Sessions, and Vitter).

29 Immigration advocates complained that the Hagel-Martinez compromise would deny legal status to too many undocumented immigrants, and that enforcement provisions in Title II of the bill were unacceptably harsh on immigrants and their families. The Department of Homeland Security (DHS) and advocates of tough enforcement complained that the multiple categories of immigration relief and different types of new visas would make effective implementation impossible. DHS also criticized due process protections included in S.2611's worksite enforcement provisions.

30 In addition to the House's failure to appoint conferees, the Senate bill faced a "blue slip" challenge in the House because the Senate bill raised revenue (fines on undocumented immigrants), and constitutional rules require that revenue legislation must originate in the House. As a result, any member of the House would be empowered to block a vote on the Senate bill. The Senate could resolve the problem by amending an unrelated House revenue bill to include the Senate's immigration language, but Republican leaders failed to obtain the necessary consent from members to do so.

31 As one Senate staffer explained, "The goalposts definitely moved . . . Every morning during the floor debate, [Senators] Graham and Kyl would come to the meeting saying if we make this concession we'll get Isakson's vote, or if we make that concession we'll get Hutchison's, or whoever. [We] were willing to do it, but the Republican votes never materialized."

32 Thus, Majority Leader Mitch McConnell voted against cloture despite his

earlier support for the bill, and Sam Brownback returned to the Senate floor to reverse his already-registered yes vote.

References

Aspen Institute. 2005. *Grow Faster Together or Grow Slowly Apart: How Will America Work in the 21st Century?* Aspen, Co: Aspen Institute. http://www.aspeninstitute.org/atf/cf/%7BDEB6F227–659B–4EC8–8F84–80F23 CA704F5%7D/DSGBROCHURE_FINAL.PDF (accessed October 27, 2006).

Baker, Stewart. 2006. "Immigration Enforcement at the Workplace: Learning from the Mistakes of 1986." Statement Before the Subcommittee on Immigration, Border Security and Citizenship, U.S. Senate Judiciary Committee, Washington, DC, June 19.

CNN 2006. "House Hearings Threaten Immigration Bill." http://www.cnn.com/2006/POLITICS/06/20/immigration.hearings/index.html (June 21, 2006).

Coalition for Immigration Security. 2006. "Open Letter to President and Members of Congress." http://www.aila.org/content/default.aspx?docid=20069 (December 18, 2006).

Craig, Richard B. 1971. *The Bracero Program: Interest Groups and Foreign Policy.* Austin: University of Texas Press.

Dorval, Chris, and Andrea LaRue. 2006. "Immigration Fails as Wedge Issue for GOP; Succeeds in Expanding Base for Democrats." *Immigration 2006.org.* http://www.immigration2006.org/index.html (December 18, 2006).

Dunn, Timothy J. 1996. *The Militarization of the U.S.–Mexico Border, 1978–1992.* Austin: Center for Mexican American Studies, University of Texas at Austin.

Freeman, Gary P. 1995. "Modes of Immigration Politics in Liberal Democratic States." *International Migration Review* 29(4): 881–902.

Fuchs, Lawrence H. 1990. *The American Kaleidoscope: Race, Ethnicity, and the Civic Culture.* Hanover, NH: Wesleyan University Press/University Press of New England.

Gaouette, Nicole. 2006. "House GOP Not Budging on Border." *Los Angeles Times,* May 24, A1.

Gimpel, James G., and James R. Edwards, Jr. 1999. *The Congressional Politics of Immigration Reform.* Boston: Allyn and Bacon.

Givens, Terri. 2005. *Voting Radical Right in Western Europe.* New York: Cambridge University Press.

Greenspan, Alan. 1999. "Testimony Before the House Ways and Means Committee on State of the Economy." January 20, 1999. Federal News Service.

Hakim, Peter. 2006. "Is Washington Losing Latin America?" *Foreign Affairs* 85(1): 39–53.

Hatton, Timothy J., and Jeffrey Williamson. 1998. *The Age of Mass Migration: Causes and Economic Impact.* New York: Oxford University Press.

Helton, Arthur C. 2002. *The Price of Indifference: Refugees and Humanitarian Action in the New Century.* New York: Oxford University Press.

Hernández, Silvia, et al. 2005. "Mexico and the Migration Phenomenon." *Working Group on Prospects and Design of Platforms for the Construction of a Mexican*

Migration Policy. October 2005. http://www.consejomexicano.org/download.php?id=71026,747,7 (November 15, 2006).

Hill, Gladwin. 1951. "Million a Year Flee Mexico Only to Find Peonage Here." *New York Times,* March 25, 1.

Hoskin, Marilyn. 1991. *New Immigrants and Democratic Society: Minority Integration in Western Democracies.* New York: Praeger Publishers.

Huntington, Samuel P. 2004. "The Hispanic Challenge." *Foreign Policy* 14 (March/April): 30–45.

Inter-American Development Bank. 2006. "Migrant Remittances as a Development Tool." http://www.iadb.org/mif/remittances/index.cfm (April 17, 2006).

Kessler, Alan E., and Gary P. Freeman. 2005. "Public Opinion in the EU on Immigration from Outside the Community." *Journal of Common Market Studies* 43(4): 825–850.

Kondracke, Morton. 2006. "Message of 2006: Moderates Fed Up With Polarization." *Roll Call,* November 9, 20.

Loescher, Gil, and John A. Scanlan. 1986. *Calculated Kindness: Refugees and America's Half-Open Door, 1945 to the Present.* New York: The Free Press.

Lowell, Lindsay, Julia Gelatt, and Jeanne Batalova. 2006. "Immigration and Labor Force Trends: The Future, Past, and Present." *Insight* #17. Washington, DC: Migration Policy Institute.

McDonald, Peter, and Rebecca Kippen. 2001. "Labor Supply Prospects in 16 Developed Countries, 2000–2050." *Population and Development Review* 27(1): 1–32.

Massey, Douglas, Joaquín Arango, Graeme Hugo, Ali Kouaouci, Adela Pellegrino, and J. Edward Taylor. 1998. *Worlds in Motion: International Migration at the End of the Millennium.* Oxford: Oxford University Press.

Meyers, Deborah W. 2005. "US Border Enforcement: From Horseback to High-Tech." *Migration Policy Institute Task Force Policy Brief,* November 7.

Meyers, Eytan. 2004. *International Immigration Policy: A Theoretical and Comparative Analysis.* New York: Pagrave-Macmillan.

Mitchell, Christopher. 1992. "U.S. Foreign Policy and Dominican Migration to the United States," in Christopher Mitchell, ed., *Western Hemisphere Immigration and United States Foreign Policy,* pp. 89–123. College Park, PA: Pennsylvania State Press.

Money, Jeannette. 1999. *Fences and Neighbors: The Political Geography of Immigration Control in Advanced Market Economy Countries.* Ithaca: Cornell University Press.

National Science Foundation. 2004. *Science and Engineering Doctorate Awards: 2003* (NSF 05–300). Arlington, VA: National Science Foundation.

Ottaviano, Gianmarco, and Giovani Peri. 2005. "Rethinking the Gains from Immigration: Theory and Evidence from the US." *NBER Working Paper 11672.* Cambridge, MA: National Bureau of Economic Research.

Reimers, David M. 1998. *Unwelcome Strangers: American Identity and the Turn Against Immigration.* New York: Columbia University Press.

Rosenblum, Marc R. 2003. "The Intermestic Politics of Immigration Policy: Lessons from the Bracero Program." *Political Power and Social Theory* 16: 139–182.

Rosenblum, Marc R. 2004a. "Beyond the Policy of No Policy: Emigration from

Mexico and Central America." *Latin American Politics and Society* 4(1): 91–125.

Rosenblum, Marc R. 2004b. *The Transnational Politics of U.S. Immigration Policy.* La Jolla, CA: University of California, San Diego Center for Comparative Immigration Studies.

Rosenblum, Marc R. 2007. "U.S.–Mexican Migration Cooperation: Obstacles and Opportunities," in James Hollifield, Pia Orrenius, and Thomas Osang, eds., *Migration, Trade, and Development: Conference Proceedings,* pp. 91–119. Dallas: Federal Reserve Bank of Dallas.

Rosenblum, Marc R., and Idean Salehyan. 2004. "Norms and Interests in U.S. Asylum Enforcement." *Journal of Peace Research* 41(6): 677–697.

Rudolph, Christopher. 2006. *National Security and Immigration: Policy Development in the United States and Western Europe since 1945.* Stanford: Stanford University Press.

Salehyan, Idean, and Kristian Gleditsch. 2006. "Refugees and the Spread of Civil War." *International Organization* 60(2): 335–366.

Saxenian, AnnaLee. 2001. "Silicon Valley's New Immigrant Entrepreneurs," in Wayne A. Cornelius, Thomas J. Espenshade, and Idean Salehyan, eds., *The International Migration of the Highly Skilled: Demand, Supply, and Development Consequences in Sending and Receiving Countries.* La Jolla, CA: UC-San Diego Center for Comparative Immigration Studies.

Schoultz, Lars. 1992. "Central America and the Politicization of U.S. Immigration Policy," in Christopher Mitchell, ed., *Western Hemisphere Immigration and United States Foreign Policy,* pp. 157–219. College Park, PA: Pennsylvania State Press.

Shanks, Cheryl. 2001. *Immigration and the Politics of American Sovereignty, 1890–1990.* Ann Arbor: University of Michigan Press.

Stepick, Alex. 1992. "Unintended Consequences: Rejecting Haitian Boat People and Destabilizing Duvalier," in Christopher Mitchell, ed., *Western Hemisphere Immigration and United States Foreign Policy,* pp. 125–155. College Park, PA: Pennsylvania State University Press.

Sum, Andrew, Neeta Fogg, Ishwar Khatiwada, and Sheila Palma. 2004. "Foreign Immigration and the Labor Force of the U.S." *Northeastern University: Center for Labor Market Studies.* http://www.nupr.neu.edu/7–04/immigrant_04.pdf (October 27, 2006).

Teitelbaum, Michael S. 1984. "Immigration, Refugees, and Foreign Policy." *International Organization* 38(3): 429–450.

Teitelbaum, Michael S., and Myron Weiner, eds. 1995. *Threatened Peoples, Threatened Borders: World Migration and U.S. Policy.* New York: W.W. Norton and Co.

Tichenor, Daniel J. 2002. *Dividing Lines: The Politics of Immigration Control in America.* Princeton: Princeton University Press.

Wadhwa, Vivek, AnnaLee Saxenian, Ben Rissing, and Gary Gereffi. 2007. "America's New Immigrant Entrepreneurs." *Master of Engineering Management Program, Duke University; School of Information, U.C. Berkeley.* http://memp.pratt.duke.edu/downloads/americas_new_immigrant_entrepreneurs.pdf.

White House. 2005a. "President Fact Sheet: Securing America through Immigration Reform." http://www.whitehouse.gov/news/releases/2005/11/2005 1128–3.html (November 28, 2005).

White House. 2005b. "State of the Union Address." http://www.
    whitehouse.gov/news/releases/2005/02/20050202–11.html (February 2,
    2005).
White House. 2005c. "Statement of Administration Policy: H.R. 4437 Border
    Protection, Antiterrorism, and Illegal Immigration Control Act of 2005."
    http://www.whitehouse.gov/omb/legislative/sap/109–1/hr4437sap-h.pdf
    (December 15, 2005).

2 Immigration Policy and the Latino Community Since 9/11 [1]

Michele Waslin

Introduction

Immediately prior to the September 11, 2001 terrorist attacks, U.S. President George W. Bush and Mexican President Vicente Fox met to set forth principles from which further migration discussions might proceed. Their deliberations showed real promise in constructing comprehensive reforms in the difficult area of migration policy, including regularizing the status of millions of undocumented immigrant workers currently living in the U.S. and bringing additional temporary workers to the U.S. to fill labor shortages through a significantly reformed program (Schmitt 2001).

Within a week of President Vicente Fox's September 6, 2001 State Visit, the unthinkable happened: 19 foreign nationals engineered the worst terrorist attacks in our nation's history. By February 2003, Mexican Foreign Minister Luis Ernesto Derbez said that a plan to legalize undocumented workers could take up to 30 years, and that "our societies are not yet ready to sign [a deal] but what they are ready for is the concept" (Reuters 2003). The years immediately following the terrorist attacks witnessed a complete halt of legalization negotiations and a deterioration in the treatment of immigrants living in the U.S. The language of legalization and immigration reform was almost entirely replaced by national security concerns, attempts to restrict the flow of immigrants at the border, and enhanced immigration enforcement in the U.S. interior.

In a very short time following the terrorist attacks, the U.S. moved from the brink of comprehensive immigration reform to enacting immigration policies based on national security concerns. Of course, the direction of immigration policy in recent years cannot be solely attributed to terrorism. The years since 9/11 have also witnessed a surge in immigration advocacy activity, from both the restrictionist and pro-immigrant camps. Restrictionist, or anti-immigrant, forces have strengthened and become more vocal, fueling anti-immigrant policies and legislation at the federal level and resulting in additional negative consequences on immigration policy and immigrant communities. [2] In some cases the attacks have been physical; the Anti-Defamation League proclaimed "Extremists Declare 'Open Season' on Immigrants: Hispanics Target of

Incitement and Violence" (Anti-Defamation League 2006). Pro-immigrant forces have also aligned and pushed for comprehensive immigration reform. Strange-bedfellows coalitions including business, labor unions, ethnic organizations, faith-based institutions, and civil rights groups have joined hands in support of immigration reform. The spring of 2006 witnessed the largest ever mobilizations by immigrants and their supporters. Witnesses estimated 20,000–40,000 in Washington, DC, 100,000–300,000 in Chicago, 350,000–500,000 in Dallas, and even 3,000 in Schuyler, Nebraska (Wange and Winn 2006). These and other activities have had a significant impact on the immigration debate of the twenty-first century.

However, the events of 9/11 continue to affect immigration policy and, as a result, the Latino community in the U.S. As immigration policy is now inextricable from counterterrorism policy, at least in the political discourse, immigrant communities continue to experience negative consequences, and advocates on all sides of the immigration debate must adapt to the new reality and rhetoric. This chapter examines the evolution of U.S. immigration policy since September 11 and specifically its effect on the Latino community in the U.S.

The Terrorist Attacks, New Immigration Policies, and U.S. Latinos

The terrorist attacks had a profound influence on immigrant communities. While many foreign nationals were included among the victims and heroes of the attacks, in the immediate aftermath, family members of some immigrant workers were hesitant to report missing loved ones out of fear of the Immigration and Naturalization Service (INS); the identities of some of these workers will never be known (Ching 2001; Tutek 2006). Furthermore, many immigrants and their family members, due to restrictions on eligibility for public services, were unable to access public assistance programs intended to aid the survivors of the attacks (New York Immigration Coalition n.d.). Many more immigrant workers found themselves among the unemployed as a result of cutbacks in travel and other affected industries. In addition, despite strong statements from leaders urging racial and ethnic tolerance, reports of violence, harassment, and hate crimes against Arab Americans, Muslim Americans, Latinos, and other minorities mistaken for "terrorists" were distressingly common.[3]

In the immediate aftermath of the attacks, some people called for severe restrictions on immigrant admissions to the U.S. and the further curtailment of the rights of immigrants already in the country. Immigration restrictionists took advantage of the opportunity to push forward their agenda—the same anti-immigrant agenda they had advocated for decades—under the guise of preventing terrorism. Preying upon the legitimate fears of ordinary Americans, anti-immigrant groups and opportunistic political leaders have portrayed ordinary immigrants as terrorists and have sought to deny immigrants the opportunity to make the U.S. their home and exercise their rights (National Council of La Raza 2002).

The ability of anti-immigrant forces to use security rhetoric to their advantage was evident early on. One of the first victims of the new environment was the extension of 245(i), a provision of the Immigration and Nationality Act which allowed persons to pay a fine to adjust their legal status in the U.S. rather than leaving the country for consular processing and risking bars to re-entry. Extension of 245(i) was passed on the House floor on September 11, 2001, but it was quickly labeled an "amnesty for terrorists" by restrictionist groups, and the extension has never become law (Dinan 2002).

Another of the first signals of things to come was the creation of the Department of Homeland Security (DHS) in December 2002. The Homeland Security Act abolished the Immigration and Naturalization Services (INS) and incorporated immigration services and enforcement into DHS.[4] Since its creation, INS and its predecessors have been housed in the Departments of Treasury, Commerce, Labor, Justice, and now Homeland Security, each move symbolic of the lens through which immigration is seen at the time. Placing immigration within a national security agency was a clear, physical as well as political, manifestation of the new reality that the border and migration were to be viewed first and foremost as issues of national security.

The post-9/11 period is neither the first time that real or perceived threats to the nation have led to reductions in the civil rights and civil liberties of the foreign-born, nor is it the first time immigration has been seen through the lens of national security. Beginning as early as the Enemy Alien Act and the Alien and Sedition Acts of 1798, the U.S. has continually banned groups or individuals based on some perceived threat to U.S. security—security being defined in an appropriate manner to suit current threats (Cole 2003). More recently, national security has been defined to include the trafficking of drugs and persons, and immigration laws and policies—particularly along the U.S.– Mexico border—have reflected those perceived threats.[5] The terrorist attacks of September 11 changed the U.S.'s view of national security and redefined the face of those who were threatening the United States. New threats include immigrants, regardless of country of origin, and the U.S.–Mexico border has become a key front on the U.S.'s war against terrorism.

The U.S. government's response to the terrorist attacks has had far reaching effects on its policy agenda and on a wide variety of communities across the nation. While the post-9/11 immigration policies appeared to be targeted at Arab-American and Muslim-American communities, many of the newly enacted policies have had detrimental effects on Latinos that will continue to be felt for many years. Since 35 million Latinos make up the nation's largest minority, and because 40 percent of the Latino population is foreign-born (National Council of La Raza 2001), these changes have caused serious concerns in the Latino community. Furthermore, since many Latinos live in mixed-status households[6] and communities—meaning that undocumented immigrants, lawful residents, and U.S. citizens live interdependently—even measures that are aimed at the undocumented population have huge spillover effects on the larger Latino community.

The following are the major post-9/11 policies and laws that have had a negative effect on the U.S. Latino community.

New Change of Address Requirements

In an early move touted as a counterterrorism device and indicative of the direction of immigration policy, the Department of Justice (DOJ) announced that it would renew enforcement of Section 265(a) of the Immigration and Nationality Act, a rarely enforced 50-year-old law requiring all noncitizens to report a change of address within 10 days of moving. The law also attaches criminal penalties to failure to submit a change of address, and may even lead to deportation. The first high-profile application of the law was the case of a Palestinian man who was stopped for driving four miles over the speed limit and then placed in removal proceedings for failing to file a change of address form (Bixler 2002). This policy subjects millions of Latino (and other) immigrants to deportation simply because they were unaware of this rule at the time they moved.

Even those who correctly submit the forms may experience problems, because the immigration service has not been able to process the forms that it has received by mail. In July 2002, the press reported that the INS had 200,000 unprocessed change of address forms stored in boxes in an underground storage facility. Immediately afterward, the number of forms received by the INS skyrocketed from 2,800 per month to 30,000 per day. The nearly one million additional forms that the INS/DHS received were now also sitting in storage, exposing a large number of immigrants to potential deportation for allegedly failing to comply with the law. It is unclear how enforcement of Section 265(a) aids in the war against terrorism, since presumably domestic terrorist cells have no incentive to comply with the law. What is clear is that this policy has provided the DHS with more information than they can handle, and has the potential to criminalize the activities of millions of immigrants, or to be used selectively against particular individuals or groups.

State and Local Police Enforcement of Federal Immigration Law

Another immigration enforcement tactic originally touted as a security measure has been to enlist state and local law enforcement officers in a variety of "cooperative" activities. The 9/11 Commission Report stated that "there is a growing role for state and local law enforcement agencies. They need more training and work with federal agencies so that they can cooperate more effectively with those federal authorities in identifying terrorist suspects" (9/11 Commission 2004: 390). Unfortunately, the proposed policies allowing local police departments to enforce federal civil immigration law may in fact hinder terrorist and other criminal investigations by alienating immigrant populations.

In June 2002, Attorney General John Ashcroft declared that state and local police have the authority to enforce civil and criminal immigration violations of immigration law. In the months since that announcement, state and local police have been called upon to catch violators of the new registration and change of address requirements. This new policy was based on an originally unreleased Office of Legal Counsel (OLC) opinion (it was released years later as the result of a lawsuit) that declared that state and local police have the "inherent authority" to enforce civil and criminal immigration violations of immigration law, indicating that the DOJ had reinterpreted the law and over-turned decades of legal precedent (Waslin 2003). The legality of the policy is still hotly debated.

In the meantime, several developments have led to increased use of state and local police to enforce federal immigration laws. Section 133 of the Illegal Immigration Reform and Immigrant Responsibility Act of 1996 (IIRIRA) allows the Attorney General to enter into agreements to delegate immigration powers to local police, but only through negotiated Memoranda of Under-standing (MOUs). These MOUs are negotiated between DHS and local authorities, and include delegation of authority to a limited number of police officers (Waslin 2003). The states of Florida and Alabama currently have MOUs—Florida's is more narrowly defined, and Alabama's is quite broad. In addition, several cities and counties have entered into MOUs with the DHS to allow their police forces limited authority to enforce immigration laws.

Congress has also attempted to expand state and local police immigration enforcement authority. The "Clear Law Enforcement for Criminal Alien Removal" (CLEAR) Act was first introduced in the House of Representatives in 2003; it was re-introduced in the 109th Congress along with companion legislation in the Senate. The bill would confirm the inherent authority of state and local police to enforce all criminal and civil immigration laws and provide financial incentives for compliance. In addition, the bills would criminalize all immigration violations and enter the names of violators into the National Crime Information Center (NCIC) database. CLEAR Act provisions have also been introduced as amendments to other pieces of legislation.

The mere suggestion that local police may have the authority to enforce immigration law sent a chill through Latino and immigrant communities, resulting in increased unwillingness to cooperate with law enforcement, to report crimes, and to come forward as witnesses. Millions will be affected by this rule as law enforcement officers, who are untrained in immigration law, stop and question Latinos and other Americans who "look" or "sound" like they might be foreign. Unlike federal immigration officials, police depart-ments do not have training in or understanding of the complexities of immi-gration law, which could result in erroneous arrests, mistakes, and civil rights violations. These problems will result in the erosion of trust and communica-tion between the police and large segments of the community. In fact, many police departments across the country publicly opposed the DOJ proposal and have stated that they will not involve themselves in immigration enforcement because they recognize the detrimental effects that the loss of community trust can have (National Immigration Forum 2002). All of these problems result in less safe neighborhoods. In summary, the policy some see as a "force multiplier" in the war against terror has enormous negative implications for the Latino community and for all Americans.

Restrictions on Identification Documents

Policies surrounding the issuance and acceptance of identification documents have been emphasized since the terrorist attacks. This is another clear instance where concerns over public safety have been eclipsed by national security rhetoric.

The issue of restrictions on eligibility for driver's licenses has been one of the most important and broadly felt problems for the Latino community because driver's licenses are necessary for participation in many facets of daily life, including driving, banking, renting an apartment, and establishing service for utilities. Prior to September 11, many states made efforts to improve road safety by broadening access to driver's licenses to undocumented immigrants who live and work in the community so that they may obtain proper driver training and vehicular insurance. However, the revelations that some of the 19 terrorists had state-issued driver's licenses caused many states to propose and enact restrictions on immigrant access to driver's licenses, despite the fact that all of the 19 had other valid documents, such as passports, that could serve as identification (Waslin 2002). Not only have these practices prohibited many undocumented immigrants from getting licensed, but many legal residents and even U.S. citizens have been caught in the restrictions because of harassment and discrimination, or because poorly conceived policies may deny licenses to lawful residents.[7]

The *9/11 Commission Report* also made the linkage between driver's licenses and terrorism and recommended that the federal government set standards for the issuance of forms of identification, including driver's licenses (9/11 Commission 2004). This gave Congress the go-ahead to pass federal legislation regulating driver's license issuance. Severe driver's license restrictions were included in the House version of the Intelligence Reform Act of 2005, although the less forceful Senate restrictions were included in the final legislation.[8] In May 2005, the REAL ID Act[9] was signed into law, repealing the provisions of the Intelligence Reform Act and imposing strong federal regulation of state-issued driver's licenses and ID documents. Specifically, the REAL ID Act provides that, beginning in 2008, no federal agency will accept driver's licenses from any state unless the state's licenses are in complete compliance with the federal law. The Act's requirements include restrictions on immigrant access to driver's licenses, such as requiring proof of citizenship or legal immigration status, and issuing distinctive licenses for immigrants on temporary visas (National Immigration Law Center 2005). Throughout the debate, Members of Congress linked the restrictions on driver's licenses to counterterrorism, proclaiming the need to stop terrorists from infiltrating U.S. society by gaining access to driver's licenses.[10]

In addition to battles over the issuance of driver's licenses, Mexican consular IDs also came under attack. Since the nineteenth century, Mexican nationals in the U.S. have been issued Mexican consular IDs (or *matriculas consulares*) to document individuals' identities. In recent years, over 60 U.S. banks and several hundred local police departments have begun to accept consular IDs as proper forms of identification. The U.S. Department of Treasury approved consular IDs as acceptable identification under Section 326 of the USA Patriot Act (Office of the Federal Register 2003), yet immigration restrictionists attacked the consular IDs, claiming that they provide "quasi-amnesty" to unauthorized migrants and pose a security threat to the U.S. (Dinerstein 2003). Legislation restricting the use of Mexican consular IDs—and any other foreign-government-issued ID—has been introduced at the federal level and in several states. These measures prevent large segments of the Latino community from establishing bank accounts and make them vulnerable to criminals who prey on immigrants known to carry cash. They also deny the legal resident and citizen members of these households the ability to accumulate assets through mainstream investments.

These attacks on identification documents have little, if any, proven impact on national security. However, the cost to immigrants and all U.S. residents is potentially huge, particularly if states implement the REAL ID Act.[11] While attempts to restrict undocumented immigrants' use of identification documents most likely would have occurred regardless of 9/11, due to increasing hostility toward unauthorized migration, the added impact of national security rhetoric on the debate all but guaranteed passage of restrictionist identification policies.

Worksite Enforcement

In addition to the "counterterrorism" measures listed above, many immigrants lost their jobs as a result of the renewed emphasis on immigration enforcement in the workplace. The Aviation and Transportation Security Act (ATSA) of 2002[12] required that all baggage screeners be U.S. citizens, thereby linking U.S. citizenship to national security, and potentially opening the door to additional restrictions on noncitizens. The new law resulted in the immediate loss of jobs for thousands of legal immigrants.[13] In addition, many Latino and immigrant workers, including janitors, food service workers, and mechanics, lost their airport jobs as a result of a series of inter-agency airport security sweeps named "Operation Tarmac." DHS worksite enforcement continues to prioritize "critical infrastructure," including military bases and public transportation. As a result of ongoing workplace raids, Latino and other unauthorized immigrant workers have lost their jobs—and no links to terrorist activity have been reported—yet no comprehensive plan to resolve the problem of unauthorized migration has been implemented.

Implications for the Debate on Comprehensive Immigration Reform

Comprehensive immigration reform,[14] another victim of the terrorist attacks, is a well-documented public policy priority for Hispanic Americans, including those who are not immigrants. The discussion initiated immediately prior to 9/11 between the Mexican and U.S. governments stalled and was never reignited. The Bush Administration, which had been vocal about its desire to pass immigration reform, became silent on the issue for several years.

Restrictionist groups quickly fine-tuned their messages to include security rhetoric and argued that cuts in legal immigration as well as enhanced enforcement measures were necessary for national security. The Center for Immigration Studies, a group that advocates reduced immigration, published reports entitled "Safety in (Lower) Numbers: Immigration and Homeland Security" and "Eternal Vigilance: Handing Out Green Cards is a Security Matter," arguing that there are "compelling reasons why a reduction in the legal admission of foreign citizens across the board—both permanent immigrants as well as temporary visa-holders, such as students, workers, and exchange visitors—is imperative for homeland security" (Krikorian 2002).

Immigrant advocates as well found it necessary to change their rhetoric; recognizing the necessity of framing issues from a security standpoint, they have argued that comprehensive immigration reform remains clearly necessary, and the current security-conscious environment should facilitate reform rather than stymie it. The broken immigration system is reframed by pro-immigrant advocates as a potential security nightmare, and immigration reform is a critical element of national security. The presence of a large undocumented immigrant population that has not entered through proper ports of entry, uses false identification documents, and fears contact with civic authorities is clearly inconsistent with U.S. security objectives. Furthermore, they argue that comprehensive immigration reform would allow the U.S. to regulate migration flows and legalize the existing workforce in a way which would allow authorities to know more reliably who is here in the U.S. and who is entering.[15] From the security perspective, the ability to conduct background checks and obtain other information from migrants who are present in, or will soon enter, the U.S. workforce is preferable to unauthorized border crossing and visa overstays.

On January 4, 2004, President Bush made a televised speech calling for comprehensive immigration reform and putting immigration reform on the front burner. Since then, proposed immigration reform activity has reflected the reality of the post-9/11 security conscious environment. Calls for increased enforcement continue to come from the same people who have always supported increased enforcement, but "close the border" has become "secure the border" as national security concerns are evoked, and members of Congress from both political parties have embraced border security as their foremost concern.

Since 2001, numerous bills have been introduced to reduce immigration, to increase immigration enforcement both along the border and in the interior of the U.S., to deny benefits to certain classes of noncitizens, and to limit the judicial review and legal channels available to immigrants, among others. While these bills would most likely have been introduced in the absence of the terrorist attacks, the rhetoric was changed to include references to terrorism and to make the linkage between immigration and terrorism. For example, with regard to the "SAFE Border Act of 2003" (H.R. 1353, 108th Congress), a restrictionist bill, Rep. Richard Baker of Louisiana stated:

> One of the many lessons of September 11th is that we cannot be too careful when it comes to our national immigration policy. It was only after these horrific attacks that we learned that most of the terrorists should not have been admitted into our country in the first place. The first step in solving this crisis is simple: we must limit, not expand, the number of people allowed into this country and the "SAFE Act" does just this.
>
> (*Congressional Record* 2004a)

Members of Congress on the other side of the immigration debate demonstrate a similar sensitivity. In his statement upon introduction of the "SOLVE Act," Senator Edward Kennedy, longtime champion of immigrants and immigration reform said:

> Since the terrorist attacks of September 11th, we can no longer tolerate policies that fail to protect and control our borders. Our borders must be safe and secure. Although no terrorists have been apprehended crossing the southern border, the conditions there are ripe for abuse. Our present enforcement policies are not effective. Our bill will replace the chaotic, deadly illegal crossings along our southwest border with orderly and safe legal avenues for immigrant workers and immigrant families. Substantially legalizing the flow of people at our borders will strengthen our security and substantially reduce criminal activities, enabling immigration enforcement agents to focus their resources on terrorists and criminals attempting to enter the country. The bill will strengthen national security by encouraging undocumented persons to come forward to become legal.
>
> (*Congressional Record* 2004b)

Thus, the impact of the terrorist attacks of 2001 continues to resonate in the immigration policy arena. At the federal and local levels, immigration policy and national security have become inextricably linked. The immigration debate in the U.S. has moved beyond a security-only discussion and comprehensive immigration reform is on the table. In May 2006 the U.S. Senate passed "The Comprehensive Immigration Reform Act of 2006" (S. 2611), also known as the McCain-Kennedy bill, which included a path to citizenship for undocumented immigrants, a new worker visa program, and the reduction of family immigration backlogs, in addition to border and interior enforcement (see Chapter 1 of this volume). However, security concerns remain a priority—and rightfully so—both in rhetoric and reality. As of 2008, the fundamental reforms that the U.S. immigration system desperately needs and that seemed imminent on September 10, 2001, have not been enacted. As a result, millions of Latino immigrants in the U.S. remain unauthorized, fearful, and vulnerable to exploitation.

Conclusion

In summary, whether they are real efforts at enhancing security, publicity stunts aimed at making people feel safer, or conscious efforts to enforce immigration laws against Latino immigrants, measures taken by the U.S. in the name of counterterrorism have had an extremely harmful effect on the country's Latino population. While the immigration restrictionists in Congress and anti-immigrant interest groups have not been entirely successful in their attempts to capitalize on anti-immigrant sentiment post-9/11, U.S. treatment of immigrants and civil liberties is decidedly worse. And, although the terrorist attacks on the U.S. were not connected to Latino immigrants in any way, the long-term consequences on the Latino community will be felt for decades. Nevertheless, if pro-immigrant advocates are able to exploit the new security-consciousness to promote comprehensive immigration reform, the impact of 9/11 on the Latino community will be decidedly more mixed. Only time will tell which scenario ultimately unfolds.

Notes

1　This chapter is based upon an earlier paper, *Counterterrorism and the Latino Community Since September 11*. National Council of La Raza Issue Brief #10, May 2003.
2　For example, see Moser (2003).
3　See American Civil Liberties Union (2002); Human Rights Watch (2002); Lawyers Committee for Human Rights (2002); Schulhofer (2002).
4　Pub. L. no. 107–296, 116 Stat. 2135 (Nov. 25, 2002).
5　See, generally, Andreas (2000).
6　According to the Urban Institute, one in ten children in the U.S. lives in a mixed-status family in which at least one parent is a noncitizen and one child is a citizen. See Urban Institute (2001).
7　In August 2006, a naturalized citizen in New Jersey was told by a DMV clerk that her documents looked suspicious and the police were called. See Llorente (2006). In 2001, a naturalized citizen's naturalization papers were not accepted as proof of citizenship and the DMV clerk demanded her passport. The DMV clerk then refused to return her driver's license so she could drive home to retrieve her passport. A police officer at the scene stated that the DMV clerk was doing the police a favor because "it's hard to tell which Latinos are legal or illegal" (Leon 2001).
8　Pub. L. no. 108–458, 118 Stat. 3638 (Dec. 17, 2004).
9　Pub. L. no. 109–13, 119 Stat. 231 (May 11, 2005).

10 For example, Rep. F. James Sensenbrenner (R-WI) argued:

> The simple fact is that if the 9/11 terrorists had not been able to enter the United States and operate freely in our country—to obtain driver's licenses (over 60 licenses for 19 hijackers), open bank accounts, rent homes and cars, and board airplanes—they would not have been able to murder our loved ones. To pretend otherwise is hypocritical; but more importantly, it is an invitation to future terrorist attacks.

> *Congressional Record*, p. H8685, October 7, 2004. It should be noted that subsequent investigations by journalists showed that the 19 terrorists did not have 60 driver's licenses.

11 For example, all persons would be required to provide proof of citizenship or legal status, all documents must be verified by the issuing agency, all transactions would be conducted in person, and license fees would increase.

12 Pub. L. 107–71, 115 Stat. 597 (Nov. 19, 2001).

13 The Service Employees International Union reported that across the country approximately 20 percent of all baggage screeners were legal immigrants, and in some airports the number was as high as 80 percent.

14 Comprehensive immigration reform is defined as a set of policy proposals aimed at fundamentally reforming the U.S. legal immigration system so that it is attuned to social and economic realities. The key elements include an earned legalization for current undocumented immigrants, the creation of a new worker visa program to regulate future migration flows, a reduction of family-based immigration backlogs, and workplace protections for immigrant and U.S. workers (Waslin 2004).

15 For example, see National Immigration Forum (2005) and Ewing (2004).

References

9/11 Commission. 2004. *9/11 Commission Report*. New York: W.W. Norton & Company, Inc.

American Civil Liberties Union. 2002. *Insatiable Appetite: The Government's Demand for New and Unnecessary Powers After September 11*. Washington, DC: ACLU.

Andreas, Peter. 2000. *Border Games: Policing the U.S.–Mexico Divide*. Ithaca: Cornell University Press.

Anti-Defamation League. 2006. "Extremists Declare 'Open Season' on Immigrants: Hispanics Target of Incitement and Violence." Anti-Defamation League. http://www.adl.org/main_Extremism/immigration_extremists.htm?Multi_page_sections=sHeading-2, April 24.

Bixler, Mark. 2002. "Minor Immigration Slip Becomes Costly to INS: Palestinian Faces Ouster on Little-used Law." *Atlanta Journal-Constitution*, July 10.

Ching Louie, Miriam. 2001. "The 9/11 Disappeareds." *The Nation*, December 3. http://www.thenation.com/doc/200/1203/louie.

Cole, David. 2003. *Enemy Aliens: Double Standards and Constitutional Freedoms in the War on Terrorism*. New York: The New Press.

Congressional Record. 2004a. April 28, p. E693.

Congressional Record. 2004b. May 4, p. S4841.

Dinan, Steven. 2002. "House Panel Rejects Alien-Amnesty Rider." *Washington Times*, May 15.

Dinerstein, Marti. 2003. "IDs for Illegals: The Matricula Consular Advances Mexico's Immigration Agenda." Washington, DC: Center for Immigration Studies.

Ewing, Walter. 2004. "From Denial to Acceptance: Effectively Regulating Immigration to the United States." Immigration Policy Center, *In Focus* 3(5)(November): 1–13.

Human Rights Watch. 2002. *Presumption of Guilt: Human Rights Abuses of Post-September 11 Detainees.* New York: Human Rights Watch.

Krikorian, Mark. 2002. "Backgrounder: Safety in (Lower) Numbers: Immigration and Homeland Security." Washington, DC: Center for Immigration Studies, October. See www.cis.org.

Lawyers Committee for Human Rights. 2002. *A Year of Loss: Reexamining Civil Liberties Since September 11.* New York: Lawyers Committee for Human Rights.

Leon, Wilfredo. 2001. "Joven Hispana es Atropellada en Oficina del DMV." *Latino* (South Carolina), December 28.

Llorente, Elizabeth. 2006. "NJ: Driver's License Renewal Turns Nightmarish for Ex-Colombian." *The Record*, August 29.

Moser, Bob. 2003. "Open Season. As extremists peddle their anti-immigrant rhetoric along the troubled Arizona border, a storm gathers." *Southern Poverty Law Center Intelligence Report.* Montgomery: Southern Poverty Law Center, Spring 2003.

National Council of La Raza. 2001. *Beyond the Census: Hispanics and an American Agenda.* Washington, DC: National Council of La Raza, August.

National Council of La Raza. 2002. *Combating Anti-Immigrant Opportunism Post-September 11.* Washington, DC: National Council of La Raza.

National Immigration Forum. 2005. "Comprehensive Reform of Our Immigration Laws." *National Immigration Forum Backgrounder.* Washington, DC: National Immigration Forum.

National Immigration Forum. 2002. "From Community Policing to Community Profiling: The Justice Department's Proposal to Have Local Police Enforce Immigration Laws." *The National Immigration Forum Backgrounder*, May 10.

National Immigration Law Center. 2005. "Summary of the Driver's License Provisions in the REAL ID Act of 2005 As Made Part of the Emergency Supplemental Appropriations Act for Defense, the Global War on Terror, and Tsunami Relief." Washington, DC: NILC, May. http://www.nilc.org/immspbs/DLs/real_id_dl_tbl_051905.pdf.

New York Immigration Coalition. 2002. "Proposals to Meet the Unmet Needs of Immigrant Victims." http://www.thenyic.org/templates/documentFinder.asp?did=100, March 11, 2002.

Office of the Federal Register, National Archives and Records Administration (NARA). 2003. *Federal Register*, May 9.

Reuters. 2003. "Mexico Says U.S. Immigration Deal May Take 30 Years." Reuters News Service, February 7.

Schmitt, Eric. 2001. "Bush Aides Weigh Legalizing Status of Mexicans in U.S." *New York Times*, July 15. http://query.nytimes.com/gst/fullpage.html?res=9COCEOD9133BF936A25754COA9679C8B63&see=&spon=&pagewanted=1.

Schulhofer, Stephen J. 2002. *The Enemy Within: Intelligence Gathering, Law*

Enforcement, and Civil Liberties in the Wake of September 11. New York: Century Foundation Press.

Tutek, Edwin Andres Martinez. 2006. "Undocumented Workers Uncounted Victims of 9/11." Newsday.com, September 7.

Urban Institute. 2001. "Children of Immigrants Fact Sheet." Washington, DC: The Urban Institute.

Wange, Ted, and Robert C. Winn. 2006. *Groundswell Meets Groundwork: Preliminary Recommendations for Building on Immigrant Mobilizations.* A Special Report from The Four Freedoms Fund and Grantmakers Concerned with Immigrants and Refugees, July. http://www.gcir.org/system/files/ Groundswell_ReportREVweb.pdf.

Waslin, Michele. 2002. *Safe Roads, Safe Communities: Immigrants and State Driver's License Requirements.* NCLR Issue Brief No. 6. Washington, DC: National Council of La Raza, May.

Waslin, Michele. 2003. *Immigration Enforcement by Local Police: The Impact on the Civil Rights of Latinos.* Washington, DC: National Council of La Raza, February.

Waslin, Michele. 2004. *Immigration Reform: Comprehensive Solutions for Complex Immigration Problems.* Washington, DC: National Council of La Raza.

3 U.S. Asylum and Refugee Policy Towards Muslim Nations Since 9/11

Idean Salehyan

Introduction

Asylum and refugee admissions, more than any other immigration category, reflect concern for human rights and the physical security of migrants. According to the UN Convention Relating to the Status of Refugees, individuals with a "well-founded fear of being persecuted" in their country of origin deserve special protection and, in particular, have the right to not be returned to unsafe conditions (Office of the High Commissioner for Human Rights 1951). Moreover, the Refugee Convention emphasizes non-discrimination against migrants on the basis of nationality, religion, ethnicity, or other social category. The United States has a long tradition of welcoming people fleeing religious, political, and ethnic persecution, as its early settlers included people fleeing wars and religious strife in Europe. Since the Second World War, the protection of refugees has been included among a "liberal consensus" on human rights and has been reinforced by international and domestic laws (Gibney 1999; Jacobson 1996; Joppke 1998).

Asylum and refugee admissions[1] are not free from geopolitical considerations, however. Humanitarian admissions criteria have also been frequently influenced by strategic foreign policy and security interests (Loescher 1993; Rosenblum and Salehyan 2004; Teitelbaum 1984). Historically, the United States was quite willing to accept refugees and asylum seekers from leftist regimes during the Cold War in order to discredit these countries for their poor human rights records, drain them of human resources, and facilitate the creation of opposition groups in the diaspora. Conversely, those fleeing gross violations of human rights in allied or friendly countries were often denied admission. Protecting "dissidents" from such countries would jeopardize bilateral relations and call U.S. support for authoritarian regimes into question.

The terrorist attacks of September 11, 2001 raised serious questions about U.S. immigration policy overall. The 9/11 hijackers entered the U.S. on visas, thousands of temporary migrants residing in the U.S. were unaccounted for, and large parts of the northern and southern borders were left unprotected. While none of the hijackers on 9/11 entered the U.S. as refugees or asylees, all aspects of U.S. immigration policies were scrutinized, including humanitarian programs, and with the creation of the Department of Homeland Security (DHS), the former Immigration and Naturalization Service (INS) received a major overhaul. As with all admissions categories, the admission of refugees selected overseas and asylees, who file claims after entry, fell considerably in the immediate aftermath of 9/11.

This chapter investigates U.S. refugee and asylum admissions after 9/11. It asks: are we witnessing a renewed "securitization" of humanitarian migration policies, and are the humanitarian goals of refugee and asylum policies tempered by security concerns stemming from the "war on terror"? Since the 9/11 hijackers, Al-Qaeda, the Taliban, and other major terrorist threats have emanated largely (though not exclusively) from the Islamic world, it makes sense to focus on policies specific to these groups. Therefore, one important hypothesis to consider is that applicants from predominantly Muslim countries face greater scrutiny and suspicion when trying to enter the United States. This chapter will begin to explore this hypothesis after a brief historical and theoretical overview of U.S. refugee and asylum policies.

Refugee and Asylum Policy in the United States

Immediately after the Second World War, the United States saw refugee resettlement as intertwined with the larger project of the reconstruction of Europe. The overarching goal was to relieve the refugee burden on U.S. allies. With thousands displaced after the war, the U.S. Congress passed a series of specific and ad hoc provisions, beginning with the Displaced Persons Act of 1948. This act approved the admission of 400,000 people, many of whom were from Eastern Europe and refused to return to communist regimes. Other refugee admissions provisions included the Refugee Relief Act of 1953 and the Refugee-Escapee Act of 1957, which was passed in response to the Hungarian uprising against Soviet control. The beginning of the Cold War clearly influenced these policies. As Loescher (1993: 59) notes, "Western governments encouraged the flow from East to West in order to weaken their rivals ideologically and to gain political legitimacy in their Cold War struggle."

In the meantime, the United Nations adopted the Convention Relating to the Status of Refugees, which defined the term "refugee" as a person fleeing persecution on the basis of "race, religion, nationality, and membership of a particular social group or political opinion." The convention was rather limited in scope and only applied to people displaced before 1951—the remaining Second World War refugees scattered across Europe. However, the United States chose not to ratify the treaty, preferring instead its own definition of "refugee," which was limited to those escaping communist countries or countries in the Middle East and rejected the broader UN definition. Thus, even official policies had an undeniable geopolitical aim. Escapees from communism were seen as people who were "voting with their feet," thus affirming the virtues of liberal democracy and capitalism over communism.

In another clear instance of immigration policy as foreign policy, the U.S.

actively encouraged the emigration of Cubans after the 1959 socialist revolution. Again, this was to embarrass the Cuban regime, but it also allowed a vibrant exile opposition movement to take root. The U.S. used Cuban exiles to launch the failed Bay of Pigs invasion in 1961 and, later, to broadcast opposition messages through Radio Martí. In a move that is still controversial to this day, in 1966 the U.S. passed legislation granting Cuban refugees permanent resident status if they physically reach U.S. soil. This is sometimes referred to as the "wet foot/dry foot" policy, as those caught at sea may be returned to Cuba, while those who reach shore are permitted to stay. No other country's nationals have such a special privilege in U.S. immigration policy.

The limited U.S. refugee definition remained on the books after the passage of the 1965 Immigration and Nationality Act (INA), which was a watershed moment in U.S. immigration policy as it removed the pernicious national origins quotas that favored European immigration. Then, in 1968, the U.S. ratified the Protocol to the UN Refugee Convention, which bound it to the terms of the 1951 treaty while eliminating its temporal restrictions. This move committed the United States to abide by the broader UN definition of "refugee," although necessary legislation to implement the treaty would not come for over a decade. Debate over U.S. humanitarian admissions policies escalated after the 1975 withdrawal from Vietnam, which prompted one of the largest refugee inflows in U.S. history. Congress demanded a more routine and orderly system for managing refugee and asylum claims.

The 1980 Refugee Act dealt with humanitarian admissions in a comprehensive manner and was a major turning point in U.S. refugee and asylum policy, as it finally removed the "fleeing from communism" qualification of the refugee definition and implemented the UN standard instead. Furthermore, it created a permanent admissions category for refugees selected overseas; the president, with the approval of Congress, would determine the number of refugees to be admitted from various regions in the world. Moreover, an asylum adjudication system, not subject to an annual ceiling, was established for people who presented claims to U.S. immigration officials. Human rights groups and refugee protection agencies praised the reform and hoped that it would end foreign policy bias.

However, during the Reagan administration, a de facto, if not legal, bias in favor of those fleeing leftist and enemy regimes would continue. Refugee admissions favored those from countries such as Vietnam, Cambodia, and Iran, while discrimination against applicants from U.S. allies drew fire from human rights advocates (Mitchell 1992; Zucker and Zucker 1991). For instance, Nicaraguan and Cuban refugees fleeing leftist regimes faced much higher asylum approval rates than those fleeing friendly governments in El Salvador, Guatemala, and Haiti, despite widespread violence and human rights violations in these countries. Since the U.S. provided billions of dollars in foreign aid to these states, admitting asylum seekers—thereby acknowledging persecution—would undermine strategic relations and suggest complicity. Indeed, the U.S. State Department would often issue "advisory opinions" to immigration judges to influence the outcome of specific cases and these opinions were usually followed.

Things began to change in the 1990s, however. The fall of the Berlin Wall and the collapse of the Soviet Union signaled a significant shift in U.S. geostrategic interests. In addition, a 1990 legal settlement explicitly forbade diplomatic considerations from influencing asylum decisions as well as the use of State Department recommendations. Finally, in 1990 the Immigration and Naturalization Service created the Asylum Corps, a team of officers trained in human rights and country conditions, to be responsible for screening claims. These shifts promised to remove the foreign policy lens through which asylum and refugee admissions were viewed (Joppke 1998). While these reforms were in a generally liberal direction, demands for immigration restrictions mounted in Congress by the mid-1990s and affected asylum admissions as well. With record high numbers of asylum applicants and an administrative backlog, measures were put in place to deter and prevent fraudulent claims. Expedited removal procedures without a full hearing before a judge, increased provisions for detaining asylum seekers, and limits on appeals were among the adopted reforms.

Two Dimensions of Refugee and Asylum Policy

This historical overview suggests that a number of factors have influenced humanitarian admissions policies. Broadly, two main dimensions underscore refugee and asylum policy: a normative/humanitarian dimension and an interest-based/strategic dimension (Rosenblum and Salehyan 2004). First, the very existence of humanitarian admissions criteria reflects concern with human rights. Finnemore and Sikkink (1998: 907) argue that human rights norms involving the protection of innocents from bodily harm are especially likely to become salient among the international community. Refugee protection was one of the first international humanitarian regimes, as the League of Nations created an international refugee agency under the leadership of Fridtjof Nansen in 1921. After the Second World War, refugee protection and assistance was one of the first international humanitarian initiatives of the newly formed United Nations and the UN High Commissioner for Refugees. Even as various levels of restriction are in place for labor migration, all liberal democracies have adopted special admissions categories for asylum seekers at their gates, as well as a common refugee definition. Although the U.S. has certainly not had a perfect track record in this regard, it is undeniable that the protection of human rights is a fundamental goal of asylum policy and enforcement procedures.

Yet, refugee policies have also reflected strategic and material interests. Even determining exactly who is a refugee is not free from political biases, as governments frequently attempt to discredit "undesirable" claimants as "bogus" refugees with fraudulent claims (Crisp 1999; Neumayer 2005; Zolberg, Suhrke, and Aguayo 1989). The U.S.'s refugee definition prior to 1980 is one of the clearest instances of political bias. Relations with foreign governments, the prevention of asylum fraud, worries over the use of social services, employment competition, and worries about culturally different foreigners all influence refugee/asylum policies as well as immigration policy more generally. States have a dual responsibility to protect the rights of migrants as well as promote what is broadly perceived as their own national interests, which may lead to conflicting priorities (Gibney 1999). In the U.S., Cold War foreign policy concerns have clearly mattered for asylum admissions. Other interest-based factors have also tempered the primarily humanitarian focus of asylum policy.

In previous research conducted with Marc Rosenblum (Rosenblum and Salehyan 2004), we investigated the determinants of U.S. asylum approval rates. We looked at asylum approval rates by nationality since the passage of the 1980 Refugee Act and investigated how humanitarian concerns and strategic interests have affected asylum enforcement. We also argued that the effect of particular "strategic" variables have changed since the end of the Cold War. We demonstrated quantitatively that poor human rights records and lack of democracy in countries of origin, as we should expect, are positively related to asylum approval rates across time periods. This confirms that the first dimension—humanitarian norms—does indeed shape outcomes.

Yet we also found that during the Cold War, U.S. military aid to origin states, communism, and economic sanctions (an indicator of poor diplomatic relations), also exerted an independent influence on approval rates. After the Cold War, material/strategic interests continued to affect asylum approval rates, but the exact nature of the bias changed. Commercial ties with sending states, as measured by trade volumes, negatively affected approval rates while military and diplomatic relations were no longer significant. In addition, concern with illegal immigration in the 1990s also affected approval rates as applicants from top sources of undocumented migrants were subject to greater scrutiny, even when controlling for human rights records. Therefore, military, diplomatic, and commercial relations with sending countries, as well as preoccupation with illegal immigration, constitute the interest-based dimension of the asylum adjudication process.

September 11 and Refugee and Asylum Policies

The terrorist attacks of September 11 marked a major turning point in how ordinary Americans and the U.S. government view national security. After the fall of the Soviet Union in the 1990s, the U.S. was unmatched in terms of military power and influence; the U.S. was perceived as the clear global hegemon that no state could seriously threaten. September 11 shifted national security discourse away from an (almost) exclusive focus on conventional interstate warfare and toward a "war on terror" in which non-state terrorist threats play a major role in defining the security agenda. The Bush Administration justified actions such as the invasion of Afghanistan and Iraq, the establishment of detention/interrogation centers around the world, the creation of the Department of Homeland Security, and augmented domestic and international surveillance programs as fundamental to combating this new security threat.

The immigration system also came under heightened scrutiny. As the 9/11 hijackers came from Arab Muslim states in the Middle East on visas, serious flaws in U.S. immigration enforcement were discovered and exposed. Thousands of people in the U.S. on temporary visas were unaccounted for, millions of undocumented migrants remained off the books, and the U.S.–Mexico and U.S.–Canada borders were not secure because many thousands of undocumented migrants were able to slip across them. An overburdened and understaffed immigration service had contributed to a backlog of paperwork, which made it difficult to keep track of immigration records and monitor who was in the country; this logjam was no longer simply a bureaucratic nuisance, but a security priority. European politicians have voiced similar concerns over immigration and security, linking immigrants and asylum seekers with terrorism, Islamic militancy, and citizen fears about social stability (Levy 2005).

Many of the reforms to the immigration system in the U.S. were blanket, across-the-board changes. A number of discriminatory policies singled out persons of particular nationalities—particularly in the Arab and Muslim world, however. While the Bush Administration publicly declared that the war on terror was not a "war on Islam," actions suggested that certain categories of persons were to be given greater attention than others. Administration officials rejected the term "racial profiling," but justified their actions as a prudent use of limited resources to screen "high-risk" groups. In one of the most controversial programs, the National Security Exit-Entry Registration System (NSE-ERS), people in the U.S. on temporary visas from a list of predominantly Muslim nations were required to register with federal authorities, and those with even minor immigration infractions were subject to deportation. While some viewed such programs as justifiable, given that Al-Qaeda and similar groups emanate from the Islamic world, others saw this as unfair discrimination against thousands of law-abiding people, and as antagonizing potential allies in the fight to counter Islamic extremism and gather intelligence on terrorism suspects.

How have these developments affected refugee and asylum policies? First, it is important to note that geopolitics and security concerns have long influenced immigration policies (Rudolph 2006). Major source countries for refugee resettlement—for example, Vietnam, Laos, Somalia, and countries of the former USSR—have typically been areas where the U.S. has had military operations or major strategic concerns. As discussed above, asylum adjudications have also been seen through a foreign policy lens.

Importantly, however, the nature of U.S. security interests has changed and non-humanitarian biases in refugee/asylum admissions (if any) may have shifted, or taken on new priorities, in the post-9/11 era. During the Cold War, major security threats came from other states, particularly communist governments. Individuals fleeing these states were greeted with open arms, while those from friendly regimes were denied admission. Since 9/11, *individuals* with ties to terrorist organizations are seen as major security threats, even if their home governments are not; thus, potential migrants from U.S. allies such as Pakistan and Saudi Arabia may be cause for concern. In this new security paradigm, private actors are capable of devastating damage once thought to be reserved for states, particularly if armed with nuclear, biological, or chemical weapons (Allison 2005; Kaldor 1999; Laqueur 2000). Therefore, we may be witnessing a new dimension to refugee and asylum admissions (as with other immigrant categories). Rather than biases for or against certain *countries*, biases may be directed against particular *individuals* given their ethnic or religious background. People from Muslim nations may therefore be subject to greater scrutiny during the migration processes, regardless of the U.S. government's relationship with their home governments.

For example, the 2003 provision "Operation Liberty Shield" required the automatic detention of asylum seekers from certain countries, particularly Muslim nations, for the duration of their asylum proceedings. Human rights groups protested the detention of asylum seekers without parole as adding to the torment of people fleeing torture and persecution, and decried the discriminatory nature of the policy (Human Rights First 2003). Under pressure from non-governmental organizations (NGOs), the program was terminated the same year it was implemented. Although not specific to particular nationalities, other new asylum provisions have included automatic denial for persons providing "material support" for terrorist groups, which may be interpreted broadly to include persons who unknowingly assisted terrorist organizations— for example, through donations to charities—or who were coerced into doing so (Refugee Council USA 2005). Legislation proposed in 2006 would increase the grounds for detaining asylum seekers as well as increase the burden of proof facing asylum applicants.

Asylum and Refugee Trends

What remains to be demonstrated empirically is whether refugee and asylum admissions have indeed changed since 9/11 to reflect these security fears. While it is certainly the case that most refugees and asylum seekers to the U.S. from Muslim countries are neither part of, nor sympathize with, organizations such as Al-Qaeda, it is still possible that such migrants are subject to increased scrutiny and suspicion. Efforts such as "Operation Liberty Shield" suggest that this may be the case, even though this measure was later repealed. New administrative procedures coming from senior officials may have negatively impacted Muslim refugees and asylum seekers and/or lower-level agents may hold biases against people of certain nationalities. In either case, if ethnoreligious "profiling" is occurring, we should see evidence of a systematic bias against Muslim applicants.

First, have refugee resettlement provisions changed since 2001? Table 3.1 shows annual refugee resettlement figures. According to the 1980 Refugee Act, annual ceilings ("authorized admissions") for overseas refugee resettlement are set for five geographic regions: Africa, East Asia, Europe, Latin America/Caribbean, and the Near East/South Asia. Since these are reported in fiscal years (FY), the number for 2001 reflects decisions made in 2000, and so on. For FY 2002, the number of refugees from the Near East/South Asia was set at 15,000; by 2004, this figure had dropped to 3,000, the largest percentage decrease of all regions. Perhaps more informative are actual refugee approvals, which may be considerably lower than the authorized caps. For FY 2002, approvals were cut across the board, falling from over 66,000 in 2001 to over 18,600 in 2002. Between 2002 and 2004, numbers have rebounded for every region except the Near East/South Asia, which has witnessed a consistent decline. Indeed, the 2004 figure for this region was only about a quarter of what it was before.

This may be due in part to political developments in Iraq and Afghanistan, which have decreased resettlement numbers. In 2001, the number of resettled Iraqi refugees was 2,473; in 2004, this number fell dramatically to 66. For the same years, the number of Afghan refugees fell from 2,930 to 959. The U.S. invasion of these countries does not tell the entire story, however, as the other

Table 3.1 Refugee resettlement in the U.S., 1999–2004

	1999	2000	2001	2002	2003	2004
Authorized admissions	91,000	90,000	80,000	70,000	70,000	70,000
Africa	13,000	18,000	21,000	22,000	20,000	30,000
East Asia	10,500	8,000	6,000	4,000	4,000	8,500
Europe	61,000	44,500	37,000	26,000	16,500	13,000
Latin America/ Caribbean	2,250	3,500	3,500	3,000	2,500	3,500
Near East/South Asia	4,250	10,000	12,500	15,000	7,000	3,000
Unallocated reserve	–	6,000	–	–	20,000	12,000
Approvals	85,592	66,546	66,198	18,652	25,329	49,638
Africa	15,581	20,014	18,402	3,419	6,860	17,566
East Asia	6,728	941	277	791	2,026	15,453
Europe	55,666	32,355	32,686	7,621	11,868	8,413
Latin America/ Caribbean	2,796	2,896	2,768	2,534	1,599	5,671
Near East/South Asia	4,725	10,266	12,030	4,247	2,940	2,535
Not reported	96	74	35	40	36	–

Source: United States Office of Immigration Statistics.

Note
Years are fiscal, not calendar years.

major source country in the region, Iran, also witnessed a decline in numbers—from 6,590 in 2001 to 1,787 in 2004—despite generally unchanged
human rights conditions. At the same time, it is difficult to claim an absolute
bias against Muslim refugees as the number one source of refugees overall,
Somalia, is a predominantly Muslim country.[2] Therefore, the evidence for bias
in overseas refugee resettlement is at best inconclusive.

Second, have asylum admissions changed since 9/11? As Figure 3.1 shows,
the absolute number of people entering through the asylum system has been
down across the board since 9/11. Admissions from majority Muslim states[3]
have been declining, but this trend began before 2001; in addition, admissions
from non-Muslim states have also declined since 2001. Which group has
experienced a steeper decline? Between 2001 and 2004, asylum admissions
from non-Muslim countries declined by 43 percent (from 22,462 to 12,793)
while admissions for Muslim countries was 75 percent lower (from 6,170 to
1,534). Yet, these figures alone would be misleading unless one also considers
the number of applications across groups; it may be the case that there have
been fewer applications from Islamic countries. Between 2001 and 2004
the number of asylum applicants from Islamic countries declined 73 percent
(from 9,884 to 2,631), while applications from non-Muslim states declined
53 percent (48,575 to 22,721). Therefore, much of the decrease in admissions
may be attributed to the decline in applications.

This being said, it would also be worth considering the reasons for this
decline in applications. Perhaps Muslim applicants perceive there to be greater
discrimination against them in the adjudication process and/or feel that the
U.S. is less welcoming now than before. Some of the change may also be due
to country-specific factors. The five countries with the largest absolute decline
in applicants are Somalia (−1,630), Indonesia (−1,197), Iran (−897), Sudan
(−572), and Azerbaijan (−451), with Iraq and Afghanistan among the top
ten. Country-specific reasons that individuals are less likely to seek asylum and
refugee admissions include the following: Indonesia has transitioned to a more
open political system; the war in Southern Sudan that sent non-Muslim refugees to the U.S. has recently died down; and Azerbaijan has experienced a
decline in armed conflict. It is difficult to draw firm conclusions about this
decline in applications without a controlled statistical test taking into account
country-level factors.

Another way to consider asylum adjudication is to look at the percentage of
applicants approved. If there has been a shift in thinking since 2001 along the
lines suggested above, then approval *rates* for predominantly Muslim states
should have declined since 2001. Changes in approval rates are perhaps more
directly related to potential biases than admissions and applications because
these may be a function of a number of factors and a few influential cases can
skew the data. Approval rates, because they are measured in percentage terms,
are less sensitive to fluctuations in applications and are more readily comparable. Because of the way immigration data are organized, a full analysis of
a large number of cases is not possible here, although additional research is

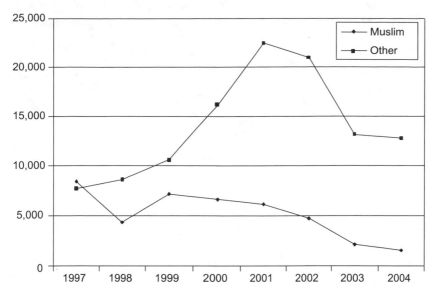

Figure 3.1 Asylum admissions.

warranted. Instead, we can examine a smaller number of cases over time to see if asylum approval figures have experienced a notable change since 2001.

Figure 3.2 illustrates asylum approval rates for Iran and Syria (states with poor relations with the U.S.), as well as Pakistan (a U.S. ally); for comparison, the graph shows the overall asylum approval rate for all nationalities. Asylum approval rates have declined somewhat since 2001, but this phenomenon is not restricted to these Muslim nationalities, as the overall approval rate has also declined. Moreover, approval rates for these nationalities are consistently higher than the overall rate (with the single exception of Syria in 2003). Indeed, several other countries with Muslim majorities—e.g., Bangladesh, Egypt, Somalia, Azerbaijan, and Malaysia—had higher than average asylum approval rates in 2004, owing largely to the poor human rights records in these regimes. These figures do not suggest an anti-Muslim bias, although a thorough statistical analysis is warranted before firm conclusions can be made.

Discussion and Conclusion

The empirical evidence presented above, if not definitive, does not support the anti-Muslim bias hypothesis. At least partly, this lack of discrimination in the refugee/asylum system may be due to liberal norms that have become embedded in the immigration policies of Western states (Hollifield 1992; Jacobson 1996; Joppke 1998). These norms prevent liberal states from discriminating against particular groups on the basis of ethnicity or religion. Albeit preliminary, the evidence presented in this chapter does not suggest

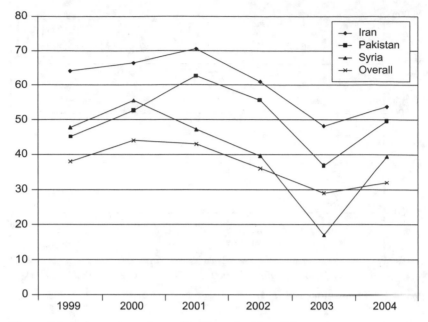

Figure 3.2 Asylum approval rates for selected nationalities.

a clear pattern of discrimination against Muslims in the U.S. refugee/asylum system, although it cannot be said that discrimination never occurs in particular instances. Discriminatory measures such as the NSEERS program and "Operation Liberty Shield" did specifically target individuals from Islamic countries, although this later initiative was quickly repealed.

The liberal thesis only goes so far, as Arab and Muslim rights groups have repeatedly complained of discrimination against them by law enforcement, immigration, and other government officials. One Iranian migrant, after having been detained as part of the NSEERS program, stated in an interview, "How can this democratic system provide this kind of dealing with innocent people? . . . Just making this judgment that every other Middle Eastern man is a terrorist is unbelievable" (Marcucci 2003). Therefore, liberal norms on immigration policy have not become taken for granted, but are instead contested and fragile. It is not inconceivable that more draconian measures, such as the internment of Japanese citizens during the Second World War, would be adopted if future attacks were to occur. Moreover, human rights groups should be concerned about the overall decline in refugee admissions as well as the U.S. failure to respond to the Iraqi refugee crisis following the 2003 invasion, which contrasts with generous admissions after failures in Vietnam and Somalia.

In addition, it seems unlikely that terrorists would attempt—as a first strategy—to enter the United States through the refugee resettlement or asylum systems. High legal and administrative hurdles, in place pre-9/11, would make this entry strategy quite doubtful. People who have been granted refugee status overseas are by no means assured of entering the United States. Of the hundreds of thousands of people who qualify for refugee status in overseas camps, only a small handful is allowed to resettle in the U.S. each year. The asylum adjudication process also seems like an unlikely candidate for potential terrorists. The administrative reforms initiated in 1996 increased provisions for detaining asylum seekers, instituted several levels of screening to determine credibility, and required that the process leave a long paper trail. Provisions are also in place to ensure that asylum seekers are fleeing government *per*secution rather than *pro*secution for legitimate offenses, such as involvement in militant activities. These bureaucratic hurdles, especially relative to other admissions categories, were likely to deter terrorists even before 2001.

This should not be taken to mean that the asylum system is free from abuse by terrorists. Immigration officials should be vigilant to spot suspected terrorists coming through the asylum process, just as with any other immigration admissions category. Ramzi Yousef, who was behind the 1993 World Trade Center bombing, abused the asylum process in order to enter the United States, although he entered prior to the 1996 reforms. Even so, such screening should occur on a case-by-case basis, rather than targeting particular nationalities or members of a certain ethnic or religious group. After all, individuals such as Jose Padilla and Richard Reid do not fit the "typical" terrorist profile. Moreover, doing so would alienate and antagonize the thousands of law-abiding Muslims in the country, as well as people across the wider Islamic world; these are groups that the U.S. should to work with—not against—to combat the global threat of terrorism.

Despite fears that the climate for Muslim immigrants in the U.S. would be unwelcoming after 9/11, a recent article published in the *New York Times* reported that more people from Muslim countries became legal permanent residents in 2005 than in any year in the last two decades (Elliot 2006). Thus, even if they oppose U.S. foreign policies, many Muslims still view the United States as the "land of opportunity" and admire its emphasis on liberty and democracy. A Pakistani woman who recently migrated to the U.S. remarked, "I got freedom in this country. Freedom of everything, freedom of thought" (Elliot 2006). Of all the immigration admissions categories, asylum and refugee admissions, even if imperfect, best exemplify the U.S. traditions of respect for human rights and political freedom.

In the war on terror, the public image of the U.S. and its "soft power" to persuade people with an appeal to values such as human rights and liberty are likely to be as important as hard military power, if not more so (Nye 2004). Protecting refugees and asylum seekers from the Muslim world, particularly when their own governments are not willing or able to do so, sends a powerful message to international audiences and discredits claims from groups such as Al-Qaeda that the West is at war with Islam. Muslim refugees from Bosnia, Somalia, Iran, Iraq, Afghanistan, along with many other nations, who come to the U.S. in search of freedom, demonstrate that democracy and human rights are not incompatible with Islamic traditions and that the protection of people from war and persecution is a common value.

Notes

1 Refugee admissions refer to individuals who are processed and screened overseas before entering the United States. Asylum seekers first enter the United States and then file for refugee protection status. Both categories must meet the same definition of a "refugee," but differ in where their claims are processed. While refugee admissions are subject to an annual ceiling, asylum admissions face no such restrictions.
2 In 2004, over 13,000 Somali refugees were resettled in the U.S., making Somalis the number one source country.
3 These are: Azerbaijan, Bosnia-Herzegovina, Kazakhstan, Kyrgyzstan, Tajikistan, Turkmenistan, Afghanistan, Bahrain, Bangladesh, Indonesia, Iran, Iraq, Jordan, Kuwait, Lebanon, Malaysia, Pakistan, Qatar, Saudi Arabia, Syria, Turkey, UAE, Yemen, Algeria, Egypt, Libya, Morocco, Somalia, Sudan, Tunisia, and Uzbekistan.

References

Allison, Graham. 2005. *Nuclear Terrorism: The Ultimate Preventable Catastrophe.* New York: Owl Books.
Crisp, Jeffrey. 1999. "Who Has Counted the Refugees? UNHCR and the Politics of Numbers." *New Issues in Refugee Research.* Working Paper 12 (June).
Elliot, Andrea. 2006. "More Muslims are Coming to U.S. After a Decline in the Wake of 9/11." *New York Times,* September 10, 2006, Section 1, p. 1.
Finnemore, Martha, and Kathryn Sikkink. 1998. "International Norm Dynamics and Political Change." *International Organization* 52(4): 887–917.
Gibney, Matthew J. 1999. "Liberal Democratic States and Responsibilities to Refugees." *American Political Science Review* 93(1): 169–181.
Hollifield, James. 1992. *Immigrants, Markets, and States: The Political Economy of Postwar Europe.* Cambridge, MA: Harvard University Press.
Human Rights First. 2003. *Asylum Protection News* 15, May 15. http://www.humanrightsfirst.org/asylum/torchlight/newsletter/newslet_15.htm (accessed September 21, 2006).
Jacobson, David. 1996. *Rights Across Borders: Immigration and the Decline of Citizenship.* Baltimore, MD: Johns Hopkins University Press.
Joppke, Christian. 1998. "Asylum and State Sovereignty: A Comparison of the United States, Germany, and Britain," in Christian Joppke, ed., *Challenge to the Nation-State: Immigration in Western Europe and the United States,* pp. 109–152. New York: Oxford University Press.
Kaldor, Mary. 1999. *New and Old Wars: Organized Violence in a Global Era.* Stanford, CA: Stanford University Press.
Laqueur, Walter. 2000. *Fanaticism and the Arms of Mass Destruction.* Oxford: Oxford University Press.
Levy, Carl. 2005. "The European Union After 9/11: The Demise of a Liberal Democratic Asylum Regime?" *Government and Opposition* 40(1): 26–59.

Loescher, Gil. 1993. *Beyond Charity: International Cooperation and the Global Refugee Crisis.* Oxford: Oxford University Press.

Marcucci, Michele. 2003. "Treatment by INS Still Haunts Immigrant." *Oakland Tribune*, headline news, February 24, 2003.

Mitchell, Christopher. 1992. *Western Hemisphere Immigration and United States Foreign Policy.* University Park, PA: Pennsylvania State University Press.

Neumayer, Eric. 2005. "Bogus Refugees? The Determinants of Asylum Migration to Western Europe." *International Studies Quarterly* 59(3): 389–410.

Nye, Joseph. 2004. *Soft Power: The Means to Success in World Politics.* New York: Public Affairs.

Office of the High Commissioner for Human Rights. 1951. United Nations Convention Relating to the Status of Refugees, Article 1. http://www.unhchr.ch/html/menu3/b/o_c_ref.htm (accessed April 9, 2008).

Refugee Council USA. 2005. "Material Support Backgrounder." http://www.refugeecouncilusa.org/finmatsupback10-31-05w.pdf (accessed September 21, 2006).

Rosenblum, Marc, and Idean Salehyan. 2004. "Norms and Interests in US Asylum Enforcement." *Journal of Peace Research* 41(6): 677–697.

Rudolph, Christopher. 2006. *National Security and Immigration: Policy Developments in the United States and Western Europe Since 1945.* Stanford, CA: Stanford University Press.

Teitelbaum, Michael. 1984. "Immigration, Refugees, and Foreign Policy." *International Organization* 38(3): 429–450.

Zolberg, Aristide, Astri Suhrke, and Sergio Aguayo. 1989. *Escape from Violence: Conflict and the Refugee Crisis in the Developing World.* Oxford: Oxford University Press.

Zucker, Norman, and Naomi Flink Zucker. 1996. *Desperate Crossings: Seeking Refuge in America.* Armonk, NY: M. E. Sharpe.

4 Post-9/11 International Graduate Enrollments in the United States
Unintended Consequences of National Security Strategies

Susan K. Brown and Frank D. Bean

Introduction

As Joseph S. Nye (2002: 9) has so cogently noted, a country's "soft" power (or its capacity "to get others to want what it wants" through means other than military force) depends on its culture, especially its educational system and the strength of its science and technology sectors. Science and technology are particularly important because economic growth in knowledge-based societies arguably hinges on technological innovation (Freeman 2005). While the mechanisms by which technology spurs growth are debated (Barro and Sala-i-Martin 2003; Lindert 2004), inventions such as wrought iron, steam power, the generation of electricity, and the internal combustion engine have historically generated major economic expansions (Easterlin 1996; Galbraith 1995, 1997). The invention of the computer and the Internet may ultimately contribute as much as these others to the economy, although not every analyst agrees on this point (Madrick 2002). Regardless, national science and technology policies generally seek to protect and sustain high-technology innovation to foster international economic competitiveness. Such relative economic strength reflects aspects of culture that contribute to the development and maintenance of soft power.

The pursuit of policies that neglect technological innovation invites the possibility of long-term relative reductions in soft power. Economic decline can eventually lead to slippage in national security stemming from societal weakness (Prestowitz 2005). It is thus useful to conceptualize policies—including those that govern the admission of immigrants and temporary non-immigrants who help support a strong, internationally competitive economy—as examples of factors that foster soft rather than hard (or military) power (Nye 2004), and thus as policies that have implications for national security. Obviously, both hard and soft sources of power are needed in the United States if the country is to retain its position as the world's leading superpower. Here, however, we focus on soft kinds of power, and within that category on education and science and technology and on the role that immigrants and non-U.S.-born visitors play in this important soft power arena. In particular, we note the irony that the imposition of "hard" national security measures can erode "soft" power and thus in turn the very security such measures were designed to enhance. In the post-9/11 U.S. case, the implementation of hard post-9/11 visa criteria for the admission of international science and technology students may have undermined, at least in the short term, the country's soft power.

This has arguably contributed to the development of increased opportunities for other countries to enhance their relative technological and educational competitiveness. Although the United States remains globally pre-eminent in technology, Europe and China are benefiting from the spread of new technologies, shifts in the world's population distribution, changes in where scientists and engineers seek graduate training, and relative declines in U.S. support for basic research. The first of these, the global diffusion of technology itself, provides a clear example of the importance of national strategies for graduate education and basic research. The installation of fiber-optic cable around the world in the late 1990s made high-speed, low-cost broadband connectivity available in almost every corner of the world (Friedman 2005) and has leveled the playing field for the development and deployment of science and engineering talent and ideas.

Developing adequate policies and strategies for sustaining technological innovation requires an understanding of the roles a number of factors may play in building such strength. In this chapter, we examine five factors in the case of the United States and make comparisons with Europe, where they are particularly revealing:

1   The United States' open and flexible immigration system, which has allowed talented individuals to come to the country to study and work;
2   A superb higher educational system that has attracted scientific and engineering (S&E) graduate students and postdoctoral scholars;
3   A high priority on basic research, as well as applied research and product development—an emphasis that has supported graduate-student and postdoctoral research programs;
4   A vital and dynamic U.S. high-tech industry that has converted innovation into useful products, thereby creating demand for highly skilled science and engineering workers;
5   A relatively global monopoly, at least until recently, in these factors (especially S&E higher education on the one hand and investment in basic research and high-tech product development on the other).

This chapter assesses the connections among these factors and gauges their relative importance for developing technological strength in highly developed countries. We focus mostly on the U.S. case, sometimes in juxtaposition with data from Europe and China. More specifically, we seek:

1   To highlight the importance of high-skilled migration, both permanent

and temporary, for the vitality of the U.S. economy in general and for the high-technology science and engineering sector in particular;

2   To point out interdependencies between temporary high-skilled migration (involving S&E graduate students and workers on H-1B visas) and high-skilled permanent migration in order to clarify how and why U.S. immigration policy, along with other factors, carries implications for flows of foreign-born science and engineering graduate students;

3   To examine and explain patterns and trends in the application, admission and enrollment of science and engineering graduate students in the United States;

4   To assess research and development spending, in the United States, Europe, and elsewhere, because the degree of such investment strongly affects both innovation and the likelihood that the world's extremely talented students will continue to study and relocate in Western countries.

In the concluding section, we note that the growth of higher education and high-tech employment in Europe and China, developments that increase world competition for top-flight students and workers (Freeman 2005), may be changing the dynamics of high-skilled migration to developed countries, thus generating attendant implications for economic growth and potentially the degree to which such growth supports or undermines national security.

International Migration and the U.S. Workforce

High-skilled international migrants play a prominent role in the U.S. economy. The foreign-born are just as likely as natives to complete college and more likely to hold advanced degrees, especially in the case of immigrants who have come to the country since 1990 (Hansen 1996; Martin and Midgley 2003). The importance of such immigrants for the economy cannot be captured simply by noting that 13.1 percent of the U.S. population was foreign-born in 2003. Instead, focusing on the adult workforce helps to highlight the significance of immigrant labor in the U.S economy. According to the U.S. Bureau of the Census (2003), 14.4 percent of the working adult population is foreign-born; furthermore, 17.2 percent of the young adult worker population (those under the age of 45 and thus most likely to be involved in the newer sectors of the economy) is foreign-born. Even more dramatic, among highly skilled young workers (with Ph.D. degrees and working in science and engineering), the percentage is a whopping 52.0 percent (Freeman 2005). Such figures illustrate the importance of international migrants in general, and of younger, highly skilled workers in science and engineering in particular, for U.S. economic productivity and growth.

Three main flows of foreign-born persons augment the high-skilled workforce in the United States. The first consists of people who enter via the policy provisions of the regular legal immigration system, namely the employment preference categories. The second consists of temporary non-immigrants who enter with H-1B visas, which run for three years, are renewable once, and are designed for those in high-skilled specialty occupations. A third, less direct, augmentation consists of international students. Although they are not initially in the workforce, many of the entrants in this group stay in the country and ultimately contribute to the high-skilled workforce. About one-fourth of these international students are S&E graduate students (National Science Foundation 2004). Also prominent are postdoctoral scholars, many of whom, like the graduate students, stay in the country and thus also contribute to the high-skilled workforce. Even more critically, international S&E graduate students and postdoctoral scholars hold important research positions that are vital to the country's basic research effort. We show below trends in graduate flows and discuss their implications for the nation's workforce and research and development activities.

High-Skilled Legal Immigration

Before 1992, the United States gave considerably more weight to family reunification than to employment as a basis for granting legal immigrant visas. This was evident not only in the numbers of legal permanent resident (LPR) slots granted under these alternative auspices, but also in the fact that four family-preference categories existed for obtaining legal permanent resident admissions but only two employment-preference categories. In the late 1980s, concerns that the U.S. economy needed more high-skilled workers led Congress to pass the 1990 Immigration Act, which President George H. Bush signed in November and which began to affect immigration statistics by fiscal year 1992. This legislation, together with the 1986 Immigration Reform and Control Act (IRCA), constituted the most far-reaching shift in the country's immigration laws since the 1965 amendments to the Immigration and Nationality Act, which abolished national origin quotas as bases for immigrant admission (Bean and Stevens 2003). The main goals of the 1990 legislation were to increase the diversity of the country's immigrants and to allow the entry of greater numbers of skilled workers (Sorensen et al. 1992).

The new employment-based immigration system raised the number of slots available for workers and their families from about 56,000 to 140,000. The law arranged these visas into five categories, which are still in effect. The first consists of priority workers, or persons of extraordinary ability in the sciences and arts. Professionals with advanced degrees are in the second category, and professionals who have a bachelor's degree as well as other skilled and some unskilled workers are in the third category. The fourth consists of special immigrants, such as religious functionaries, and the fifth category consists of investors who will invest at least $1 million, or at least $500,000 in rural or high-unemployment areas. The new law thus opened the door wider to employment-based immigrants and substantially changed the composition of employment-based immigration. Under the first three employment provisions of the new law, more spots were allotted to professionals and skilled workers and fewer to unskilled workers. The latter group, now limited to 10,000, received scarcely half the number it had before 1990 (Fix and Passel 1991).

Figure 4.1 shows the numbers of legal permanent residencies granted to high-skilled workers (principals) in each fiscal year since 1985. The bars depicting the number of visas underrepresent, perhaps substantially, the true volume of high-skilled migration to the United States for at least two reasons. First, the vast majority of U.S. immigrants still enter under the family reunification categories. Many of these immigrants have high levels of education (Sorensen et al. 1992), although these entrants do not show up in statistics about the numbers of high-skilled employment immigrants. Second, the immigration statistics for high-skilled employment LPRs include the spouses and children of principals. However, in order to emphasize principals, Figure 4.1 excludes spouses and children, who have constituted about half of all high-skilled LPRs over the past several years. No doubt many of the spouses also hold advanced degrees and are themselves employed.

By showing the overall numbers of high-skilled immigrants (those in the first three categories) in particular fiscal years, not the numbers of such persons newly admitted to the country in those years, Figure 4.1 also misrepresents when the immigrants first came to the country. In fact, well over 80 percent of each of the fiscal year totals consists of persons who had adjusted their statuses. In 2004, for example, 87.5 percent of the principals in the first three employment preference categories and their spouses were "adjusters" rather than

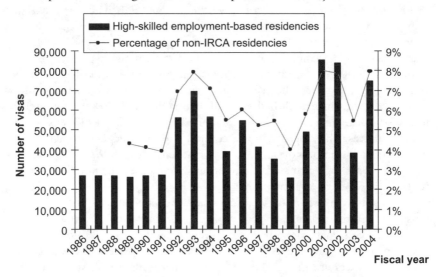

Figure 4.1 U.S. high-skilled employment-based residencies, number by year and as a percentage of non-IRCA residencies. (Number gives estimate of principals alone.)

Source: Immigrants admitted by type and selected class of admission: fiscal years 1986–2004. Office of Immigration Statistics; Table 4 of *Yearbook of Immigration Statistics: 2004* http://www.dhs.gov/xlibrary/assets/statistics/yearbook/2004/table4.xls (accessed June 19, 2008).

"new arrivals" (U.S. Citizenship and Immigration Services 2005). Most of these were changes from student or H-1B temporary worker visas (or even sometimes from unauthorized status, which itself often results from overstaying either a student or H-1B visa). Thus, the figures for the most part involve high-skilled people who had already been in the country under student or H-1B visas. This is one of the chief reasons it is important to examine trends in all three of these kinds of admissions taken together.

Student or H-1B visas are thus perhaps the chief pathways by which high-skilled foreign-born persons enter the U.S. immigration system and ultimately gain legal permanent residency (Usdansky and Espenshade 2001). The possibility of obtaining legal permanent residency status on the basis of education and skills provides an incentive for foreign-born persons to come to the United States as graduate students and H-1B workers, illustrating what is often an interdependency between temporary and permanent forms of entry to the country. What many observers may not realize, however, is that a ceiling on permanent high-skilled slots creates a squeeze whenever greater numbers of temporary entrants seek permanent status than the ceiling can accommodate. Such squeezes are almost inevitable, because in recent years Congress has been far more likely to increase temporary slots than to raise the ceiling on permanent slots (Lowell 2001).

The large increase in the numbers of high-skilled, employment-based legal permanent residents after the 1990 Immigration Act is evident in the yearly totals in Figure 4.1, although levels jump around somewhat from year to year, partly because lag times in the processing of applications vary from year to year. In any event, by the 2000s, about twice as many high-skilled principals were receiving employment-sponsored legal status each year, a figure that constituted about 8 percent of the total number of legal immigrants coming to the country outside the special legalization provisions of the 1986 Immigration Reform and Control Act (IRCA).[1] If we compare only principals, the percentage of high-skilled employment-based principals would be even higher, about 16.0 percent. In addition, if the data were available to include in the category of high-skilled principals those family-based principals with high levels of education who are also employed, the percentage of principals with high levels of education would be greater still, perhaps reaching 20–25 percent.

The relatively high levels of high-skilled immigration during the early 2000s after the economic boom of the late 1990s reveal the sometimes problematic feature of the cap on employment-based permanent immigration (the slight fluctuations in the numbers in Figure 4.1 after 2000 may be more a reflection of application processing variations than of changes in either the demand for such workers or the demand for such visas among potential immigrants). The high levels thus mean that demand in those years probably continues to outstrip supply (Lowell 2001), even in a relatively stagnant economy (except perhaps in 2003, which may represent a delayed manifestation of the dampening effects of 9/11 on interest in adjusting to legal permanent resident status). But because, under current law, the number of employment-based legal permanent residents cannot change, and because many high-skilled employment immigrants have previously held either student or H-1B visas, the latter especially are growing enormously (as we show below). For these reasons, the demand for high-skilled employment-based legal status appears recently to have been outrunning supply. The important point here is to note that this may be troublesome in the near future, especially if the business cycle swings upward.

Temporary High-Skilled Migrants

Because many employment-sponsored slots are granted to persons who have previously held H-1B temporary visas, it is instructive to examine trends in the numbers of such visas granted. The 1990 Immigration Act defined skills for the first time on the basis of education (Usdansky and Espenshade 2001: 34–37). In addition to increasing the number of employment-based slots substantially (allowing them to almost triple to 140,000 by 1992), and raising the number of employment-based preference categories from two to five, the law introduced a special category of high skilled-temporary worker through its adoption of the H-1B visa for non-immigrants. The number of such visas was set at 65,000 annually. H-1B workers were to be paid the prevailing wage for their job and were permitted to stay three years (renewable for another three years). In addition, no cap was set for their spouses and minor children, unlike in the case of regular employment-based visas (Usdansky and Espenshade 2001). For example, for H-1B visas, the 65,000 ceiling applies to principals, but by the time spouses and children are included, this generates many more than 65,000 entrants. By contrast, the 140,000 ceiling for permanent employment residencies, which includes principals as well as their spouses and children, generates only about 70,000 principals annually. A new development (as of May 2005) is that 20,000 more H-1B visas will be issued to foreign students who have completed a graduate program in an American university (these visas will not be included in the 65,000 visa cap).

The impetus for the 1990 legislative changes was a growing concern during the late 1980s about looming shortages of high-skill and specialty workers—fears that were fueled by think-tank and government studies like the Hudson Institute's "Workforce 2000" report and the 1990 report of the Council of Economic Advisors predicting that high-skilled labor squeezes were likely soon to develop (U.S. Congress 1991). In 1997, for the first time, the 65,000 ceiling on H-1B visas set in 1990 proved insufficient to meet demand. Up until then the number of such visas had not been an issue, but after that point there were pressures to increase the ceiling. In response, Congress in 1998 raised the number to 115,000 visas for 1999 and 2000. In fiscal year 1999–2000, however, the new supply of H-1B visas still ran out by June, with the result that in October of 2000 Congress rushed to extend the limit to 195,000 for an additional three-year period.

The strong growth in the number of H-1B admissions began in the mid-1990s, rising from about 100,000 in 1994 to about 400,000 in 2004 (U.S. Department of Homeland Security 2007). Interestingly, its initial trend was counter-cyclical with that of high-skilled employment-sponsored immigrants; that is, as the number of H-1B admissions went up during the late 1990s, the number of high-skilled employment immigrants went down, reflecting a substitution of temporary workers for legal permanent resident workers in the early stages of the H-1B expansion (Lowell 2001). However, by the early 2000s, the rising levels of temporary H-1B workers undoubtedly were creating greater demand for legal permanent resident status as H-1B recipients confronted the expiration dates of their three-year stays. This trend is likely only to grow. Time and time again, in place after place around the world, temporary migration programs have begotten permanent migration (Cornelius, Martin, and Tsuda 2003). It is thus no shock that the same pattern seems to be emerging with high-skilled migration to the United States. Current limits on high-skilled permanent immigration may now be too low to meet the needs of the economy. (The numbers declined in 2005, when the temporary increase expired.) If so, it would not be at all surprising to see growing unauthorized migration of the highly skilled in the next few years.

Graduate-Student Enrollments in Science and Engineering

Given the importance of science and technology in the global economy and the importance of international migration among the highly skilled, trends in international enrollment of science and engineering (S&E) students are of particular interest, especially since graduates who remain in the United States to work comprise a major source of high-skilled foreign-born workers. Enrollment trends are also important because the entry requirements for foreign-born students were tightened after 9/11; the greater subsequent difficulty in obtaining visas probably lowered such enrollments. We seek here to address a number of important questions about these trends. First, to what extent does the available evidence indicate a recent decline in the enrollment of science and engineering graduate students in the country? Second, to what extent does any observed decline result from the inability of science and engineering students to acquire appropriate visas because security requirements were tightened in the wake of 9/11? Third, to what extent does any observed decline derive from factors other than difficulties in obtaining visas? Fourth, what can we learn about possible trade-offs between "hard" and "soft" strategies of protecting national security from these trends?

It is important to emphasize the difficulty of definitively answering these questions based on evidence obtained from analytical studies because of limited data. For example, information collected on the visa status of graduate students (even in some very rough sense) did not distinguish first-time from continuing students until 2001, meaning that only a very short time series of information about first-time enrollments is now available, even though this information is crucial for discerning the influence of current conditions on enrollment trends. Moreover, some of the relevant data have only slowly become available. Despite such limitations, it is nonetheless possible to discern important clues, both from the patterns involved in the trends and from the results of other research studies, about the forces driving recent graduate student enrollment trends. This helps to answer the above four questions, at least in a preliminary way. We address each of the four below, after first describing the changes in graduate student enrollments over the past decade or so.

Changes in International Graduate Student Enrollments

The numbers of foreign-born students in the United States began to increase after the Second World War. By 1954, 34,232 (or 1.4 percent) of higher education enrollments were international students on temporary visas. This, of course, is a conservative estimate of foreign-born students because immigrants who had become legal permanent residents would not be counted as international students. In short, the percentage of foreign-born enrollments was undoubtedly even higher than this figure indicates. By 2002, international enrollments had grown to 613,221 (or 4.1 percent) of the total, a conservative figure given that by the early 2000s about 18,000 students each year were converting their status from that of student visa to legal permanent resident (U.S. Citizenship and Immigration Services 2005). Since 1970, Europe and other OECD countries, as well as many less developed countries, particularly China, have been closing the graduate education gap with the United States. Several European countries (Netherlands, Norway, Finland, United Kingdom, and France) surpassed the United States in the proportion of degrees granted per 24-year-old (National Science Foundation 2004; OECD 2004). Moreover, higher fractions of students in many European countries and China enrolled in science and engineering than in the United States (Freeman 2005).

While many international undergraduate students may eventually change their status and stay in the United States, it is graduate students, especially those in science and engineering, that are immediately and more directly involved in U.S. research and development endeavors through their participation in university research projects. Figures 4.2 and 4.3 show the trends since 1993 and 2000, respectively, in both total and first-year graduate student enrollments in the United States for two categories of students—citizens and permanent residents on the one hand and temporary residents on the other. As of this writing, 2005 is the last year for which we have data broken down by citizenship, temporary visa status, first-time enrollment, and gender. For that year, nearly 140,000 graduate students were in the country on temporary visas (an apparently unknown number of permanent residents and naturalized citizens were also here, but these two different kinds of students cannot be

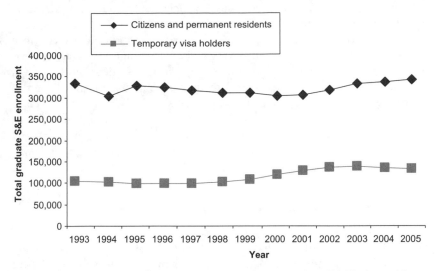

Figure 4.2 Graduate enrollment in science and engineering (S&E), by residency and visa status, 1993–2005.

Source: National Science Foundation, Division of Science Resources Statistics, Survey of Graduate Students and Postdoctorates in Science and Engineering, 2005.

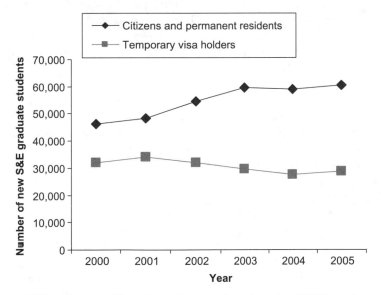

Figure 4.3 Enrollment of first-time science and engineering (S&E) graduate students, by residency and visa status, 2000–05.

Source: National Science Foundation, Division of Science Resources Statistics, Survey of Graduate Students and Postdoctorates in Science and Engineering, 2005.

examined separately because the National Science Foundation's statistical reports lump these together with native citizens).

Foreign-born graduate S&E enrollment has risen by about 50 percent since 1996 but has leveled off; foreign-born science and engineering graduate students now make up almost a quarter of all foreign-born student enrollments in the United States (including undergraduate enrollments), and nearly half of all science and engineering graduate enrollments. This rise has also been characteristic of both men and women. As many observers have noted, international graduate enrollments have become an ever larger and more integral part of the nation's research and development (R&D) programs (Freeman 2005; National Research Council 2005).

Have There Been Declines since 9/11 because of Changed Visa Review Procedures?

Since 2000, the National Science Foundation (NSF) has also been reporting information on first-time enrollments of foreign graduate students. These first-time data are more sensitive to the influence of contemporaneous events like 9/11 than total enrollments, since students already enrolled in long-term programs would be less affected by such occurrences or the policy shifts they spawn. Figure 4.3 shows the first-time S&E enrollments for both permanent and temporary students. The results reveal three important patterns. First, the very narrow gap in 2000 between temporary (foreign-born) and permanent/ citizen (mostly native-born) first-time graduate student enrollments suggests that by the end of the 1990s foreign-born graduate students constituted an even larger fraction of the total number of science and engineering enrollments (about 40 percent) than previously, demonstrating how rapidly the foreign-born have become a larger share and more integral part of S&E enrollments and R&D in the country.

Second, and most important, the results show enrollments declined after 2001 for first-time foreign-born graduate S&E students, with a drop of 6,565 students, or a decline of 19.2 percent, by 2004 before rebounding by 1,100 students in 2005. Third, and significantly, this decrease does not represent a broader, more general pattern since it does not characterize permanent resident/citizen (mostly native-born) first-time enrollees. In other words, the decline shows up only among foreign-born first-time enrollees, suggesting a significant negative impact from the more arduous and often intimidating visa screening after 9/11. The National Research Council (2005) recently reached this conclusion as a result of a thorough investigation of graduate enrollment trends.

Annual percentage changes in science and engineering applications, admissions, and enrollments reported by the Council of Graduate Schools (CGS) show overall international graduate student applications down nearly 30 percent from 2003–4, and those for S&E international graduate students down over 35 percent for the same years (Figure 4.4) (Brown and Doulis 2005;

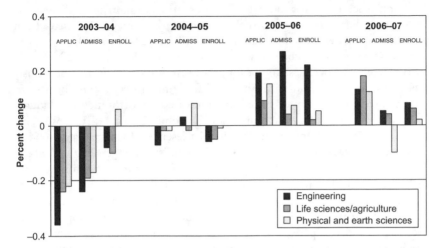

Figure 4.4 Changes in applications, admissions, and enrollment of new international graduate students in science and engineering, 2003–07.

Source: Council of Graduate Schools.

Brown and Syverson 2004). Smaller declines occurred in admissions and enrollments. Applications for 2005, however, declined only slightly, and overall admissions and enrollments were up slightly from the previous year. Applications, enrollments, and admissions bounced back in 2006 and generally continued to rise in 2007. Even so, the collective number of international graduate applications were 19 percent lower in 2006 than in 2003 (Redd 2007a, 2007b).

Because most students apply to and may be admitted by more than one school, and because the least committed students may be the ones most discouraged from applying, the greater decreases in applications and admissions do not necessarily represent proportionate decreases in yield, or enrollments, as the figures in fact make clear. The National Research Council (2005) study also concluded that no clear evidence had emerged by that time indicating a decrease in the quality of international S&E graduate students enrolling after 9/11. As far as overall S&E graduate student enrollments were concerned, however, a decline clearly occurred post-9/11, and changes in visa review procedures seemed definitely to have been responsible for a substantial portion of the drop, at least in the first two years after 2001. Moreover, by 2006 the decrease had not yet bounced back to pre-9/11 levels, despite the substantial reduction in the time required to process visa applications and the lengthening of the student visa period from one to four years.

Are Other Factors also Contributing to the Decline?

Other factors thus may have contributed to the continuing deceleration of foreign S&E graduate enrollments, even after the substantial improvements that took place in processing visas for international graduate students. The CGS data in Figure 4.4 suggest such additional forces may indeed have been at work. A small decline in applications occured from 2004 to 2005, even after the new visa processing changes were implemented. Moreover, the NSF data reveal enrollment declines among foreign-born women, who had previously been moving upward in their share of first-time foreign enrollments. In addition, widespread reports of recently increased opportunities for graduate S&E education in Britain, the European Economic Union (EEU), Australia, India, and China suggest a greater global presence of alternatives for S&E graduate study than used to be the case (Economist Intelligence Unit 2004).

Analysts have also noted the rise in international opportunities for graduate S&E education outside the United States (especially in Europe and China) started before 9/11 and has grown steadily since then (Brown and Doulis 2005). What may be new, however, is the attractiveness of these opportunities after the negative experiences many visa applicants underwent after 9/11. These may have led to the development of negative perceptions about the United States, with this in turn contributing to a boost in the demand among prospective foreign-born S&E graduate students for the pursuit of graduate studies in locales other than the United States. In short, just as other countries started to strengthen their supply of graduate S&E educational opportunities, their attractiveness may have received an unanticipated boost from the new security practices by the United States, perhaps influenced additionally by other aspects of U.S. foreign policy that have been unpopular abroad. While at the moment we lack definitive evidence over the past two or three years that foreign-born S&E graduate students are opting in large numbers not to come to the United States, this possibility must be given serious consideration.

The influence of changes in demography and other circumstances, like the strength of the S&E job market, the nature of S&E working conditions, and the relative availability of attractive alternatives (i.e., jobs that pay well and offer good working conditions), also influence native graduate student enrollments (Bean and Brown 2005). This is particularly true among native males, whose labor supply appears more sensitive to U.S. labor market conditions than that of international males. Freeman (2005) has convincingly shown that, during the 1990s, pay levels in S&E deteriorated even as training requirements (length of graduate study and/or postdoctoral apprenticeship) became more onerous. The U.S. research and development community has been able to cope with this handicap by relying even more heavily on foreign-born S&E talent than before. In other words, native graduate enrollments seem likely to have declined not because research projects were competitively substituting foreign-born talent for native-born talent, but because a significant portion of the native-born talent pool pursued more attractive alternative careers. In fact, one study by the NSF shows that growth in enrollment of international graduate students in S&E actually stimulates rather than discourages the enrollment of U.S.-born whites and underrepresented minorities (Regets 2007).

What Are the Trade-Offs?

The U.S. trends in S&E graduate enrollments examined above suggest a notable irony: given the strong likelihood that their decline began before 9/11 and strengthened after 9/11 owing to factors related to increased international competition for high-skilled talent, a growth in competitiveness that comes mostly from Europe and China, a strong possibility exists that U.S. efforts to increase "hard" security after 9/11 (i.e., to prevent the entry of potential terrorists) may have weakened "soft" security (i.e., the potential vitality of the scientific and technological innovation that undergirds the robustness of the U.S. economy). A further irony is that this potential deterioration in "soft" security might have gone unnoticed had it not been for the immediate and severe decline in graduate S&E enrollments after 9/11, after which the need to change the procedure for screening visas became quickly obvious. Thus, 9/11 occasioned a scrutiny of enrollment trends that showed yet other factors contributing to decreases in foreign enrollments.

Investment in Research and Development

Because most of the nation's basic research is conducted in universities, and because international graduate students and postdoctoral scholars constitute such a large part of science and engineering graduate enrollments and research, international students are vital to this country's research and development efforts (Fossum et al. 2004). The United States competes with other countries for top-flight talent to work on this research, and within the United States S&E fields compete with other industries and occupations for the best students. Success in attracting both foreign and native-born talent clearly depends both on the numbers of research assistant and postdoctoral positions available and on the pay scales associated with such study and work. At least since the Second World War, the United States has enjoyed a preeminent position in the world with respect to the total volume of spending on research and development. As Figure 4.5 reveals, the U.S. far outspends all other countries in terms of total gross expenditures on R&D. In 2002, the second largest expenditure (in purchasing power parity dollars) was Japan at slightly more than $100 billion, which was only about 40 percent of the U.S. total (UNESCO 2004).

Clearly, U.S. expenditure on R&D is related to the enormous size of its economy. However, when examined in relative terms, the United States does not fare so well. As Figure 4.6 reveals, when R&D investment is expressed as a percentage of gross domestic product (GDP), the United States ranks no better than seventh in the world in the priority devoted to investment in research and development. Moreover, the trend in relative investment in R&D in the United States has turned downward since 2001, dropping 8.1 percent (UNESCO 2004). The increased emphasis given to R&D by other countries is clearly discernible in the data in Figure 4.7, which show increases in such

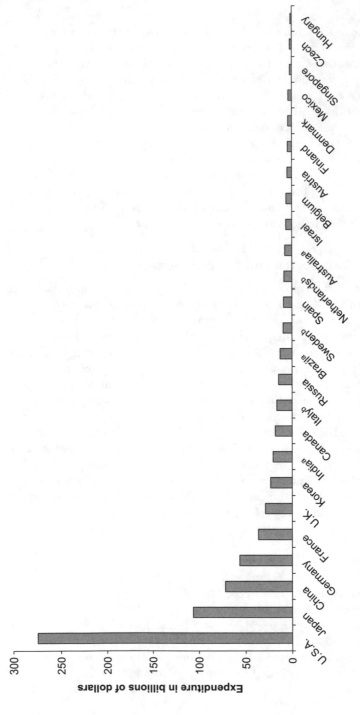

Figure 4.5 Total gross expenditure on R&D, in purchasing power parity, 2002 US$.

Source: UNESCO Institute for Statistics.

Notes
a Data from 2000.
b Data from 2001.

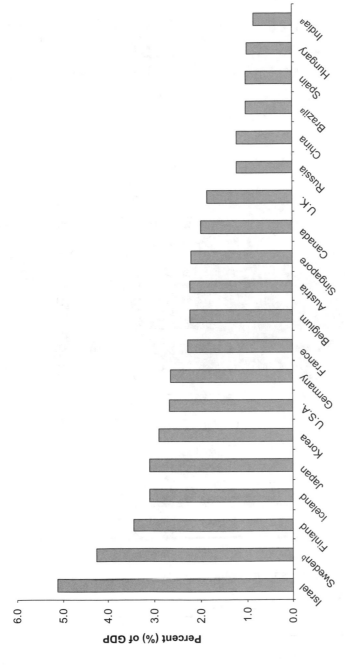

Figure 4.6 Percentage of GDP spent on R&D in 2002 for selected countries.

Source: UNESCO Institute for Statistics.

Notes
a Latest available data from 2000.
b Latest available data from 2001.

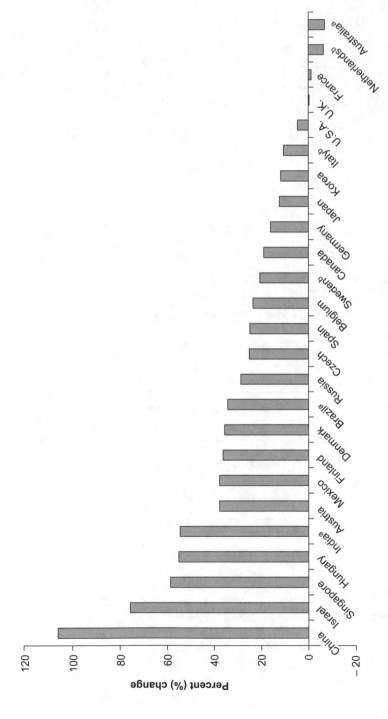

Figure 4.7 Change from 1996 to 2002 in percentage of GDP spent on R&D for selected countries.

Source: UNESCO Institute for Statistics.

Notes
a Data from 2000.
b Data from 2001.

relative investment since 1996. The United States has scarcely changed at all during this period, and has actually declined since 2001, with the result that the American share of global R&D investment has fallen from 39.6 to 36.4 percent since the mid-1990s (UNESCO 2004).

Moreover, the effects of the decline in relative R&D spending in the United States are likely even more dramatic than the statistics suggest, for two reasons. First, long-term trends in R&D investment are down in particular for government spending as opposed to industry spending (Auyang 2004). This matters because the government is much more likely than industry to support spending on basic research, the kind of investment that appears to have constituted the main wellspring of innovation in the American economy for the last 60 years (Economist Intelligence Unit 2004; Fossum et al. 2004; Freeman 2005). Industry spending is much more likely to target applied problems, or find new ways to better convert innovation into viable products, rather than innovation per se (President's Council of Advisors on Science and Technology 2002). The relative decline in basic research spending is thus even more severe than the numbers on both research and development taken together indicate. Second, the overall relative stagnation in R&D in general, and the decline in government basic research spending in particular, would have been far worse except for major increases in life science research spending over the past ten years. Specifically, the research budgets of the National Institutes of Health approximately doubled from 1995–2004 in constant dollars (Brainard and Field 2005; Freeman 2005), a rise that serves to mask the declines and stagnation in other kinds of government basic research investment (Auyang 2004).

The past ten years or so have thus witnessed a significant relative drop in almost all categories of U.S. investment in basic research. This decline ranges from basic defense-related spending under the auspices of the Defense Advanced Research Project Agency (DARPA) to physical science, computer science and engineering basic research spending under the auspices of the NSF (Fossum et al. 2004; Kling 2005; Markoff 2005). To be sure, the research budgets of the United States are still higher than those of other countries in terms of the absolute levels of dollars, but the relative priority the country has given to research and development over the past several years, and within that category to basic research in particular, is noticeably less than it was in the not-too-distant past.

Does investment in R&D make a difference to the economy? As Richard B. Freeman (2005: 1), the distinguished Harvard labor economist, states:

> Leadership in science and technology gives the US its comparative advantage in the global economy. US exports are disproportionately from sectors that rely extensively on scientific and engineering workers and that embody the newest technologies. In 2003, with a massive national trade deficit, the smallest deficit relative to output was in high technology industries . . . In a knowledge-based economy, leadership in science and technology contributes substantially to economic success.

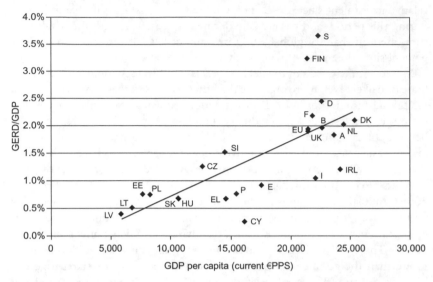

Figure 4.8 European Gross Domestic Expenditure on Research and Development (GERD) as a percentage of GDP against GDP per capita, in Euros, 1999.

Source: Commission of the European Communities (2003).

The relationship between science and technology leadership and economic dynamism is reflected in the positive association between per capita gross domestic product and the relative investment in research and development. Figure 4.8 shows this association for the countries of the European Economic Union. Some may think there is ambiguity about the direction of causality in this relation—whether it is rich countries that can afford to invest in R&D, or whether it is relatively high R&D countries that become rich. But even if it were the case that only rich countries could afford R&D, and not the other way around, this would beg the question of what helps countries become rich in the first place and what now sustains high economic growth in increasingly global and ever more knowledge-based economies. Recent studies indicate that investment in basic research enhances economic growth through innovations that contribute to increased productivity (Branstetter and Ogura 2005; Kortum 1997; Kortum and Lerner 2000; President's Council of Advisors on Science and Technology 2004).

Conclusions

This chapter has examined declines in the U.S. enrollment of science and engineering graduate students and postdoctoral scholars since 9/11. Such enrollments take place in the United States in the context of relatively low ceilings on the annual numbers of legal high-skilled employment visas available. However, reductions over the past three years in first-time graduate student enrollees do not appear to result from such low ceilings but rather from changes in visa application procedures and time delays involved in post-9/11 security checks. But the fact that such enrollments have been slow to bounce back to their earlier levels, even though major visa processing improvements have been made, suggests that the recent enrollment declines do not derive from 9/11 problems alone (although some portion of such decreases undoubtedly does). Rather, a large part seems to have stemmed from recent increases in opportunities in Europe and elsewhere for graduate science and engineering study and employment, as well as from the United States becoming relatively less attractive as a destination for science and engineering study. Ironically, the changes behind such developments have occurred at about the same time as, or perhaps even a bit before, 9/11, meaning that the data emerging in the aftermath of 2001 may have obscured some of the other reasons for the drop in foreign student involvement in the U.S. R&D sector.

Unless decreases in U.S. graduate international S&E enrollment prove short-lived, they will carry important implications for the country's research and development programs and thus the country's soft power and national security. Some observers may notice an up-tick in native enrollments the past few years and think that this native upswing after 9/11 may continue, thus helping substantially to resolve any current and future shortages. Such a conclusion would be premature at best, because changes in native enrollments may be primarily the result of a demographic fluctuation that has generated growth in the size of native cohorts of 20- to 24-year-olds (Bean and Brown 2006). However, this rise in the pool of native persons from whom S&E enrollments are drawn is temporary. When the children of baby boomers pass the age of graduate school, these increases in the enrollment of natives will probably turn around, unless women and minorities enter science and engineering in far greater numbers than they ever have before.

The recent drops in international enrollments, then, together with what are likely to be further declines in native enrollments, may constitute a potential threat to future U.S. economic growth. Ironically, these declines also appear to be exacerbated by decreases in relative U.S. spending on basic research. The United States faces the challenge, particularly in a difficult fiscal environment, of avoiding negative spirals by which declines in basic research spending beget declines in international graduate S&E enrollments, which in turn beget further declines in the country's basic research infrastructure, which in turn may undermine economic growth and thus one of the country's most important sources of soft power. Declines in soft power may be just as likely to reduce national security as reductions in hard power.

Drawn to the United States by its strength in innovation and technology, foreign graduate students and workers have played a vital role in the U.S. economy and its maintenance of soft power. But this attractiveness may now be diminished because more alternatives for graduate S&E study and R&D employment are available in Europe and China. Moreover, negative experiences with visa applications and unpopular U.S. foreign policies have tarnished the image of the United States. At the same time, science and engineering graduates in this country continue to receive relatively poor pay and to work under unappealing conditions. A very real possibility is not merely that talented natives may continue to forge careers outside science and engineering, but also that talented foreigners in increasing numbers will continue to be drawn to Europe and China for S&E education and R&D employment. If the United States attends mostly to, and spends disproportionately on, hard national security strategies and gives them higher priority than maintaining strength in the conditions that constitute important bases of soft security, science and engineering capabilities and technological leadership may shift to Europe and China at even more rapid rates than now appear to be the case.

Note

1 IRCA included provisions allowing unauthorized migrants to legalize (that is, to become legal permanent residents) one year after obtaining temporary legal status. IRCA-based applicants for legal immigrant visas began entering the U.S. immigration system in substantial numbers starting in 1989, and their flow tapered off after 1992. We exclude IRCA immigrant LPRs because they came about through entirely different mechanisms than other immigrant LPRs.

References

Auyang, Sunny. 2004. *Engineering—An Endless Frontier.* Cambridge, MA: Harvard University Press. Online supplement at http://www.creatingtechnology.org/R&D.htm.

Barro, Robert J., and Xavier Sala-i-Martin. 2003. *Economic Growth.* Cambridge: MIT Press.

Bean, Frank D., and Susan K. Brown. 2005. "A Canary in the Mineshaft? International Graduate Enrollments in Science and Engineering in the United States." Paper presented at the Forum on the Impact of Foreign Graduate Student Enrollment on the Economy, Universities, and Security. The Beckman Center of the National Academy of Sciences, University of California, Irvine. October 16–17.

Bean, Frank D., and Gillian Stevens. 2003. *America's Newcomers and the Dynamics of Diversity.* New York: Russell Sage Foundation.

Brainard, Jeffrey, and Kelly Field. 2005. "For Science Programs, Bush Budget Proposes Mostly Cuts." *Chronicle of Higher Education*, February 18, A25.

Branstetter, Lee, and Yoshiaki Ogura. 2005. "Is Academic Science Driving a Surge in Industrial Innovation? Evidence from Patent Citations." Working Paper 11561. Cambridge, MA: National Bureau of Economic Research. http://www.nber.org/papers/w11561.

Brown, Heath A., and Maria Doulis. 2005. "Findings from 2005 CGS International Graduate Admissions Survey I." *Council of Graduate Schools.* Washington, DC.

Brown, Heath A, and Peter D. Syverson. 2004. "Findings from U.S. Graduate Schools on International Graduate Student Admissions Trends." Washington, DC: Council of Graduate Schools.

Commission of the European Communities. 2003. "Investing in Research: An Action Plan for Europe." Working Paper, Brussels. http://europa.eu.int/comm/research/era/3pct/index_en.html.

Cornelius, Wayne A., Philip L. Martin, and Takeyuki Tsuda. 2003. *Controlling Immigration: A Global Perspective.* Stanford, CA: Stanford University Press.

Easterlin, Richard A. 1996. *Growth Triumphant: The Twenty-First Century in Historical Perspective.* Ann Arbor: University of Michigan Press.

Economist Intelligence Unit. 2004. "Scattering the Seeds of Invention: The Globalisation of Research and Development." Special Report, *The Economist,* London, New York, Hong Kong.

Fix, Michael, and Jeffrey S. Passel. 1991. "The Door Remains Open: Recent Immigration to the United States and a Preliminary Analysis of the Immigration Act of 1990." *Urban Institute Working Paper* PRIP-UI-14. Center for Research on Immigration Policy, Washington, DC: The Urban Institute.

Fossum, Donna, Lawrence S. Painter, Elisa Eiseman, Emile Ettedgui, and David M. Adamson. 2004. *Vital Assets: Federal Investment in Research and Development at the Nation's Universities and Colleges.* Santa Monica: The RAND Corporation.

Freeman, Richard B. 2005. "Does Globalization of the Scientific/Engineering Workforce Threaten U.S. Economic Leadership?" Working Paper 11457. Cambridge, MA: National Bureau of Economic Research. http://www.nber.org/papers/w11457.

Friedman, Thomas L. 2005. *The World is Flat: A Brief History of the Twenty-First Century.* New York: Farrar, Straus and Giroux.

Galbraith, John Kenneth. 1995. *A Journey through Economic Time.* Boston: Houghton Mifflin Company.

Galbraith, John Kenneth. 1997. *The Great Crash 1929.* New York: Mifflin.

Hansen, Kristin A. 1996. "Profile of the Foreign-Born Population in 1995: What the CPS Nativity Data Tell Us." Paper presented at the Annual Meeting of the Population Association of America, New Orleans, May 6–8, 1996.

Kling, Jim. 2005. "DARPA and the Decline of U.S. Computer Science Research." *Science,* June 24.

Kortum, Samuel. 1997. "Research, Patenting, and Technological Change." *Econometrica* 65: 1389–1419.

Kortum, Samuel, and Joshua Lerner. 2000. "Assessing the Contribution of Venture Capital to Innovation." *Rand Journal of Economics* 31: 674–692.

Lowell, B. Lindsay. 2001. "The Foreign Temporary Workforce and Shortages in Information Technology," in Wayne A. Cornelius, Thomas J. Espenshade, and Idean Salehyan, eds., *The International Migration of the Highly Skilled: Demand, Supply, and Development Consequences in Sending and Receiving Countries,* pp. 131–160. La Jolla, CA: UC-San Diego Center for Comparative Immigration Studies.

Madrick, Jeffrey. 2002. *Why Economies Grow: The Forces That Shape Prosperity and How We Can Get Them Working Again.* New York: Basic Books.

Markoff, John. 2005. "Pentagon Redirects Its Research Dollars." *New York Times,* April 2, C1.

Martin, Philip, and Elizabeth Midgley. 2003. "Immigration: Shaping and Reshaping America." *Population Bulletin* 58(2): 1–40.

National Research Council. 2005. *Policy Implications of International Graduate Students and Postdoctoral Scholars in the United States.* Washington, DC: The National Academies Press. http://www.nap.edu/catalog/11289.html.

National Science Foundation. 2004. *Science and Engineering Indicators.* NSB 04–01. Arlington, VA: Division of Science Resources Statistics, National Science Foundation.

National Science Foundation. 2006. *Graduate Students and Postdoctorates in Science and Engineering: Fall 2004.* NSF 06–325. Arlington, VA: Division of Science Resources Statistics, National Science Foundation.

Nye, Joseph. 2002. *The Paradox of American Power: Why the World's Only Superpower Can't Go It Alone.* New York: Oxford University Press.

Nye, Joseph S. 2004. *Soft Power: The Means to Success in World Politics.* New York: Public Affairs.

Organisation for Economic Cooperation and Development (OECD). 2004. *Education at a Glance: 2004.* Paris.

President's Council of Advisors on Science and Technology. 2002. "Assessing the U.S. R&D Investment." Special Report, Executive Office of the President, Washington, DC.

President's Council of Advisors on Science and Technology. 2004. "Sustaining the Nation's Innovation Ecosystems." Special Report, Executive Office of the President, Washington, DC.

Prestowitz, Clyde. 2005. *Three Billion New Capitalists: The Great Shift of Wealth and Power to the East.* New York: Basic Books.

Redd, Kenneth E. 2007a. *Findings from the 2007 CGS International Graduate Admissions Survey. Phase II: Final Applications and Initial Offers of Admission.* Washington, DC: Council of Graduate Schools. http://www.cgsnet.org/portals/0/pdf/R_IntlAdm07_II.pdf.

Redd, Kenneth E. 2007b. *Findings from the 2007 CGS International Graduate Admissions Survey. Phase III: Final Offers of Admission and Enrollment.* Washington, DC: Council of Graduate Schools. http://www.cgsnet.org/portals/0/pdf/R_intlenrl07_III.pdf.

Regets, Mark C. 2007. *Research Issues in the International Migration of Highly Skilled Workers: A Perspective with Data from the United States.* Working Paper SRS 07–203. Arlington, VA: Division of Science Resources Statistics, National Science Foundation.

Sorensen, Elaine, Frank D. Bean, Leighton Ku, and Wendy Zimmerman. 1992. *Immigrant Categories and the U.S. Job Market: Do They Make a Difference?* Washington, DC: Urban Institute Press.

UNESCO. 2004. Population Division, UNESCO Institute for Statistics.

U.S. Bureau of the Census. 2003. "Census 2000, Five-Percent Public Use Microdata Sample (PUMS)." http://www.census.gov/Press-Release/www/2003/PUMS5.html, October 7.

U.S. Citizenship and Immigration Service. 2005. *Yearbook of Immigration Statistics* (various years). Washington, DC: U.S. Government Printing Office. http://uscis.gov/graphics/shared/statistics/yearbook/YrBkPur.htm.

U.S. Congress. 1991. United States Code Congressional and Administrative News. 101st Congress, 2nd Sess., 1990, vol. 8, Legislative History: Public Laws 101–625 to 101–650, Proclamations, Executive Orders, Tables and Index. St. Paul, MN: West Publishing.

U.S. Department of Homeland Security. 2007. *Yearbook of Immigration Statistics: 2006*. Washington, DC: U.S. Department of Homeland Security, Office of Immigration Statistics.

Usdansky, Margaret L., and Thomas J. Espenshade. 2001. "The Evolution of U.S. Policy Toward Employment-Based Immigrants and Temporary Workers," in Wayne A. Cornelius, Thomas J. Espenshade, and Idean Salehyan, eds., *The International Migration of the Highly Skilled*, pp. 23–53. San Diego: Center for Comparative Immigration Studies, University of California at San Diego.

Part II
Europe

5 Migration, Security, and Legitimacy
Some Reflections

Christina Boswell

Introduction

The belief that 9/11 led to the "securitization" of migration policy is fairly widespread amongst scholars and commentators on migration issues. The central claim is that the terrorist attacks on the U.S. and the subsequent bombings in Madrid and London provided an opportunity for governments, politicians, and the media to correlate terrorism with immigration. Immigrants were portrayed as a security threat, legitimizing the introduction of more draconian measures to restrict and control migration. James Hampshire (see Chapter 6 of this volume) offers an eloquent articulation of this argument.

In the discussion that follows, I would like to challenge this received wisdom about the securitization of migration. This chapter argues that, despite some initial attempts to link terrorism and migration, political discourse on migration control in these countries has remained surprisingly untouched by the anti-terrorism agenda.[1] By and large, there is very little evidence of attempts to securitize migration in Europe through explicitly linking irregular migrants and new entrants to terrorism. This conclusion appears to contradict the expectations of theories on the securitization of migration. In particular, it challenges their underlying assumption that states and political elites have a fundamental interest in portraying migration as a security threat in order to legitimize more stringent control measures.

The obvious explanation for the absence of securitization is provided by theories of embedded liberalism. Scholars such as James Hollifield (1990), Christian Joppke (1999), and Yasmin Soysal (1994) have argued that liberal democratic states are constrained from pursuing overly restrictive approaches to migration because of their commitment to liberal and human rights norms. So prima facie, these accounts might offer an answer to the puzzle as to why states do not attempt to link migration to terrorism. Yet theories of embedded liberalism are also problematic. They fail to explain the source of resilience of liberal institutions in the face of political pressures for restriction. If governments are willing and able to mobilize support for "securitarian" migration policies, why should they be concerned to respect liberal norms that constrain them from so doing? Moreover, arguments about rights did not appear to feature strongly in the discourse on migration after 9/11. Instead, as I shall argue, any interest that states may have had in securitizing migration were not constrained by liberal norms, but rather by a number of more pragmatic considerations.

Instead of relying on the concept of embedded liberalism, this chapter offers a rather different explanation for the apparent absence of securitization that revolves around a theory of how states perceive the preconditions for political legitimacy. Rather than understanding states as either power maximizing (the securitization thesis), or as vulnerable to liberal institutional constraints (the embedded liberal thesis), I argue that states are fundamentally concerned with securing public legitimacy. In the area of migration policy, this implies the need to meet a number of often conflicting functional requirements: not just being seen to guarantee security and respect human rights norms, but also creating the conditions for economic growth and, importantly, offering a plausible narrative about the societal impacts of government policies.

The chapter begins by briefly outlining the claims of the two main contenders for explaining migration policy after 9/11—securitization, and embedded liberalism. It goes on to assess their aptitude in explaining developments in debates on migration control in Europe by examining post-9/11 debates on migration control in three European cases—Germany, Spain, and the U.K. The discussion focuses on the level of declaratory politics (i.e., the rhetoric of governments, party politics, and the mass media in relation to migration control). It does not consider the rather different dynamics at the level of praxis, or policy implementation (see Boswell 2007a). The final part of the chapter examines the implications of these findings for theories of securitization and embedded liberalism. It argues that discourse on migration policy is best understood in terms of the state's interpretation of the tasks it needs to fulfill in order to secure legitimacy.

Two Theses about Migration Control after 9/11

The first contender for explaining migration policy after 9/11 comes from the so-called Copenhagen School, or "critical security studies" literature. A number of scholars have argued that states have a basic interest in securitizing migration issues for two main reasons. First, it provides an opportunity for consolidating categories of collective identification and helps mobilize support for the relevant political community, generating greater loyalty or patriotism through the definition of a common threat (Bigo 2002; Huysmans 1995, 1998, 2000). Second, it legitimizes the state in its attempt to introduce more restrictive measures. By linking migration and terrorism, the state becomes justified in introducing policies that would otherwise not have been considered legitimate (Buzan et al. 1998: 24–25). In short, the theory hypothesizes that states are interested in maximizing state control through taking advantage of opportunities to securitize migration.

Underlying this account is a strong assumption that states have an interest in maximizing societal control. The premise is that states are driven by a desire both to expand the scope of their societal intervention through acquiring competence in new areas and to multiply the instruments for achieving control, including establishing new forms of regulation and surveillance. Such theories find their inspiration in Foucauldian concepts of biopolitics and panopticism: the notion that the modern state seeks to increase its control through expanding knowledge and surveillance of the populations they seek to govern (Foucault 1975: 195–198; 1994: 67–85; for an application to migration policy, see Huysmans 2006). The securitization thesis argues that states are able to legitimize these techniques of governance through creating a sense of risk or unease. This type of securitizing discourse has a performative impact, contributing to the reconfiguration of political alliances and expectations about legitimate state interventions.

Proponents of the securitization thesis have applied it to account for increasingly restrictive discourse and practice on migration control in Europe since the 1980s (Buzan et al. 1998), and especially after 9/11 (Berthelet 2002; van Krieken 2005; Zucconi 2004). These authors claim that the terrorist attacks provided an opportunity to correlate migration with terrorism, thereby mobilizing popular loyalty to the state, and legitimizing the adoption of more draconian migration control practices.

Most proponents of the securitization thesis are less clear when it comes to defining the state or its relationship to the political system. Some theorists distinguish between the levels of political discourse and practice (Bigo 2002, 2005: 67–68; Buzan et al. 1993; Huysmans 2000). This implies drawing a distinction between the dynamics of securitization within the political system (characterized by party political competition to mobilize electoral support) and the administration (the state apparatus concerned with the elaboration and implementation of policy—see Luhmann 1981; Poggi 1990). However, the assumption is that both the party political leadership of the state and its bureaucratic apparatus have an identical interest in securitization.

The embedded liberalism thesis challenges this unity of politics and administration. On this account, liberal institutions—including parts of the state apparatus—act as a constraint on attempts at securitization. While this thesis does not necessarily deny that parts of the political system and administration may have an interest in expanding societal control, they by no means have unlimited scope for doing so. A range of formal and informal norms and practices impedes excessively restrictive migration policies.

It is easy to find concrete examples of such liberal institutions. They include: 1) constitutional provisions on human rights and equality; 2) arrangements for the separation of powers and independent judiciaries; and 3) regional and international treaties and conventions on human rights or the rights of refugees and migrants. These arrangements may limit the state's margin of maneuver in the area of migration policy, typically constraining the introduction of more restrictive or exclusionary policies. Arguably, bureaucratic organizations with some degree of autonomy in determining the scope of rights holders or welfare recipients can also exercise some influence in reining in tendencies towards the exclusion of newcomers (Guiraudon 2000, 2003; Rosenhek 2000: 53).

However, the focus on liberal institutions does beg the question of the origins of this apparent capacity to resist political interests, where these latter come into conflict with liberal norms. Once the state becomes interested in pursuing more restrictive policies, what prevents it from rolling back liberal institutions? The obvious answer is that the state risks losing legitimacy if it blatantly disregards liberal norms. The preservation of judicial independence and/or the continued separation of powers are likely to be important features of a legitimate democratic system. Likewise, respect for equal rights and norms of justice are important sources of legitimation in liberal democratic states. The state cannot simply disregard these norms and practices where they conflict with its own political interests.

The problem with this account, however, is that state concerns about legitimacy may not be a very reliable guarantee of liberal institutions in the context of attempts to securitize migration. As we saw, securitization involves the use of discourse that justifies disregarding liberal norms in order to ensure effective protection from threats. And proponents of the securitization thesis rightly observe that mobilization of support for restriction on the grounds that migration is a security threat has indeed been effective in legitimizing disregard of human rights norms in liberal democracies. So securitization appears to trigger a process whereby liberal norms are deprived of their constraining force; securitization succeeds precisely insofar as it is able to trump embedded liberal considerations. It brings about what James Hampshire terms a "disembedding" of liberalism (see Chapter 6 of this volume).

If the power of liberal norms is located in the state's concern to retain legitimacy, we need to refocus the question. Instead of inquiring into the nature of liberal institutions, or some inherent property that accounts for their resilience, we need to consider the configuration of political and institutional pressures from the perspective of the state. The question becomes that of what sorts of factors influence how the state (in this context understood as the political component of the state, i.e., its elected leadership) defines the preconditions for legitimacy. Under what conditions will the state consider it important to prioritize its role as security provider versus its role as protector of individual rights? In other words, when and why will an interior minister, a home minister, or a head of state consider it expedient to encourage securitarian discourses that might trump liberal constraints? Conversely, under what conditions might it be considered wiser to downplay this type of rhetoric, or to retreat from confrontation with liberal institutions? Examining these questions through the lens of the state is not intended to attribute it absolute autonomy in determining policy; indeed, a central assumption is that the state's actions are fundamentally shaped by how it interprets the preconditions for legitimacy. The system of politics is constantly engaged in reading signals from its environment to try to gauge how best it can retain support (Luhmann 1981).

I shall compare these three different conceptions of the state in more depth later in the chapter. In the meantime, I would like to analyze discourse on migration in Europe after 9/11, to see what we can gauge about state interests and patterns of political mobilization on migration issues. The empirical analysis focuses on migration discourse before and especially after September 11, 2001. Indeed, the impact of 9/11 on discourse on migration policy provides a fascinating case for exploring the determinants of responses to migration. Did 9/11 offer an opportunity for securitization, and did political leaders use this opportunity? If so, this would lend support to the securitization thesis. Alternatively, did such attempts at securitization fail to emerge, or prove to be unsustainable? In this case, can the absence of securitization be attributed to embedded liberalism, or to other sorts of factors linked to the state's quest for legitimacy?

Discourse on Migration after 9/11

Before considering the effect of 9/11 on public debates on migration, it is worth briefly sketching predominant patterns of discourse prior to the terrorist attacks. This will provide a better basis to gauge the influence of 9/11 on those debates.

While there were important variations between different European countries, one can discern three general trends in the framing of migration control issues in Europe. The first was the notion that large numbers of illegal migrants were desperate to enter European countries. Potential or actual migrants were portrayed as impoverished and unscrupulous, keen to reach Europe at any cost. This kind of framing has been especially prominent in Southern European countries with porous sea borders, as well as sections of the U.K. media and public. This is a clear example of securitization in political rhetoric, with states responding with a range of highly visible and often symbolic security measures to reassure the public that they were being protected from a tangible threat.

The second way of framing the problem of border control focused on the social and economic impact of irregular stay and employment. This is more typical for Northern European countries with a longer history of welfare state protection. Concerns tend to revolve around the abuse of welfare provisions and social services, the costs of asylum systems, and the fear that irregular workers will undercut the domestic labor force. Typical policy responses include employer sanctions, monitoring of asylum or immigration abuse through identity cards and control of access to social services, as well as restrictive asylum systems.

A third way of framing migration control issues has focused on the problem of smuggling and trafficking of persons. Politicians and the media have raised concerns about forced labor in prostitution or sweatshops and the use of highly dangerous smuggling routes. The networks involved are characterized as sophisticated international criminal structures often engaged in drugs or arms trafficking. Because of the clear linkages to organized criminality, the issue has been seen as a legitimate area for engagement by police agencies, including at EU level.

These three patterns of framing imply rather different constructions of the problem of border control and irregular migrants, and imply diverging policy responses. What unites the three characterizations, however, is the emphasis on exclusion as the preferred solution. Whether the concern is about floods of destitute migrants, abusers of the welfare state, or sinister trafficking gangs, the proposed remedy is to bar entry, or to deport unwanted immigrants. Correspondingly, the rhetoric and public policy debate at both national and EU level has focused predominantly on a repertoire of policy measures aimed at excluding migrants: limiting entry through restrictive visa policies, carrier sanctions, and border control; curtailing overstay through detention and deportation; and imposing various penalties to deter irregular entry, labor, or abuse of asylum systems. EU policy has also focused on cooperation with neighboring countries to stop irregular emigration, and to facilitate the return of irregular migrants to countries of origin or transit.

Debates on Migration after 9/11

How, if at all, did the terrorist attacks of 9/11 influence this pattern of framing migration control issues? In the immediate aftermath of the attacks, there was only rather limited intelligence on the perpetrators, leaving considerable scope for different ways of framing the question. There were several attempts to address the security threat through migration control policies. The U.K. Home Secretary David Blunkett insisted that Britain would not "offer hospitality to terrorists," and announced provisions to facilitate the detention and removal of foreign nationals (*Hansard* 2001). The German Interior Minister Otto Schily made similar statements to the effect that asylum seekers and refugees suspected of terrorist activities should immediately be deported, while EU member states announced the strengthening of external border controls, and the reintroduction of periodic checks at the borders between Schengen countries (Council of the European Union 2001).

However, the linkage between terrorism and illegal immigration was difficult to sustain, and from late 2001 onwards references to terrorism are almost wholly absent from debates on irregular migration and migration control in Europe. This emerges quite clearly if one looks at press reporting on migration issues in European countries from 2002 onwards.

In Germany, both 9/11 and the Madrid bombings of March 11, 2004 occurred at a time of quite heated debate on a new Immigration Law. Shortly after the U.S. attacks, the SPD Interior Minister Otto Schily decided to delay the debate to make certain the bill was "watertight" against terrorism. The focus was on facilitating the deportation of asylum seekers suspected of involvement in terrorist activities, as well as so-called "hate preachers" and extremist organizations that were considered to be inciting religious hatred and violence.

However, with the exception of a few isolated comments from the government, opposition parties, and the media, discourse on migration control in Germany remained largely untouched by the issue of terrorism. The main critique of the draft Immigration Law remained concerns about increasing labor migration during a period of high unemployment in Germany, and the problem of the perceived poor performance of foreign nationals in education and the labor market. To be sure, the press was quite preoccupied with the problem of Al-Qaeda "sleeper cells" operating in Germany, and radicalization amongst Germany's roughly three million Muslims (*Frankfurt Allgemeine Zeitung* 2002). But these questions were for the most part linked to problems of integrating ethnic minorities already present in Germany. They were not raised in respect of problems of irregular immigration and migration control. Arguments for restricting migration and ensuring better control of the entry and stay of irregular migrants were by and large based on socioeconomic, rather than security, concerns.

The absence of any linkage between migration control issues and terrorism is even more pronounced in the case of Spain. In the aftermath of the Madrid bombings of March 11, 2004, the vast majority of suspects held in connection with the attacks were Moroccan (BBC News Online 2004). Morocco was the major source country for Spain's growing stock of *sin papeles*[2]—in April 2004 it was estimated that there were around 200,000 irregular migrants of Moroccan origin living in Spain (Bárbulo 2004). Morocco was also the most important transit country for irregular migration from Africa; indeed, from summer 2004 onwards, concerns about irregular migration started to focus on the attempts of a number of people to cross into the Spanish enclaves of Ceuta and Melilla in Moroccan territory.

And yet in spring 2004, days after the Madrid attacks, Spain's new Prime Minister Zapatero announced a marked shift in migration policy away from a focus on security issues, instead emphasizing labor market and economic needs. That summer, he put forward plans for a major amnesty for irregular migrants resident in Spain, which resulted in the legalization of more than 700,000 migrants between February and April 2005, the largest group of whom were Moroccan (19.3 percent) (Granda 2004). To be sure, this relatively open approach was complemented with a fairly "securitarian" approach to border control. But there is no evidence that the government made any attempt to link the problem of irregular entry with the threat of terrorism: quite a remarkable fact, given the apparent incentives to do so after March 11.

Probing the U.K. Case: Migration Control and the Anti-Terrorism Act

The absence of any serious attempts to link migration control issues to terrorism may appear quite anomalous. Why did politicians and the media not exploit concerns about terrorism to mobilize support and legitimize more extensive powers for migration control? One possible answer is that the profiles of international terrorists that emerged after 9/11 did not correspond in any obvious way with the established frame for irregular migrants in Europe. The debate on Al-Qaeda networks from autumn 2001 onwards depicted terrorists as single-minded fanatics, who were able to cleverly exploit European rules on entry and stay to achieve their fundamentalist goals, but who otherwise had little regard for the welfare or employment benefits European countries might have to offer.[3] The typical image was of a network of sleeper cells operating in highly organized way, involving well-trained individuals with access to ample resources. This hardly fits the image of large numbers of destitute and desperate migrants arriving on the shores of Southern Europe, or the "economic migrants" keen to cheat welfare systems and steal low-skilled jobs from native workers. It was also fairly incongruous with images of organized criminal networks involved in trafficking women and children for prostitution— although, of the three types of irregular migration, this was the one most frequently associated with terrorist activities.

Perhaps even more undermining for such a linkage, though, were the emerging revelations that European nationals were involved in terrorist attacks. In this sense, any discursive opportunities to link migration and terrorism were constrained not just by a lag in adapting established patterns of framing the migration control problem, but also by the growing body of information on the profile of the European Muslims involved. We can elucidate this point through considering in more detail a case where a European government did attempt to draw such a linkage, and was thwarted for these reasons: the U.K. Anti-Terrorism, Crime and Security Act (ATCSA) of 2001.

The ATCSA was introduced into Parliament in November 2001, as a direct response to the attacks of 9/11. Part 4 of the Act explicitly covered immigration and asylum, setting out provisions to facilitate the deportation of foreign nationals suspected of being international terrorists, or their detention in cases where their removal or departure was prevented by law or practical considerations. These provisions were controversial for a number of reasons, not least because the provisions on detention without trial implied a derogation from the European Convention on Human Rights (House of Lords and House of Commons 2004). More tellingly for our discussion, however, were two sets of criticism advanced by the so-called Newton Report of December 18, 2003, issued by a special Review Committee mandated to review Part 4. The first criticism related to what the committee considered to be an unwarranted focus on foreign nationals:

> The Home Office has argued that the threat from al Qaeda-related terrorism is predominantly from foreigners, but there is accumulating evidence that this is not now the case. The British suicide bombers who attacked Tel Aviv in May 2003, Richard Reid ("The Shoe Bomber"), and recent arrests suggest that the threat from UK citizens is real. Almost 30% of Terrorism Act 2000 suspects in the past year have been British. We have

been told that, of the people of interest to the authorities because of their suspected involvement in terrorism, nearly half are British nationals.

(Privy Counsellor Review Committee 2003: 53–54)

The report therefore strongly urged the government to "deal with all terrorism, whatever its origin or the nationality of its suspected perpetrators" (p. 11). The Home Secretary accepted this point in Parliament:

> On 11 September 2001, the threat that arose was from overseas nationals—the people that were involved in the attacks on that day . . . Since that period, there has been a continued involvement of UK nationals as well in that approach, and increasingly so.
>
> (*Hansard* 2005)

The second concern was that even assuming the provisions targeted the right group, it was not clear that the focus on deportation of those who could be removed would reduce the terrorist threat. Again, to quote the Newton Report:

> Seeking to deport terrorist suspects does not seem to US to be a satisfactory response, given the risk of exporting terrorism. If people in the UK are contributing to the terrorist effort here or abroad, they should be dealt with here. While deporting such people might free up British police, intelligence, security and prison service resources, it would not necessarily reduce the threat to British interests abroad, or make the world a safer place more generally. Indeed, there is a risk that the suspects might even return without the authorities being aware of it.
>
> (Privy Counsellor Review Committee 2003: 54)

As the Conservative Shadow Home Secretary David Davis commented in Parliament, "releasing people whom we believe to be international terrorists to travel the world seems to be a peculiar policy" (*Hansard* 2004). Indeed, Home Secretary Clarke subsequently defined the new goal as "to prevent an individual from continuing to carry out terrorist-related activities" (*Hansard* 2005).[4]

The debate involving Part 4 of the ATCSA and the Newton Report therefore illustrates rather well some of the cognitive and practical obstacles to pursuing the linkage between terrorism and migration control. It was becoming increasingly clear that a large proportion of suspected terrorists were European nationals, rendering instruments of migration control largely irrelevant in the fight against terrorism. And even where terrorist suspects were involved in such activities, exclusion did not seem to be an effective instrument for suppressing their activities. To be sure, the popular media was often less interested in these niceties. In tabloid reporting, one often finds a loose grouping of foreigners and terrorists as part of the same problem. But debate within

Parliament required more precision, and politicians had little choice but to respond to new information. The focus of activities therefore shifted increasingly towards monitoring and intelligence gathering on suspects, including British nationals. The watchword became surveillance, rather than exclusion through entry control or deportation.

Although I have so far stressed cognitive factors as a determinant of the framing of migration control issues in political discourse, it is also important to bear in mind that the securitization of migration control issues would have conflicted with a number of the policy goals of European governments. While concerns about irregular migration were high on the migration policy agenda, many European governments were simultaneously attempting to generate public support for the introduction of more liberal policies on labor migration. Center-left governments in the U.K. and Germany had recently introduced new programs for high-skilled migrants, and were loosening access to the labor market for foreign students. The Social Democratic government in Spain, as we saw, was keen to regularize illegal workers to meet the demand for labor in the Spanish economy. More generally, European governments had an obvious interest in keeping mobility open for the purposes of business, tourism, and study. So there was no strong incentive to encourage a linkage between terrorism and migration policies that could have negative repercussions for business-friendly policies on entry and access to labor markets.

Implications for Theories of Migration Policy

Thus far I have emphasized the role of political and cognitive factors in constraining attempts at securitization. It appears that European governments were unwilling or unable to sustain linkages between migration control and terrorism because of conflicting political interests, as well as the difficulties in sustaining a coherent account of the causal linkages between the two. How do these insights fit with existing theories of migration policy?

The analysis of European migration discourse post-9/11 should lead us to question the plausibility of the securitization thesis. In particular, it casts doubt on this theory's assumptions about state interests in the area of migration. To be sure, populist political actors frequently mobilize public support through strategies of securitization, but states and political parties with a realistic prospect of securing power are often more circumspect about promoting such linkages.

The first reason for caution is that securitization can create unfeasible expectations about the state's capacity to control migration. By depicting migration policy as part of a counterterrorism strategy, states are effectively raising the stakes of migration control. If they fail to deliver on targets of migration control, they expose themselves to quite serious accusations about their capacity to provide security. Politicians with any experience of migration policy implementation are quite aware of the structural constraints in meeting such targets in areas such as border control, enforcing rules on irregular work and stay, or deporting irregular migrants and rejected asylum seekers. Awareness of the difficulties in meeting such targets is likely to encourage caution about linking such objectives to internal security and counterterrorism. Any subsequent failure to meet these goals would risk a loss of legitimacy.

Pursuing a strategy of securitization may also jeopardize other goals of the state, such as ensuring a sufficient supply of migrant labor to guarantee the conditions for economic growth (Favell and Hansen 2002). Center-left governments in Germany, Spain, and the U.K. have all recently been keen to promote more expansive policies on labor migration in order to fill skills and labor gaps. Again, such goals are integral to state legitimation in the area of economic growth. In light of this goal, it would be unwise to draw attention to any potential correlations between labor migration and the entry of potential terrorists that could undermine public acceptance of labor migrants.

The third reason why European states appear to have resisted the securitization of migration control relates to cognitive constraints. As we saw most clearly in discussion of the U.K. case, governments need to offer coherent and credible accounts of the causes and nature of the terrorist threat and of the sorts of state interventions that can best respond to them. This ruled out simply equating terrorists with immigrants. While this type of linkage may remain possible for populist fringes within the political debate—be these far-right parties, or the populist tabloid press—it is not a sustainable option for mainstream political parties and governments. These latter need to maintain some degree of epistemic authority (Herbst 2003).

This analysis leads to the conclusion that there is no reason to expect politics to be driven exclusively by an interest in encouraging public unease or introducing more stringent security measures. Governments and rival political parties may seek to securitize migration control under certain conditions, but there is no inevitability about this, and there is good reason to expect it will not be a sustainable political strategy for governments or mainstream opposition parties.

The obvious alternative to the securitization thesis would be to opt for a neo-institutionalist account. Such an account would emphasize the role of liberal institutions in constraining excessively restrictive approaches. But my account also questions the assumptions of this "embedded liberalism" approach. These accounts tend to attribute explanatory power to various institutionalized norms and practices, such as constitutional and treaty provisions, and court rulings. They locate the force of this liberal constraint in the embeddedness of liberal practices; such commitments are difficult or impossible to opt out of, because of their codification in robust institutional arrangements, often nested in international agreements (Hollifield 1992). These liberal norms also reflect the attitudes of members of liberal democracies, who are socialized into a deep commitment to liberal democratic values.

Previous experience with migration and refugee policy, however, suggests that neither of these sources of commitment to liberal values is particularly robust. Where states and other political actors have a strong interest in rolling back human rights commitments, they are often able to bypass international and national commitments. To be sure, states will be concerned about whether their actions meet certain public expectations about legitimacy. But they can and often have been able to retain public legitimacy whilst quite blatantly disregarding human rights norms in relation to migrants or refugees (see, for example, Schmidtke 1999). The existence of liberal institutions in itself provides no watertight guarantee that states will not pursue quite draconian measures.

Moreover, analysis of this discourse on migration control in Germany, Spain, and the U.K. does not suggest that human rights or liberal arguments played a pronounced role in constraining securitization. Rather, the factors mitigating against the linkage between migration and terrorism appeared to be interests in generating support for more liberal labor migration policies, and cognitive constraints to sustaining this correlation. I also suggested that states might draw back from promoting this linkage because of the risk of creating unmanageable public expectations about migration control. In the U.K. case, in particular, it is unlikely that human rights arguments in themselves would have led to the serious questioning of provisions on the detention of foreign suspects. A far more compelling argument in parliamentary debates was the fact that this provision was failing effectively to address the threat of terrorism.

Is there an alternative way of explaining migration discourse after 9/11 and the relative absence of securitization? The problem with both the securitization thesis and embedded liberalism is that they rely on overly simplistic assumptions about the state. In one case, states are essentially concerned with maximizing power through security and control. In the other, liberal institutions successfully act as a constraint on such tendencies.

As I suggested earlier, the question we should be asking ourselves instead is that of the conditions under which states act as power maximizers or respecters of liberal values. This is ultimately a question of how states consider they will best secure public legitimacy (Boswell 2007b). A state may believe that it will engender support through taking a tough line on immigration, despite human rights considerations. The German and U.K. governments certainly took steps in this direction in the immediate aftermath of 9/11. A number of new policies on asylum seekers and foreign terrorist suspects did imply derogation from human rights commitments (see Chapter 6 in this volume). But states were also concerned not to lose support for failing to pursue migration policies that boost the economy. This was clearly the case in Spain and the U.K., where center-left governments were keen to mobilize support for more liberal labor migration policies. A blanket association of terrorism with new migrants could have jeopardized this agenda. States, political parties, and the mass media are also concerned about losing legitimacy through straying too far from factually accurate accounts—the cognitive constraint I mentioned earlier. They must provide plausible accounts about the causal impact of their (proposed) policies on the phenomena in question. We saw a clear example of how this cognitive requirement undermined the U.K. government's attempts to link terrorism with migration control.

Looking at political rhetoric on migration through the lens of the state's imperative of securing legitimacy certainly lacks the theoretical neatness of either the securitization thesis or embedded liberal accounts. We cannot infer trends in political discourse from any immanent features of states or liberal institutions. Rather, the way in which states and rival political actors mobilize support on migration issues depends on their perception of how best they can generate support. This can only be gauged through empirical research on how states interpret public opinion and the preconditions for securing legitimacy.

Conclusion

In contrast to the U.S. case, discourse on migration control in Europe does not appear to have become securitized as a result of 9/11 or the subsequent terrorist attacks in Madrid and London. Initial attempts to construct a causal linkage between irregular entry, illegal migration, and terrorism proved impossible to sustain. A combination of cognitive constraints and conflicting political interests in the area of migration served to impede initial attempts at securitization, at least in the case of migration control policies.[5]

This analysis should lead us to challenge the securitization thesis and its assumptions about states as power-maximizing entities. The account also questions whether embedded liberal accounts can explain the absence of securitization. I have argued that it was not so much the existence of liberal institutions that provided a check on securitization. In the U.K. case, far more important was the cognitive constraint implied by revelations about the profile of terrorist suspects. These undermined the plausibility of drawing causal linkages between migration control and counterterrorism. In both the U.K. and Spain, a strong interest in mobilizing support for more liberal labor migration policies also provided disincentives to play on anxieties about immigration. In Germany, political parties and the mass media had ample arguments for generating opposition to the proposed new immigration law, and little interest in adding the terrorist threat to their list.

I have suggested in this chapter that the best way of explaining these dynamics is in terms of the state's perception of the preconditions for securing public legitimacy. States need to be seen to be guaranteeing the security of their citizens, and their actions must accord with public expectations about rights. But they also need to ensure that migration policy meets goals of economic growth and welfare, and, moreover, they must be able to offer a plausible narrative about the societal impacts of their policies. While in some cases governments or their party-political rivals may derive legitimacy from strategies of securitization, this may also carry its own risks. And, importantly, these risks are not generated by any inherent properties of liberal institutions. Instead, the constraint to securitization can be located in more pragmatic considerations on the part of political leaders: the implied conflict with other functional requirements of the state, especially in the area of economic policy; the risk of a loss of legitimacy by failing to meet public expectations on migration control; and the need to advance a credible narrative of the nature of the terrorist threat, and appropriate responses to it. These considerations were clearly deemed more important for shoring up legitimacy than the expected gains from securitizing migration.

Notes

1 The discussion is limited to migration control—i.e., policies to exclude irregular migrants or other unwanted foreign nationals through entry restrictions, border control, detention, and deportation. The chapter does not discuss the question of whether there has been a securitization in policies on immigrant integration or inter-ethnic relations.
2 Literally, "without papers."
3 See, for example, Hooper (2001).
4 For a more detailed account of the government's retreat from this initial position, see James Hampshire's contribution to this volume (Chapter 6).
5 The situation is somewhat different in the case of discourse on the Muslim community in European countries, and problems of immigrant "integration."

References

Bárbulo, Tomás. 2004. "Los marroquíes piden a Zapatero un consejo islámico que controle imames y mezquitas." *El Pais*, April 7.
BBC News Online. 2004. "Madrid Blasts: The Islamic Connection." March 30. http://news.bbc.co.uk.
Berthelet, Pierre. 2002. "L'Impact des événements du 11 septembre sur la création de l'espace de liberté, de sécurité, et de justice." *Cultures et Conflits* 42(2). Online at http://www.conflicts.org/index795.html (accessed January 28, 2006).
Bigo, Didier. 2002. "Security and Immigration: Toward a Critique of the Governmentality of Unease." *Alternatives* 27: 63–92.
Bigo, Didier. 2005. "Frontier Controls in the European Union: Who Is in Control?" in Didier Bigo and Elspeth Guild, eds., *Controlling Frontiers: Free Movement Into and Within Europe*, pp. 49–99. Aldershot: Ashgate.
Boswell, Christina. 2007a. "Migration Control after 9/11: Explaining the Absence of Securitization." *Journal of Common Market Studies* 45(September): 589–610.
Boswell, Christina. 2007b. "Theorizing Migration Policy: Is There a Third Way?" *International Migration Review* 41(1): 75–100.
Buzan, Barry, Ole Wæver, and Jaap de Wilde. 1998. *Security: A New Framework for Analysis*. Boulder, CO: Lynne Rienner.
Council of the European Union. 2001. *Presidency Note, European Union Action Following the Attacks in the United States*. Brussels, October 24 (13155(01)).
Favell, A., and Hansen, R. 2002. "Markets Against Politics: Migration, EU Enlargement and the Idea of Europe." *Journal of Ethnic and Migration Studies* 28(4): 581–601.
Foucault, Michel. 1975. *Discipline and Punish: The Birth of the Prison*. London: Allen Lane.

Foucault, Michel. 1994. *Essential Works of Foucault 1954–1984*, vol. 1, *Ethics*, ed. Paul Rabinow. London: Penguin.

Frankfurter Allgemeine Zeitung (FAZ). 2002. "Viele Angebote, undeutliche Erwartungen." January 22.

Granda, Elsa. 2004. "El Gobierno perdonará a los empresarios que regularicen a extranjeros 'sin papeles'." *El País*, August 22.

Guiraudon, Virginie. 2000. "European Integration and Migration Policy: Vertical Policy-Making as Venue Shopping." *Journal of Common Market Studies* 38: 251–271.

Guiraudon, Virginie. 2003. "The Constitution of a European Immigration Policy Domain: A Political Sociology Approach." *Journal of European Public Policy* 10(2): 263–282.

Hansard. 2001. United Kingdom Parliamentary Debates, October 15.

Hansard. 2004. United Kingdom Parliamentary Debates, February 25.

Hansard. 2005. United Kingdom Parliamentary Debates, February 22.

Herbst, Susan. 2003. "Political Authority in a Mediated Age." *Theory and Society* 32(4): 481–503.

Hollifield, James F. 1990. "Immigration and the French State: Problems of Policy Implementation." *Comparative Political Studies* 23(4): 56–79.

Hollifield, James F. 1992. *Immigrants, Markets and States: The Political Economy of Postwar Europe*. Cambridge, MA: Harvard University Press.

Hooper, John. 2001. "Double Life of Suicide Pilot: War on Terrorism." *Observer*, September 23.

House of Lords and House of Commons. 2004. "Review of Counter-Terrorism Provisions." Eighteenth Report of Session 2003–04, HL Paper 158 HC 713, August 4.

Huysmans, Jef. 1995. "Migrants as a Security Problem: Dangers of 'Securitizing' Societal Issues," in Robert Miles and Dietrich Thränhardt, eds., *Migration and European Integration: The Dynamics of Inclusion and Exclusion*, pp. 53–72. London: Pinter.

Huysmans, Jef. 1998. "Security! What Do You Mean? From Concept to Thick Signifier." *European Journal of International Relations* 4(2): 226–255.

Huysmans, Jef. 2000. "The European Union and the Securitization of Migration." *Journal of Common Market Studies* 38(5): 751–777.

Huysmans, Jef. 2006. *The Politics of Insecurity: Fear, Migration and Asylum in the EU*. London: Routledge.

Joppke, Christian. 1999. *Immigration and the Nation-State: The United States, Germany, and Great Britain*. Oxford and New York: Oxford University Press.

Luhmann, Niklas. 1981. *Political Theory in the Welfare State*. Berlin: Walter de Gruyter.

Poggi, Gianfranco. 1990. *The State: Its Nature, Development and Prospects*. Cambridge: Polity.

Privy Counsellor Review Committee. 2003. "Anti-Terrorism, Crime and Security Act 2001 Review: Report." London: The Stationery Office.

Rosenhek, Zeev. 2000. "Migration Regimes, Intra-State Conflicts and the Politics of Exclusion and Inclusion: Migrant Workers in the Israeli Welfare State." *Social Problems* 47(1): 49–67.

Schmidtke, Oliver. 1999. "Illiberal Policies in Liberal Societies: Some Remarks on Hollifield's Thesis of the Immigration Dilemma in Liberal Societies," in Axel

Schulte and Dietrich Thränhardt, eds., *International Migration and Liberal Democracies*, pp. 87–100. Münster: Lit Verlag.

Soysal, Y.N. 1994. *Limits of Citizenship: Migrants and Postnational Membership in Europe*. Chicago and London: University of Chicago Press.

van Krieken, Peter. 2005. "Terrorism and the Changing Paradigm of Migratory Movements," in Holger Henke, ed., *Crossing Over: Comparing Recent Migration in the United States and Europe*, pp. 47–76. Lanham, MD: Lexington.

Zucconi, Mario. 2004. "Migration and Security as an Issue in US–European Relations," in John Tirman, ed., *The Maze of Fear: Security and Migration After 9/11*, pp. 142–154. New York: New Press.

6 Disembedding Liberalism?

Immigration Politics and Security in Britain since 9/11

James Hampshire

Introduction

Since the attacks on the United States of September 11, 2001, terrorism has moved to the top of the political agenda in Britain. In the past five years, the British government has introduced a raft of anti-terror measures, including *inter alia* detention without trial for foreign nationals suspected of terrorist activities, restrictions on the right of assembly for public protest, and prohibitions on speech acts which "glorify" terrorism. Against a chorus of disapproval from civil libertarians, the government insists that these measures are necessary and proportionate responses to the threat from Al-Qaeda and other terrorist organizations. Then Prime Minister Tony Blair responded to his critics by arguing that Britain faced a genuinely new kind of security threat requiring special measures to protect the public from terrorism. As he stated in his speech outlining the government's response to the July 7 London bombings, "let no-one be in any doubt, the rules of the game are changing" (Prime Minister's Office 2005).

Migration is one of several policy areas that has been profoundly affected by the new concern with terrorism. Whilst the connections between security and international migration predate 9/11 (see Bigo 2001; Huysmans 1995, 2000; Rudolph 2003), the attacks on New York and Washington, DC prompted a reassessment of the risks associated with migration. All 19 of the 9/11 terrorists were non-U.S. citizens, and they all exploited loopholes in immigration legislation to infiltrate the United States. In Britain, although three of the four London bombers were British-born (the fourth was a Jamaican national), they were second-generation immigrants. In this context, the increased concern about the security risks associated with migration has at least a prima facie legitimacy. However, as several scholars have argued, the "securitization" of migration may be shaped by wider fears and insecurities (Huysmans 2006; Tirman 2004) and the resulting policies can have highly negative effects on the vast majority of migrants who have no associations with terrorist organizations.

This chapter considers how the securitization of migration in Britain since 9/11 is affecting immigration politics and policy. In particular, it examines how the framing of migration as a security threat has been used to challenge some of the liberal ideas and institutions that normally constrain the executive's ability to pursue restrictionist policies. In doing so, the chapter draws upon two existing literatures that address immigration politics and policy-making: comparative political science and critical security studies. Perhaps due to their different theoretical orientations (positivist and constructivist, respectively), as well as their different disciplinary locations (political science and international relations), these two literatures are rarely engaged. This is something of a missed opportunity. While political science has arguably paid too little attention to the security logics that shape migration policy (see Rudolph 2003), the critical security studies literature has tended to overemphasize them to the detriment of other factors, such as interest group lobbying, judicial activism, and the mobilization of public opinion.

Utilizing the analytical frameworks developed in these two literatures and drawing on empirical evidence from Britain, the questions I want to consider are:

1   What are the normal rules of the game in the immigration politics of liberal democratic states?
2   To what extent and in what ways is immigration being presented as a security threat?
3   How, if at all, is this changing the rules of the immigration game?
4   What kinds of policies are being legitimized by the representation of immigration as a security threat?

The chapter first outlines two influential models of immigration politics in liberal democratic states: client politics and embedded liberalism. I argue that a holistic approach that captures the insights of both of the above models is required, and I discuss the relevance of a holistic approach for the British case. I then develop a conceptual framework for the analysis of securitization, based on the critical security studies literature. Lastly, I examine the impact of securitization on immigration politics in Britain, and I assess the implications for migration policy. My central contention is that a partial securitization of migration in Britain has occurred, weakening some of the liberal constraints on restrictive immigration policymaking.

Two Models of Immigration Politics in Liberal Democratic States

The identification of a puzzle spurred recent attempts to develop models of immigration politics in liberal democratic states—to identify the "rules" of the immigration policy game. This puzzle, neatly if perhaps misleadingly known as the "gap hypothesis" (Cornelius et al. 2004), arises from an observation about the disjuncture between stated policy objectives and actual policy outcomes in labor-importing countries. In many of these countries, public discourse on immigration is broadly restrictionist, or at least control-minded, whilst policy outcomes tend to be expansionist and unpredictable. Policy "gaps" exist when the stated objectives of immigration policies are to control and manage migration, whilst immigration itself is neither successfully controlled nor managed.

In addition to the gap between policy objectives and outcomes, there is another, equally puzzling gap between public opinion on immigration and government policies. Across liberal democratic states, and especially in the reluctant Western European countries of immigration, sizeable numbers of voters oppose immigration and want it to be controlled. Analysis of European Social Survey data reveals that a substantial portion of the public in Western European countries supports restrictive immigration and asylum policies (Ivarsflaten 2005; see also Lahav 2004).[1] This suggests that there is a considerable electoral dividend for acting (or at least appearing to act) tough on immigration, and indeed politicians often do adopt restrictionist stances and promise their electorates ever-tighter border controls. Yet this only furthers the conundrum: if sizeable numbers of voters support restrictive immigration policies and their representatives promise such policies, why are outcomes so often expansionist? Why, in other words, doesn't restrictionist political rhetoric translate into restrictionist policy outcomes?

Various competing explanations have been put forward to answer these questions. Globalization theorists argue that the immigration policy gap is the product of a globalized world in which national sovereignty has been diminished and the state no longer has the capacity to control migration (Sassen 1996, 1999). In this view, migration is part and parcel of the global economy, no less a defining feature of globalization than capital mobility, international trade flows, or information communications technologies. Porous borders are inevitable and the state is increasingly powerless to prevent the transnational movement of people. A related literature argues that migrants appeal to international human rights law, premised on "universal personhood," thus undermining the state's ability to distinguish between citizens and aliens (Jacobson 1997; Soysal 1994). Whilst migration is undoubtedly an important feature of the global economy, these arguments significantly underestimate the extent to which states—acting independently and also in concert—have not only retained but in many ways increased their capacities to control migration (see Freeman 1998; Hansen 2000: 259–261; Joppke 1999).

A more plausible explanation for the gap, and one which directs our attention to the domestic structural logic of immigration politics, is Gary Freeman's (1995) client politics model. This model is based on a policy typology that predicts modes of politics based on how the costs and benefits of a given policy are distributed. Both the costs and benefits of a policy can be either concentrated or diffuse, yielding a matrix of four distinct modes of politics: client (concentrated benefits, diffuse costs), interest group (concentrated benefits, concentrated costs), majoritarian (diffuse benefits, diffuse costs), and entrepreneurial (diffuse benefits, concentrated costs) (see Freeman 1995 for elaboration). Freeman argues that "client politics is the dominant mode of immigration politics" (2002: 80–81) in liberal democratic states because the benefits of migration policies tend to be concentrated, whilst the costs tend to be diffuse. Those who stand to gain from expansive migration policies, primarily employers seeking cheap labor and ethnic groups, are a concentrated constituency with significant resources and a capacity to mobilize to advocate their interests. Those who bear the costs of immigration, however, are in no such position. Mass publics who compete with migrants for employment and housing face collective action problems and thus find it difficult to mobilize their discontent to influence policy. This leads to a form of politics in which immigration clients are able to exercise a disproportionate influence over policy-making. Thus immigration policy is influenced by those who stand to gain from it, and client-driven expansionist policies emerge in a context of restrictive public opinion.

The client politics model offers an accurate description of some features of migration policymaking in certain countries, but, as critics have observed, it has several shortcomings. First, it fits much better with the classic countries of immigration—Australia, Canada, and above all the United States—than it does with the reluctant European countries of immigration. In Europe, the two major clients who lobby for liberal immigration policies—namely employers and ethnic lobby groups—have been less prominent and less entrenched in immigration policy networks than in the United States (Joppke 1998, 1999). Second, as an interest-based model grounded in political economy, client politics helps account for one dimension of migration policy, namely labor migration, but it is much less suitable for explaining asylum policy, where employers' associations are not active lobbyists and the "interests" involved are very different. Thus, in order to explain why liberal states accept asylum-seeking migrants we need to turn our attention to different actors and institutions, and the resulting mode of politics is unlikely to be clientelist. Admittedly, Freeman (2006) has now refined his model to account for different migration policy types, but the point remains that it is difficult to explain many aspects of immigration politics, including asylum, using his framework.

Finally, the client politics model fails to account sufficiently for the importance of period- and context-specific factors (Freeman claims that his model is "structural" and therefore relevant, mutatis mutandis, to all liberal democracies), particularly the way in which migration is discursively framed and how immigrants are represented in the public domain. As Roger Brubaker states, "there are competing representations of immigrants, and the relative rhetorical and organizational power of purveyors of these competing representations varies across contexts" (Brubaker 1995: 906–907). Such discursive framing is hardly inconsequential, as it fundamentally affects how relevant actors perceive the costs and benefits of migration; in other words, it shapes their perceived interests. Critics of Freeman insist that we should attend to "the extent and way immigration is politicized and publicly mediated, and how certain positions are made to appear more feasible, reasonable, and legitimate, compared to alternative definitions of political reality" (Statham and Geddes 2006: 251). As I argue below, the recent framing of migration as a security threat affects immigration politics precisely by making certain restrictionist policies appear both more necessary and legitimate. These criticisms are not meant to suggest that Freeman's model is redundant—indeed, I shall argue below that there are some clientelist features of labor migration policy in Britain, as in other European countries—only that it should be supplemented with other analytical approaches.

The second model that I want to consider focuses less upon interest-based politics in the context of liberal democracy than upon liberal ideas and their institutionalization in liberal democratic states. The "embedded liberalism" model holds that liberal states accept unwanted immigration and extend rights to immigrants because of the influence of embedded liberal ideals, such as universal human rights standards, and because domestic, and to a lesser extent international, courts are able to constrain governments intent on pursuing restrictive policies (Hollifield 1992a, 1992b; Joppke 1998). As with client politics, this model considers the domestic conflict between restrictionist and expansionist actors, but unlike client politics, which pits employers against publics, here the chief restrictionist actors are state executives while the main expansionist actors are courts and judiciaries. This approach offers a more promising way of explaining immigration policy gaps in areas such as family reunion and asylum, where interest-based mobilization is limited but where liberal norms are important. The central contention is that courts mobilize liberal norms to constrain the restrictionist impulses emanating from democratic politics, especially state executives: "constitutionally guaranteed fundamental freedoms have been successfully invoked by independent courts to protect migrants against vindictive state executives. This is a case of 'self-limited' sovereignty, in which liberal norms circumscribe the ability of democratic governments to control the entry and stay of people on their national territory" (Guiraudon and Joppke 2001).

Note that embedded liberalism has both an ideational and institutional dimension: liberal values are discursively embedded in the public political culture and they are institutionally embedded through constitutional courts and judiciaries. If these constraints are weakened, for example, if liberal ideals are subverted in public debate or the power of independent courts is curtailed, then a "disembedding" of liberalism might be said to have occurred. For sovereignty to be effectively self-limited, liberal norms and values should be sufficiently robust to command wide public appeal and thereby delimit political discourse. Furthermore, the courts that deal with immigration cases must be independent of executives, and executives must accept the authority of courts and be prepared, most of the time, to adhere to their rulings. This is likely to be the case in the normal pursuit of liberal democratic politics, but under extraordinary conditions—whether real or perceived—it is at least possible that liberal values might become disembedded. Below I shall suggest that the framing of migration as a security issue has significantly undermined these conditions, and that the British government has been able to increase its powers of exclusion by appealing to the "extraordinary" nature of the terrorist threat.

To sum up, both of the models outlined above have significant explanatory force, but they are of varying use in different countries, at different times, and in different migration policy domains. Client politics accurately describes the politics of labor migration in settler countries, and helps explain the gap between public resistance to increased immigration in those countries and the tendency for the number of permanent settler visas to have increased. Embedded liberalism accurately describes the politics of family migration and asylum seeking in many European countries, and thus helps to explain gaps between popular attitudes and public discourse on the one hand and policy outcomes on the other. The explanatory power of the two models derives from the different causal factors that they adduce. Whilst the client politics model draws our attention to the role of economic interests in immigration politics, the embedded liberalism model highlights the role of liberal norms and values, especially universal human rights, and the institutional venues in which those rights are protected.

Given the complexity of immigration politics, I propose that any satisfactory explanatory framework should be holistic; that is to say, it must account for the role of interests, institutions, and ideas, and for the way in which these three categories of explanatory variable interact (cf. Hansen and King 2001; Lieberman 2002). A holistic approach will recognize that migration policies are powerfully shaped by mobilization around (economic) interests, but also that institutional and ideational constraints weigh heavily in the policymaking equation. It will also recognize that multiple actors operate in a number of policy arenas, both domestic and international, to shape migration policies (Lahav and Guiraudon 2006). Lastly, it will not overlook the importance of situational factors, including such factors as the historical legacies of past migrations, different imagined communities of citizenship and nationhood (Brubaker 1992), and the path-dependent effects of previous policy decisions (Hansen 2002). If accounting for such a range of variables demands that parsimony give ground to complexity, then this is something we should accept. We might not be able to capture all of the variables within a single model, but a holistic approach can nevertheless seek to identify and theorize the respective influence of the different variables. In this vein, Guiraudon and Joppke (2001) have suggested that immigration politics in liberal democratic states can be understood in terms of a series of "control dilemmas" in which political, economic, and legal factors interact to shape policymaking. The migration policies that we should expect to arise from a contested political field in which all of these factors play a role will likely exhibit both restrictionist and expansionist tendencies, and it should be no surprise if we find gaps between stated objectives and policy outcomes.

Immigration Politics in Britain

How do the control dilemmas between employers' interest in labor, the restrictionist imperatives of elected governments, and expansionist judiciaries play out in the British case? How useful are client politics and embedded liberalism in explaining gaps in immigration policy in Britain? Until very recently, many scholars doubted that Britain fitted either of the two models particularly well. Postwar British governments had implemented immigration controls well before the pan-European immigration stop in the mid-1970s and they had been unusually successful in constructing a restrictionist immigration regime. Furthermore, neither employers' associations nor courts appeared to have exercised significant influence over Britain's powerful executive. In short, there wasn't much of a gap between policy objectives and outcomes: politicians promised immigration controls and, by and large, they delivered them. Britain, in the words of Gary Freeman, was a "deviant case" (Freeman 1994; cf. Geddes 2003: 29).

Yet, since the election of the Labour government in 1997, profound changes have taken place in British immigration policies. Without doubt the most striking change has been in the area of labor migration. Britain now has a relatively liberal immigration regime that actively recruits migrants to meet labor and skills shortages in different sectors of the economy, ranging from low-skilled workers in agriculture, construction, and hospitality sectors, to high-skilled economic jetsetters in finance and banking. In the international competition for labor, Britain has emerged as a market leader. That underlying demographic and economic factors have driven this new openness to labor migration is clear (Layton-Henry 2004; Spencer 2003). What is less obvious is whether labor migration policymaking has evolved in a more clientelistic direction, as Freeman's model would suggest.

In a recent (2006) article, Statham and Geddes query the relevance of the client model for Britain. They argue that immigration politics in Britain remains an elite-led highly institutionalized field in which organized interests play a marginal role. However, whilst their data demonstrate that this is indeed the case in the field of asylum policy, they do not present findings for the field of labor migration policy. Although more research needs to be conducted in this area, some evidence indicates that the labor migration policy field is becoming increasingly clientelistic. The leading employers' association, the Confederation of British Industry (CBI), has actively lobbied government for a more liberal and flexible approach to labor migration linked to skills shortages, as have multinational companies (Confederation of British Industry 2002). Certainly, employers have endorsed the expansion of the work permit system and, most recently, the creation of a points-based labor migration system. Of course, it is possible that an autonomous executive could arrive at a soliciting strategy without the influence of immigration clients, but it seems more likely that employers are beginning to exert their influence on this area of policy. What cannot be doubted is that labor migrants are now wanted migrants, something that is unlikely to change so long as demand for labor remains strong.

If labor migration has become wanted migration and we see evidence of nascent clientelism in this policy field, what of the embedded liberal constraints on restrictive policymaking in other fields such as family and asylum migration? Again, Britain has often been seen as deviant here too. The British executive is one of the least constrained in the democratic world, and without a codified constitution or entrenched bill of rights to draw upon, the judiciary has been historically less activist than in other liberal democracies. In his article on why liberal states accept unwanted immigration, Joppke explicitly contrasts Germany and Britain in this regard. Joppke argues that Germany, "with both a strong constitution celebrating human rights and the moral burdens of a negative history," represents an "extreme case of self-limited sovereignty, making it one of the most expansive immigrant-receiving countries in the world" (1998: 292). Britain, on the other hand, has successfully managed to control unwanted immigration due to the absence of a codified constitution protecting individual rights and the concomitant weakness of the courts relative to the executive. The conflicting imperatives of controls and rights exist in both countries, but "whereas in the German case the rights came to predominate over the controls imperative, in the British case the opposite happened" (p. 287).

Joppke certainly has a point, but he overplays his argument. Despite the lack of a codified constitution in Britain, domestic courts have successfully constrained the government on several occasions, both with regard to immigration controls and immigrant rights. In the words of Statham and Geddes, Joppke "overstates the autonomy and power of the national judiciary relative to the political system when discussing Germany, and understates it when discussing Britain" (2006: 255). Indeed, courts have recently overturned restrictionist government policies in several important cases. For example, in February 2003, the Court of Appeal upheld a High Court ruling that the government's attempt to remove welfare benefits from asylum applicants under Section 55 of the Nationality, Immigration and Asylum Act of 2002 was "inhumane" and "unlawful."[2] The government appealed this decision to the House of Lords, but the ruling was unanimously upheld (5–0).[3] In a further example of the judiciary's ability to frustrate government restrictionism, this time on remote border controls, an Appellate Committee of five Law Lords ruled in December 2004 that government attempts to cut asylum applications by preventing people (mostly Roma) from boarding flights to Britain at Prague Airport was unlawful.[4] As I argue below, the courts have additionally mounted a rearguard action against the government's more recent counterterrorism policies aimed at foreign nationals. These examples illustrate the power of the judiciary to check executive power, particularly in the areas of asylum policy and the rights of foreign nationals.

It is also important to recognize that liberal ideas are not exclusively embedded in national institutions. International law plays a role, not so much as an external constraint upon national sovereignty (as postnationalists argue), as a source of liberal norms which can be mobilized by domestic political actors including judiciaries and non-governmental organizations (Gurowitz 1999). As a member of the European Union, Britain is bound to observe European law, including the European Convention on Human Rights (ECHR), which has led to several defeats for governments pursuing restrictionist migration policies.

Perhaps the most important piece of ECHR jurisprudence on the rights of migrants is *Chahal* v. *U.K.* (1996).[5] In this case, the European Court of Human Rights ruled that the British government could not deport an Indian national, Mr. Chahal, although the government had argued that his presence was not conducive to the public good. If he was returned to India, Mr. Chahal faced a real risk of death or torture in custody, contrary to Article 3 of the ECHR, which provides that "no one shall be subjected to torture or to inhuman or degrading treatment or punishment." The British government contended that the effect of Article 3 should be qualified in a case where a state sought to deport a non-national on grounds of national security. The Court rejected this argument, asserting that Article 3 was absolute and could not be qualified even in times of national emergency. The Chahal case has become a central piece of European jurisprudence and British courts have repeatedly referred to it in their recent conflicts with the government over deportation (see below). The current government has made plain its frustrations with the Chahal ruling and, at the time of writing, is trying to change it by intervening in a case before the European Court.

In sum, immigration politics in Britain has become less deviant than it was as little as ten years ago. An emerging clientelism in the labor migration policy field and court activism in the asylum policy field mark out some of the main fault lines of British immigration politics. In the remainder of this chapter, I want to consider how the framing of migration as a security issue affects these political dynamics. In order to do so, I first outline a conceptual framework derived from the critical security studies literature.[6]

Securitization, Migration, and Liberal Democracy

At the heart of critical security studies is the concept of securitization. This concept refers to the process by which a policy issue is represented as a security threat. According to Ole Wæver (1995), policy issues are not inherently about security or not about security; rather, a policy issue is (or is not) framed as a security issue by actors who seek to present it as a threat. Whilst the securitization of some policy issues—for example, nuclear armaments or counterterrorism—is so entrenched as to seem almost inevitable, other issues have only more recently been constructed as security threats, often by actors who seek to promote their issue on the political agenda. A case in point is the environment, where non-governmental organizations have sought to represent environmental change as a security threat, often in the hope that this will increase awareness and a sense of urgency about tackling environmental problems (Buzan et al. 1995; Graeger 1996).

Attempts to securitize a policy issue occur through speech acts that represent the issue as a threat to the security of a referent object. According to Barry Buzan et al. (1998: 21), a policy issue is securitized when it is "presented as posing an existential threat to a designated referent object (traditionally, but not necessarily, the state, incorporating government, territory, and society)." When the former is successfully presented as posing an "existential" threat to the latter—that is to say, when the intended audience of the securitizing statements accept the purported threat—then a successful securitization has taken place. For example, if politicians present immigration as a security threat to the nation, and this is widely accepted in public discourse, then immigration has become securitized.

Crucially, securitization is not simply about making discursive linkages between a given policy issue and security. It is additionally about justifying extraordinary measures to combat the threat thus identified. Securitizing actors seek to challenge the normal order of things, suspending the operation of standard procedures: "'security' is a move that takes politics beyond the established rules of the game and frames the issue either as a special kind of politics or as above politics" (Buzan et al. 1998: 23). The invocation of a security threat is further used to bestow legitimacy on policies which would otherwise appear illegitimate: "the special nature of security threats justifies the use of extraordinary measures to handle them … a state representative declares an emergency condition, thus claiming a right to use whatever means are necessary to block a threatening development" (Buzan et al. 1998: 21). Thus, if immigration is successfully securitized we would expect to see extraordinary policies being justified with reference to the putative threat that immigrants pose.[7]

I argue that a government-led securitization of migration has indeed occurred in Britain since 9/11, and that this has been used to legitimize extraordinary policies especially in the field of asylum and migrants' rights. The securitization of migration has partially "disembedded" some of the ideational and institutional constraints on restrictive policymaking. This process of disembedding has occurred in two interrelated ways: firstly, politicians have invoked security concerns to challenge the liberal ideals that normally delimit migration policymaking; secondly, they have sought to weaken some of the legal constraints on migration policymaking—at both the domestic and international level—by challenging judicial rulings and, in some cases, by legislating so as to limit the ability of courts to challenge executive decisions.

But we should be wary of viewing everything through a security lens. The economic and demographic factors that inform labor migration policy, as well as the liberal norms and institutions that shape asylum and family migration policy, are not simply trumped by security concerns. To treat security as *the* defining logic of immigration is surely to overstate the case. In this respect I agree with Boswell (2006: 4), who argues that we should avoid "narrowing the focus of observation to the search for one rather specific type of issue framing." Although the findings of this chapter conflict with her claim that there has been an "absence of securitization," she is right to point out that encouraging unease about migrants will not always be in the political elite's interest, especially if doing so would "create unfeasible expectations about the state's capacity to control migration, or where it would conflict with other goals of the liberal state" (Boswell 2006: 4). As I shall argue below, it is precisely such "other goals," including the ongoing interest in certain types of labor migration, that have limited the extent of securitization and its effects.

Security and Migration Policy in Britain since 9/11

Since 9/11, the British government has introduced a raft of counterterrorism measures and also repackaged some pre-existing policies as ways of tackling terrorism.[8] Migration policy has not escaped this wider trend, and migration has been increasingly, although by no means exclusively, framed in security terms. In this section I show how the securitization of migration has provided the context for a series of extraordinary policies that have significantly increased the government's powers of exclusion. In their pursuit of these policies, senior ministers have openly questioned liberal ideals, and the role of the judiciary in constraining the executive's powers has been publicly challenged on a number of occasions. References to the exceptional or novel circumstances in which we supposedly find ourselves have justified illiberal policies throughout.

In what follows I focus on government speech acts (ministerial statements, speeches, and parliamentary debates) in the debates surrounding two pieces of legislation that came in the aftermath of 9/11 and July 7. This focus is not meant to suggest that government is the only actor that has made discursive linkages between migration and security over the last five years. The mass media, particularly the tabloids, and the anti-immigration pressure group MigrationWatch, have also made securitizing moves, representing migration in general as a security threat or emphasizing the migrant status of particular individuals accused of terrorist activities. Nevertheless, and in line with Statham and Geddes's (2006: 266) argument that migration policy discourse in Britain is elite-directed, I submit that the securitization of migration has been largely government-led.

My aim is to show how migration has been linked with security in political debate, how embedded liberal ideas have been challenged by senior government figures, and how these "securitising moves" (Wæver 1995) have been used to justify extraordinary policy measures. These measures relate mostly to asylum, border control, and the rights of foreign nationals, and include increased powers to detain and deport foreign nationals, restrictions on asylum claims, a lower threshold for deprivation of citizenship, and new border control measures, including biometric technologies.

The government's immediate legislative response to the 9/11 attacks was to pass the Anti-Terrorism, Crime and Security Act (ATCSA) of 2001. In the parliamentary debates leading up to the ATCSA 2001, abuse of the asylum system and the removal and exclusion of aliens suspected of terrorist activities became prominent themes.[9] The threat of terrorism was strongly associated with resident foreign nationals. On October 4, then Prime Minister Tony Blair outlined the government's legislative response to the attacks. One of the main goals of the legislation was to "increase our ability to exclude and remove those whom we suspect of terrorism and who are seeking to abuse our asylum procedures."[10] The connection between foreign nationals suspected of terrorism and abuse of the asylum system was repeated in parliamentary debates over the following days and weeks.[11]

In the febrile political atmosphere following 9/11, the ATCSA passed through Parliament in just over four weeks.[12] Many of its provisions were unrelated to migration, but at its heart was a controversial proposal on the detention and deportation of foreign nationals suspected of involvement in terrorism. Part 4 of the ATCSA allowed the Home Secretary to certify a foreign national as a "suspected international terrorist" and detain him or her indefinitely without charge or trial. Whilst the 1971 Immigration Act already provided powers of deportation on national security grounds, because of the 1996 Chahal ruling prohibiting deportation to a country where a person might face torture, the government now sought powers of indefinite detention for those who could not be deported. The government argued that it was necessary to imprison people who, on the Home Secretary's "reasonable suspicion," posed a security threat to the country, but against whom it was not possible to bring criminal proceedings. Sixteen foreign nationals were subsequently certified and detained in Belmarsh high-security prison. Under the legislation, the Home Secretary's decision could be appealed to the Special Immigration Appeals Commission (SIAC), a court originally established in 1996 to hear deportation appeals. SIAC appeals against detention are held in secret, with security-vetted lawyers, and appellants are not presented with any "closed material" (evidence gained from secret intelligence) that is used in their case.

Part 4 of the ATCSA required a derogation from Article 5 of the European Convention on Human Rights (ECHR), which provides a right to liberty, and it was extremely controversial as a result. The government justified its derogation from the ECHR by claiming that the country faced a "public emergency," something that no other European state felt compelled to do.[13] Ministers began to claim that it was necessary to rethink traditional liberal commitments to civil liberties, arguing that we were living in exceptional times which required exceptional responses. This line of thought was succinctly captured by then Home Secretary, David Blunkett, as he presented the bill to Parliament: "Those who drew up the European Convention and the refugee convention could not have dreamt of the act that took place on 11 September, but they did envisage some act of that kind that would at some point require us to be able to take the necessary steps."[14]

It is remarkable just how closely the introduction and acceptance of Part 4 conforms to securitization theory. Following the attacks on the United States, migrants were associated with the threat of terrorism in parliamentary debates (as well as in the popular media), a public emergency was announced, and an extraordinary policy, which sanctioned detention without trial, was passed.

Part 4 did not go unchallenged, however. Civil liberties groups, notably Liberty and Justice, as well as media commentators and academics, heavily criticized the government's willingness to suspend civil liberties in the fight against terrorism. In 2003, the Privy Counsellor committee set up to review the operation of ACTSA recommended that Part 4 should be repealed "as a matter of urgency." The Newton Report argued that counterterrorism measures should not discriminate between citizens and non-citizens, nor should they require derogation from the ECHR (Privy Counsel 2003). In a similar vein, the Joint Committee on Human Rights questioned the detention policy and whether circumstances justified it. In its sixth report on the ATCSA, the Joint Committee said that it continued "to doubt whether the very wide powers conferred by Part 4 are . . . strictly required by the exigencies of the situation" (House of Lords 2004). The government, however, was unmoved, claiming that the nation continued to face a state of emergency that justified extraordinary powers. David Blunkett argued that the internment powers were an "essential component" of the government's counterterrorism strategy.

The government's policy finally met its match in the courts, as the embedded liberalism thesis would predict. Several of the men certified and detained under the ATCSA challenged the lawfulness of their detention. Their first appeal to the SIAC was successful; the court ruled that Part 4 of the ACTSA was unlawful on the grounds that it was both disproportionate and discriminatory. The Home Secretary then appealed this decision to the Court of Appeal, which reversed the SIAC decision and upheld the legality of the men's detention. In a final attempt to challenge their detention, the nine appellants then went to the House of Lords, which, as the highest court in the English legal system, overturned the previous decision and ruled that the policy of detention without trial was contrary to human rights law. The Law Lords ruled that the discriminatory nature of the legislation, which allowed only foreign nationals to be indefinitely detained without charge, was incompatible with the ECHR. In his ruling, Lord Nicholls of Birkenhead said: "Indefinite imprisonment without charge or trial is anathema in any country which observes the rule of law."[15]

In response, the government legislated again, creating a system of "control orders" that can be applied to all persons, irrespective of nationality, and that allow suspected terrorists to be placed under house arrest. But these have also recently been successfully challenged in the courts, much to the annoyance of the government. This episode illustrates the power of the judiciary to invoke liberal norms and constrain the government's ability to detain foreign nationals;

it also indicates the executive's increasing desire to challenge rulings that limit its pursuit of counterterrorism legislation.

As these court appeals and counterappeals were unfolding, the discursive linkage between security and migration began to weaken. This was partly due to a growing acceptance that the terrorist threat did not originate solely from foreign shores. The arrest of Richard Reid, the so-called "Shoe Bomber," in December 2001, and the revelation that British citizens had carried out suicide bombings in Tel Aviv in May 2003, amply illustrated the potential threat from British nationals. As the Newton Report observed, nearly half of the people suspected of involvement in terrorist activities by the security services were British nationals (Privy Counsel 2003: 53–54). The report argued, and the Home Secretary subsequently accepted, that the initial bias towards foreigners was misplaced and more efforts were required to address internal threats. The focus of the public debate shifted, and between 2002 and 2005 the migration–terrorism nexus was largely absent from parliamentary debates on immigration legislation. In 2003, several exchanges were related to the security threat posed by asylum seekers following a counterterrorism operation in Manchester in which a police officer was killed, but this was the exception that proved the rule.[16] Above all, in the 2002 debates on the Nationality, Immigration and Asylum Bill security was not mentioned at all. The initial framing of migration as a security threat had given way to a more familiar admixture of positive and negative framings around labor migrants and asylum seekers respectively.

In a bleak irony, the London suicide bombings on July 7, 2005—perpetrated by four British nationals—prompted a second wave of securitizing statements about migrants, as well as a slew of restrictionist policies legitimized by reference to the terrorist threat. In the aftermath of the attacks, before the identities of the bombers were known, some media pundits immediately drew connections between immigration control and security. Writing in the *Daily Mail* on July 8, Melanie Phillips claimed that "in the light of the clear danger from terrorists slipping into this country from abroad, the Government's failure to secure our borders defies belief" (Phillips 2005: 20). Once the identities of the men had been released, the public debate evolved into a more incredulous and self-seeking disquisition about so-called "homegrown" terrorism, but lingering associations between immigrants and terror remained. Although three of the four suicide bombers were British nationals, they were the children of immigrants, and several of the suspects in the attempted London bombings on July 21 were foreign nationals or naturalized citizens who had come to Britain as asylum seekers.

The government's response to the attacks contained several measures to bolster its powers of exclusion. Just one week after the bombings, the Home Secretary, Charles Clarke, announced that new terror legislation would include proposals to impose additional conditions on those seeking asylum or leave to remain in the United Kingdom (Clarke 2005). In a statement to Parliament on July 20, Clarke made a classic securitizing move, linking the present threat to the need for a special policy:

in the circumstances that we now face, I have decided that it is right
to broaden the use of these [exclusion and deportation] powers to deal
with those who foment terrorism, or seek to provoke others to commit
terrorist acts . . . [existing] powers need to be applied more widely and
systematically both to people before they come to the UK and when they
are here.[17]

Clarke announced the he would draw up a list of "unacceptable behaviours"
and that a database of individuals who have "demonstrated the relevant
behaviours," whether in the United Kingdom or abroad, would be made
available to immigration officials and entry clearance officers through the
existing warnings index. The list published on August 5 covers any non-U.K.
citizen who uses any medium (including speeches, published material, and
websites) to express views that: foment, justify, or glorify terrorist violence in
furtherance of particular beliefs; seek to provoke others to terrorist acts;
foment other serious criminal activity or seek to provoke others to serious
criminal acts; or foster hatred which might lead to inter-community violence in
the U.K.

The use of the list of unacceptable behaviors as a basis for immigration
control constitutes a significant increase in the Home Secretary's and thus the
executive's discretionary power to refuse entry and right to remain in Britain.
The list goes well beyond the normal liberal democratic powers of territorial
exclusion. Whilst it is almost universally accepted that liberal states can legiti-
mately exclude individuals on the grounds of proven criminality or threat to
national security, the list of unacceptable behaviors allows the minister and
immigration officials to exclude those who pose only an indirect threat—for
example, by having written a pamphlet which, in the Home Secretary's
judgment, "glorifies" terrorism.

On the same day as the list was published, the Prime Minister issued a major
policy statement outlining the government's "comprehensive framework for
action" in response to the London bombings. Five of the twelve measures
detailed in the statement relate to migration: 1) new powers of deportation;
2) primary legislation to ensure that "anyone who has participated in terrorism
or has anything to do with it anywhere will automatically be refused asylum,"
3) new powers to strip those "engaged in extremism" of their British citizenship; 4) new conditions for the acquisition of citizenship; and, lastly, 5) a
promise to "bring forward the proposed measures on the security of our borders" (Prime Minister's Office 2005). The statement ends with an invocation
of Britain's traditional "respect and tolerance towards others" followed by a
warning to those who would abuse such openness: "coming to Britain is not
a right. And even when people have come here, staying here carries with it a
duty. That duty is to share and support the values that sustain the British way
of life. Those that break that duty and try to incite hatred or engage in violence
against our country and its people, have no place here" (Prime Minister's
Office 2005). The four new measures that the Prime Minister outlined would

be added to the Immigration, Asylum and Nationality Bill, which had recently been introduced to Parliament.[18]

The Immigration, Asylum and Nationality Bill was primarily developed from two government policy documents published prior to 7 July.[19] With the exception of some of the border control proposals (including extended provisions for immigration officials and subcontractors to search aircraft, ships, and vehicles at ports of entry, as well as powers to enable immigration officers to verify passengers' identity documents and demand biometric data), the original bill did not contain significant security-related measures. This is important as it demonstrates clearly the effect of the London bombings. On September 15, and then again on October 12, the Home Secretary wrote to his counterparts in the opposition parties setting out draft clauses to be added to the bill.[20] The new measures outlined in the letter include a "streamlined" appeals process against deportation in national security cases, a clause to "clarify our ability to deny asylum to terrorists," and new powers relating to acquisition and deprivation of citizenship. Quite clearly, then, the securitization of the long-planned immigration legislation was a direct response to the bombings and the measures that the Prime Minister had promised in his August statement.

The Immigration, Asylum and Nationality (IAN) Act received royal assent on March 30, 2006. A full discussion of its clauses and their implications is beyond the scope of this chapter. Suffice it to say that, in addition to the border control measures mentioned above, the IAN Act 2006 includes a number of restrictionist measures relating to deportation, asylum, and deprivation of citizenship:

- The Act requires that any appeal against a decision to make a deportation order on national security grounds should normally only be brought from outside the United Kingdom.
- The Act outlines a new construction of "acts contrary to the purposes and principles of the United Nations." This now includes "acts of committing, preparing or instigating terrorism (whether or not the acts amount to an actual or inchoate offence)" and acts of encouraging or inducing others to do so. The Home Secretary is empowered to reject an asylum claim on these grounds, and any appeal hearing would need to begin with substantive deliberation on this issue.
- The Home Secretary is empowered to deprive a person of their British citizenship if satisfied that this deprivation is "conducive to the public good" and doing so would not leave the person stateless. This is a much lower threshold than the previous requirement in the 1981 British Nationality Act that "the person has done anything seriously prejudicial to the vital interests of the United Kingdom or a British overseas territory."[21]

These various control measures thus widen the executive's powers of exclusion from territory, from asylum, and from citizenship. Taken together, they amount to a significant extension of the state's discretionary powers over migrants and foreign nationals.

Conclusion

This chapter began by asking whether the securitization of migration since 9/11 has changed the rules of the immigration game. Whilst the previous sections demonstrate that there has been a tendency to frame migration as a security issue over the last five years, we should also recognize that security concerns have not wholly supplanted other logics of immigration politics. On the one hand, in its response to 9/11 and then July 7, the British government has made discursive linkages between migration and terrorism. Furthermore, the representation of migration as a security threat and the invocation of a public emergency have allowed the government to enact several extraordinary policies. Recent legislation has further empowered an already powerful executive, and the Home Secretary's discretionary powers have been significantly expanded in a number of areas. Undoubtedly, security is now a factor in the immigration policy process.

However, while these developments point to an erosion of the liberal constraints on restrictive immigration policy outcomes, other logics and goals continue to drive policy in an expansionist direction. Britain has not closed its borders to immigrants since 9/11. On the contrary, the government has pressed ahead with expansionist labor recruitment driven by demographic and economic demand-side factors, and increasingly influenced by immigration clients. The absence of security claims in the debates surrounding the 2002 Nationality, Asylum and Immigration Bill, as well as the government's recent attempts to promote its points-based system for labor migrants, illustrates how migration is far from being wholly securitized.

Moreover, the government's commitment to the migration–terrorism nexus has been rather fickle, with two bursts of legislative activity after 9/11 and July 7 separated by a period in which migration policymaking reverted to a more normal language. Thus, if the pattern after 9/11 is repeated, we should expect the migration–terrorism nexus to decline as July 7 recedes from the public mind. It is unlikely that the association now established will disappear altogether, however. Indeed, recent government statements have continued to emphasize the potential dangers, as well as the benefits, that migration presents. In an article published in the *Observer* newspaper in February 2006, Tony Blair defends the government's record on civil liberties, arguing that the "new Islamic global terrorism" is "different in nature and scale" from previous terrorist threats such as the IRA. "In theory," he writes, "traditional court processes and attitudes to civil liberties could work. But the modern world is different from the world for which these court processes were designed." What, then, is the most salient characteristic of this new world? "It is a world of vast migration, most of it beneficial but with dangerous threats" (Blair 2006: 29).

Notes

1 This proportion of pro-restriction voters ranges from 29 percent in Sweden to 67 percent in Greece (Iversflaten 2005: 27–28).
2 Court of Appeal (Civil Division), The Queen on the Application of Q & Others (Respondents) and Secretary of State for the Home Department (Appellant), [2003] EWCA Civ 364, March 18, 2003.
3 House of Lords, *Regina (Limbuela, Tesema and Adam)* v. *Secretary of State for the Home Department*, [2005] UKHL 66, November 3, 2005.
4 House of Lords, *Regina* v. *Immigration Officer at Prague Airport* and another *(Respondents)* ex parte *European Roma Rights Centre and others (Appellants)*, [2004] UKHL 55, December 9, 2004.
5 *Chahal* v. *U.K.*—22414/93 [1996] ECHR 54, November 15, 1996.
6 There are at least two distinct schools of critical security studies: the Copenhagen School, associated with the work of Ole Wæver, Barry Buzan, and others; and the Paris School, associated with the work of Didier Bigo and others. Waever et al. focus on the "politics of exception," i.e., how security threats are used to legitimize exceptional policy measures, whereas Bigo emphasizes what he calls a "governmentality of unease." For the purposes of this chapter, I am primarily drawing upon the former approach.
7 Note that I am focusing here on the discursive construction of policy issues as security threats, which takes place through political debate, rather than security practices that take place in the administrative field. See Boswell (2006) for this distinction.
8 The most egregious example is identity cards. The original argument for the cards focused on the need to combat illegal working and identity fraud, but they are now more often presented as anti-terror measures. See Perri 6 (2005).
9 See the Commons debates on September 14, October 4, October 15, November 1, and November 15, 2001. These debates are usefully summarized in Huysmans (2005).
10 Hansard, *Parliamentary Debates*, Commons, October 4, 2001, col. 675.
11 See, for example, David Blunkett and Shadow Home Secretary, Oliver Letwin's, exchange on October 15, 2001. Hansard, *Parliamentary Debates*, Commons, October 15, 2001, cols. 924–926.
12 The bill was introduced to Parliament on November 19, 2001 and received royal assent on December 13.
13 Statutory Instrument 2001 No. 3644: The Human Rights Act 1998 (Designated Derogation) Order 2001.
14 Hansard, *Parliamentary Debates*, Commons, November 19, 2001, col. 29.
15 Judgments—*A (FC) and others (FC) (Appellants)* v. *Secretary of State for the Home Department (Respondent)* [2004] UKHL 56, December 16, 2004.
16 Hansard, *Parliamentary Debates*, Commons, January 15, 2003, cols. 684ff.
17 Hansard, *Parliamentary Debates*, Commons, July 20, 2005, col. 1255.
18 The bill was introduced into the Commons on June 22 and it had its Second Reading on July 5, just two days before the London bombings.
19 The relevant documents are: Home Office (2004, 2005).
20 Charles Clarke to David Davis and Mark Oaten, September 15, 2005 and October 12, 2005. Available at http://security.homeoffice.gov.uk/news-and-publications1/publication-search/legislation-publications/proposed-legislation-letter2?view=Binary and http://security.homeoffice.gov.uk/news-and-publications1/publication-search/legislation-publications/homesec_letter_terrorism?view=Binary.
21 United Kingdom. 1981. British Nationality Act, s. 40(2).

References

Bigo, Didier. 2001. "Migration and Security," in Virginie Guiraudon and Christian Joppke, eds., *Controlling a New Migration World*, pp. 121–149. London: Routledge.

Blair, Tony. 2006. "I Don't Destroy Liberties, I Protect Them." *Observer*, February 26.

Boswell, Christina. 2006. "Migration Control in Europe After 9/11: Explaining the Absence of Securitization." Unpublished manuscript.

Brubaker, Rogers. 1995. "Comments on 'Modes of Immigration Politics in Liberal Democratic States'." *International Migration Review* 29(4): 903–908.

Buzan, Barry, Ole Wæver, and Jaap de Wilde. 1995. "Environmental, Economic and Societal Security." Working Paper 10. Copenhagen: Centre for Peace and Conflict Research.

Buzan, Barry, Ole Wæver, and Jaap de Wilde. 1998. *Security: A New Framework for Analysis*. Boulder: Lynne Rienne.

Clarke, Sean. 2005. "Government to Hold Terrorism Law summits." *Guardian*, July 14. http://politics.guardian.co.uk./terrorism/story/0,,1528655,00.html.

Confederation of British Industry. 2002. *CBI Response to the Government's White Paper on Immigration, Asylum and Nationality*, March. www.cbi.org.uk.

Cornelius, Wayne A., Takeyuki Tsuda, Philip L. Martin, and James F. Hollifield, eds. 2004. *Controlling Immigration: A Global Perspective*, 2nd ed. Stanford: Stanford University Press.

Freeman, Gary P. 1994. "Commentary," in Wayne A. Cornelius, Philip L. Martin, and James F. Hollifield, eds., *Controlling Immigration: A Global Perspective*, 1st ed., pp. 174–178. Stanford: Stanford University Press.

Freeman, Gary P. 1995. "Modes of Immigration Politics in Liberal Democratic States," *International Migration Review* 29(4): 881–902.

Freeman, Gary P. 1998. "The Decline of Sovereignty? Politics and Immigration Restriction in Liberal States," in Christian Joppke, ed., *Challenge to the Nation-State: Immigration in Western Europe and the United States*, pp. 86–108. Oxford: Oxford University Press.

Freeman, Gary P. 2002. "Winners and Losers: Politics and the Costs and Benefits of Migration," in Anthony M. Messina, ed., *Western European Immigration and Immigration Policy in the New Century*, pp. 77–96. Westport: Praeger.

Freeman, Gary P. 2006. "National Models, Policy Types, and the Politics of Immigration in Liberal Democracies." *West European Politics* 29(2): 227–247.

Geddes, Andrew. 2003. *The Politics of Migration and Immigration in Europe*. London: Sage.

Graeger, Nina. 1996. "Environmental Security?" *Journal of Peace Research* 33(1): 109–116.

Guiraudon, Virginie, and Christian Joppke, eds. 2001. *Controlling a New Migration World*. London: Routledge.

Gurowitz, Amy. 1999. "Mobilizing International Norms: Domestic Actors, Immigrants, and the Japanese State." *World Politics* 51(3): 413–445.

Hansen, Randall. 2000. *Citizenship and Immigration in Post-War Britain*. Oxford: Oxford University Press.

Hansen, Randall. 2002. "Globalization, Embedded Realism, and Path Dependence: The Other Immigrants to Europe." *Comparative Political Studies* 35(3): 259–283.

Hansen, Randall, and Desmond King. 2001. "Eugenic Ideas, Political Interests, and Policy Variance: Immigration and Sterilization Policy in Britain and the U.S." *World Politics* 53(2): 237–263.

Hollifield, James F. 1992a. *Immigrants, Markets, and States: The Political Economy of Postwar Europe.* Cambridge, MA: Harvard University Press.

Hollifield, James F. 1992b. "Migration and International Relations: Cooperation and Control in the European Community." *International Migration Review* 26(2): 568–595.

Home Office. 2004. *Confident Communities in a Secure Britain.* London: Her Majesty's Stationery Office.

Home Office. 2005. *Controlling Our Borders: Making Migration Work for Britain.* London: Her Majesty's Stationery Office.

House of Lords. 2004. Joint Committee on Human Rights, *Sixth Report: Anti-Terrorism, Crime and Security Act 2001: Statutory Review and Continuance of Part 4*, HL 38/HC 381, February 24.

Huysmans, Jef. 1995. "Migrants as a Security Problem: Dangers of 'Securitizing' Societal Issues," in Robert Miles and Dietrich Thränhardt, eds., *Migration and European Integration: The Dynamics of Inclusion and Exclusion*, pp. 53–72. London: Pinter.

Huysmans, Jef. 2000. "The European Union and the Securitization of Migration," *Journal of Common Market Studies* 38: 751–777.

Huysmans, Jef. 2005. "Nexus Terrorism–Immigration/Asylum/Refuge in Parliamentary Debates in the UK: Commons Debates since 11 September 2001." Report for ESRC Project MIDAS (Migration, Democracy, and Security) in the New Security Challenges Programme, November 2. www.midas.bham.ac.uk.

Huysmans, Jef. 2006. *The Politics of Insecurity: Fear, Migration and Asylum in the EU.* London: Routledge.

Ivarsflaten, Elisabeth. 2005. "Threatened by Diversity: Why Restrictive Asylum and Immigration Policies Appeal to Western Europeans." *Journal of Elections, Public Opinion and Parties* 15(1): 21–45.

Jacobson, David. 1997. *Rights Across Borders: Immigration and the Decline of Citizenship*, 2nd ed. Baltimore: Johns Hopkins University Press.

Joppke, Christian. 1998. "Why Liberal States Accept Unwanted Immigration." *World Politics* 50(2): 266–293.

Joppke, Christian. 1999. *Immigration and the Nation-State: The United States, Germany and Great Britain.* Oxford: Oxford University Press.

Lahav, Gallya. 2004. *Immigration and Politics in the New Europe: Reinventing Borders.* Cambridge: Cambridge University Press.

Lahav, Gallya, and Virginie Guiraudon. 2006. "Actors and Venues in Immigration Control: Closing the Gap between Political Demands and Policy Outcomes." *West European Politics* 29(2): 201–223.

Layton-Henry, Zig. 2004. "Britain: From Immigration Control to Migration Management," in Wayne A. Cornelius, Takeyuki Tsuda, Philip L. Martin, and James F. Hollifield, eds., *Controlling Immigration: A Global Perspective*, 2nd ed., pp. 297–333. Stanford: Stanford University Press.

Lieberman, Robert C. 2002. "Ideas, Institutions, and Political Order: Explaining Political Change." *American Political Science Review* 96(4): 697–712.

Perri 6. 2005. "Should We Be Compelled to Have Identity Cards? Justifications for the Legal Enforcement of Obligations." *Political Studies* 53(2): 243–261.

Phillips, Melanie. 2005. "The Failure to Secure Our Borders Defies Belief." *Daily Mail*, July 8.

Prime Minister's Office. 2005. *Prime Minister's Statement on Anti-Terror Measures*, August 5. http://www.number10.gov.uk/output/Page8041.asp.

Privy Counsel. 2003. Privy Counsellor Review Committee, *Anti-Terrorism, Crime and Security Act 2001 Review: Report*, HC 100, December 18.

Rudolph, Christopher. 2003. "Security and the Political Economy of International Migration." *American Political Science Review* 97(4): 603–620.

Sassen, Saskia. 1996. *Losing Control? Sovereignty in an Age of Globalization.* New York: Columbia University Press.

Sassen, Saskia. 1999. "Beyond Sovereignty: De-Facto Transnationalism in Immigration Policy." *European Journal of Migration and Law* 1(2): 177–198.

Soysal, Yasemin N. 1994. *The Limits of Citizenship: Migrants and Postnational Membership in Europe.* Chicago: University of Chicago Press.

Spencer, Sarah. 2003. "Introduction," in Sarah Spencer, ed., *The Politics of Migration: Managing Opportunity, Conflict and Change.* Oxford: Blackwell.

Statham, Paul, and Andrew Geddes. 2006. "Elites and the 'Organised Public': Who Drives British Immigration Politics and in Which Direction?" *West European Politics* 29(2): 248–269.

Tirman, John, ed. 2004. *The Maze of Fear: Security and Migration After 9/11.* New York: New Press.

Wæver, Ole. 1995. "Securitization and Desecuritization," in Ronnie D. Lipschutz, ed., *On Security*, pp. 46–86. New York: Columbia University Press.

7 Fortifying Fortress Europe?

The Effect of September 11 on EU Immigration Policy

Adam Luedtke

The Pre-September 11 Context

The pre-9/11 world was an optimistic one for those who favored the development of a common immigration policy for the European Union (EU). Despite the resistance and reluctance of most of the EU's national governments for more than a decade, by the turn of the century Europe was marching closer to having a unified set of immigration rules regarding whom to let in, whom to keep out, and the rights and duties for admitted immigrants (Givens and Luedtke 2004). Not only was the economic and political context favorable (i.e., left governments in power, economies strong, European integration advancing in other fields), but the EU had also already taken concrete steps towards harmonizing their immigration policies. By early 2001, Europe's border-free travel zone (the "Schengen" zone) had become a reality, and the EU's intergovernmental club, the European Council, had agreed upon an ambitious program for immigration policy unification, known as the "Tampere Conclusions" (European Council 1999).

Named after the city in Finland where the European Council had met, the Tampere program seems in retrospect to be an incredibly ambitious (and optimistic) document. Arguing that "it would be in contradiction with Europe's traditions to deny . . . freedom to those whose circumstances lead them justifiably to seek access to our territory," the Council "requires the Union to develop common policies on asylum and immigration." Amazingly, considering the rather frosty view of immigration taken by most European governments, the document stated that the aim of future policy should be "an open and secure European Union, fully committed to the obligations of the Geneva Refugee Convention and other relevant human rights instruments, and able to respond to humanitarian needs on the basis of solidarity. A common approach must also be developed to ensure the integration into our societies of [immigrants]." Regarding the rights of immigrants to equal treatment, the Conclusions went further still, holding that the EU "must ensure fair treatment" of immigrants. "A more vigorous integration policy should aim at granting them rights and obligations comparable to those of EU citizens. It should also enhance non-discrimination in economic, social and cultural life and develop measures against racism and xenophobia" (European Council 1999).

Thus, by 2001 the blueprint had been laid, and the political will (and economic impetus) seemed to exist. Answering the call of the European Council (which represents national governments), the European Commission (the supranational executive body) began drafting an ambitious portfolio of laws and policies, including common EU rules for immigrants to bring in family members, rights and obligations for long-term residence, and even plans for an EU-wide "green card" and system of labor immigration (European Commission 2001a).

If we fast-forward to 2008, however, the picture looks very different. The proposal on labor immigration and general "green cards" is languishing on the back burner, shunned by every single one of the (now 27) national governments. In 2007, a more modest plan for "blue cards" for skilled immigrants was proposed by the European Commission, but even if it passes against national opposition the system it creates would be weak at best. The family reunification law, while passed, is so restrictive in nature towards the rights of immigrants that the European Parliament made a legal challenge on the grounds that the law tramples on the human rights of immigrant children. The long-term residents law, while also passed, was universally criticized by nongovernmental organizations (NGOs) and even (in my personal interviews) by civil servants from both the EU and national governments!

Further still, French and Dutch citizens voted down the draft European "constitution," which would have taken large steps towards a common EU immigration policy (by granting more power to Brussels), in large part due to worries over Muslim immigration, terrorism, and the prospect of Muslim Turkey joining the EU (de Vreese and Boomgaarden 2005). The author was in Paris during the referendum on the Constitution and saw many posters proclaiming "No to the Constitution, No to Turkey." In the Netherlands, the murders of Pim Fortuyn and Theo Van Gogh whipped up a simmering blend of xenophobia, fear of terrorism, and fear of immigrants, all of which joined forces in contributing to the defeat of the constitutional treaty (a large setback for fulfilling the Tampere goals). Spelling out this link explicitly, one Dutch news magazine ran this headline just before the referendum: "A dark scenario . . . European constitution removes the possibility for the Netherlands to regulate own immigration. There's an emergency brake: a no-vote" (Wynia 2005).[1]

What happened between the optimism of 1999 and the failures of 2005? Can 9/11 and the general specter of terrorism really be blamed for this dramatic setback? Or are there more conventional culprits at work, such as economic recession, political infighting, and a general reluctance to let European integration proceed too far into sensitive national powers? This chapter will attempt to answer these questions by looking at evidence (both direct and indirect) of a "9/11 effect" on EU immigration policy. Directly, I will attempt to find evidence of EU justice and interior ministers shifting their attention away from immigration and towards fighting terrorism (since both issues are usually handled by the same ministry in European countries). Indirectly, I will use my interviews with national and EU civil servants (conducted mainly in fall 2004 and spring 2005) to assess whether 9/11 changed their political climate and made the job of building an EU immigration policy a more difficult one. This chapter will close by assessing whether the few EU immigration laws which did pass allowed the more generous member states to lower their standards and become stricter towards the rights and freedoms of immigrants. If so, there is a large body of literature pointing to security concerns (such as terrorism) as being the primary causal factor pushing towards these types of restrictive immigration policies (Huysmans 2005; Rudolph 2003; Simon 1989; Weiner 1995).

Since both France and Belgium had some of the most generous national immigration legislation as of 2005, I will use these countries as test cases, to determine the effect of EU immigration law and the post-9/11 climate on their policies. Both countries have a relatively large percentage of foreign-born residents (11 percent for France, 7 percent for Belgium), a large percentage of Muslim residents (9 percent for France, 4 percent for Belgium), and a strong far right anti-immigrant party in terms of polling (17 percent support in France, 18 percent in Belgium). Therefore, if there was indeed a 9/11 effect on EU immigration policy, one might expect that both countries would use EU immigration law to tighten their own (relatively) generous laws. This chapter will look for evidence of such a shift in the areas of rights for long-term resident immigrants and family reunification, respectively, since these were the two most important immigration laws coming out of Brussels. First, however, let us analyze the more direct effects of 9/11 on immigration policymaking at EU level, by seeing how the new terrorist threat affected the institutional dynamics surrounding EU immigration policymaking.

Direct Effects: The Rise of Terrorism on the EU's "Justice and Home Affairs" Agenda

Institutionally, immigration policy is in a strange position in the European Union's scheme of governance. Immigration first joined the EU's agenda in the 1992 Maastricht Treaty (Papademetriou 1996). However, due to the reluctance of national governments to allow Brussels to play a role in matters of "justice" (subjects handled by interior ministries, such as policing, border control, and immigration), all of these subjects were relegated to a third "pillar" of EU policy (the second pillar being foreign policy). This pillar contained very weak rules for decision-making, including a national veto in the Council of Ministers (the EU's prime legislative body), and the fact that any agreements would not be legally binding on member states (thus removing the European Court of Justice's traditional role of judicial review). This made the task of harmonizing immigration policy a cumbersome, bureaucratic, and ineffective process.

The fact that immigration policy was lumped in with matters of crime and terrorism made many advocates of a more "open" immigration policy nervous. Despite much talk to move immigration to the jurisdiction of the EU's directorate on social and labor policy, immigration matters remained in the Commission's new directorate created to handle matters of justice (including terrorism).

Jörg Monar is a specialist on the EU's handling of Justice and Home Affairs (JHA) and has written about the dynamics of these institutions. Despite the favorable context of Tampere, Monar shows how September 11 and its aftermath very dramatically affected the context within which immigration policy was "harmonized" among EU countries. The terrorist attacks of 9/11 "put enormous pressure on justice and home affairs' cumbersome decision-making system to produce substantial legislation in a very short time" (2002: 121). Showing how the agenda shifted away from immigration matters, Monar writes that "this test was passed quite successfully—especially in the area of judicial cooperation in criminal matters" but that "other areas—asylum and immigration, in particular—saw only slow and limited progress" (2002: 121). In fact, after it was blocked from taking steps towards a common EU immigration policy, the Belgian EU presidency wrote a highly critical report lamenting the lack of progress on implementing the Tampere agenda (cited in Monar 2002: 124):

> The Belgian Presidency's efforts in the sphere of asylum and immigration policy were to some extent disrupted by the events of 11 September. It meant that, not only did the JHA Councils in November and December give very little time to asylum and immigration issues, but also that Member States became more reluctant to engage in further harmonization at a time when several of them were in the process of toughening certain asylum and immigration rules as part of their national anti-terrorism packages. Concerned about the adoption of further national legislation which could make the development of common approaches even more difficult, the Belgian Presidency proposed the introduction of a stand-still clause, committing the Member State to forgo adopting further legislation before agreement could be reached at the EU level on some common principles and measures, but the idea was rejected at the JHA Council meeting of 16 November.

At the European Council meeting on November 21, a statement was released announcing that "terrorism is a real challenge to the world and to Europe and . . . the fight against terrorism will be a priority objective of the European Union" (cited in Apap and Carrera 2004: 8). Only ten days after the attacks, the EU passed a broad package of anti-terrorist measures. According to Apap and Carrera, writing for the top think tank in Brussels, the Center for European Policy Studies, "all of these radical measures were subject to less controversy and agreed [to] more quickly than could have conceivably been the case without the events of 11 September 2001" (2004: 8).

The national "toughening" of immigration rules as part of national anti-terrorism legislation stemmed from a new perception that terrorists or potential terrorists were exploiting national immigration and asylum rules. After all, not only had many known terrorists lived in Europe as legal immigrants (most notably the Hamburg cell of Mohammad Atta), but (much more troubling to the European press, public, and governments) many Al-Qaeda members and/or sympathizers were living in Europe as genuine refugees. Given the rather brutal tactics of some Middle Eastern governments towards fundamentalist clerics and their sympathizers, many suspected Al-Qaeda members faced genuine Geneva Convention-recognized persecution in their home countries, and thus were (apparently) legally entitled to shelter in the West.

European governments quickly moved to counteract this trend, with Britain leading the way. After September 11, the Blair government quickly passed a new immigration law, entitled the Asylum, Immigration and Nationality Act (British Government 2002). Not only did this law make it easier to deport or refuse asylum to suspected terrorists, but Section 4 of the Act allows the government to strip the citizenship of anyone who has "done anything seriously prejudicial to the vital interests of the United Kingdom" (British Government 2002). This clause was used most famously in the case of the radical cleric Sheikh Abu Hamza, who had been a British citizen since 1981, but was stripped of this citizenship in 2003 under the new rules. Citizenship policy was changed in Belgium as well, in part as a response to Al-Qaeda's assassination of the Afghan Northern Alliance leader, Ahmed Shah Masood. The two suicide bombers who posed as journalists and killed Masood both held Belgian passports, and in my interview with Joanna Apap (the immigration expert at the Center for European Policy Studies), she argued that the other member states have accused Belgium of giving away citizenship too easily. "So, there have been lots of changes in implementation. Without changing the actual law, they make practice more restrictive towards immigrants. The effect of 9/11 was strong."[2] One direct effect was to actually include references to criminal and terrorist matters in the EU's nascent immigration laws, including the directive on family reunification mentioned above. Although this Directive was first proposed in 1999, by 2003 it had been amended to include the following passage:

> Family reunification may be refused on duly justified grounds. In particular, the person who wishes to be granted family reunification should not constitute a threat to public policy or public security. The notion of public policy may cover a conviction for committing a serious crime. In this context it has to be noted that the notion of public policy and public security covers also cases in which a third country national belongs to an association which supports terrorism, supports such an association or has extremist aspirations.
>
> (European Council 2003)

On the issue of political asylum, 9/11 again shifted the emphasis of

negotiations at the European level. The Belgian EU presidency began negotiations on a common EU policy on "minimum standards and procedures for
granting and withdrawing refugee status." According to Johannes van der
Klaauw of the UN High Commissioner for Refugees (2004: 239), "since this
[negotiation] happened in the aftermath of the terrorist attacks . . . negotiations were colored by a concern to protect asylum procedures from abuse by
potential criminal and terrorist elements, to screen out undeserving claims
rapidly". According to Apap, the key question in the negotiations over the
asylum directive was: "who to grant protection to? 9/11 had a role in excluding 'criminals', terrorists, etc."[3] Progress in immigration and asylum matters
was made only by granting a wide degree of national discretion, thus blocking
the development of a truly harmonized EU policy.

Overall, 2002 saw that:

> Major (and largely unexpected) progress was made in the area of judicial
> co-operation in criminal matters mainly as a result of the terrorist attacks.
> After difficult negotiations, the Member States were able to reach political
> agreement . . . on a framework decision on combating terrorism . . . the
> Council also agreed on [a] regulation . . . authorizing the freezing of
> assets of terrorists and terrorist organizations. The framework decision . . .
> provides for a common definition of terrorist attacks . . . such as serious
> intimidation of the population and destabilization of fundamental politi-
> cal and constitutional structures. It marked a significant step forward not
> only in the fight against terrorism, but also as regards the harmonization
> of national penal laws for serious forms of international crime.
>
> (Monar 2002: 129–130)

Again, given the fact that the same EU institutions and personnel share both
the above agenda (terrorism) and immigration, the large shift in attention and
resources to terrorism and criminal matters obviously affected the progress
that could be made on immigration. This, again, led to the highly critical
report by the Belgian government, calling European governments to account
for their failure to implement the Tampere program (European Council 2001).
The fact that the Belgian presidency failed even to reach agreement on a clause
"freezing" the divergence of national immigration legislation (in response to
9/11) meant a large setback for the goal of a common EU immigration policy.
Continuing with this shift in agenda, the Spanish EU presidency of early 2002
announced that the fight against terrorism would be a priority (van der Klaauw
2004). In a speech to NATO in 2002, an official of the Spanish Ministry of
Defence had the following words to say regarding the emphasis of his country's
EU presidency:

> The Spanish Presidency is fostering a greater co-ordination within the
> European Union on judiciary matters. Progress has been made in the com-
> mon definition of the crime of terrorism and in the conditions for the

arrest and handing over of terrorists among member countries (EURO-WARRANT) which will speed up the traditional bilateral extradition procedures.

(Macias 2002)

Indirect Effects: The National Governments and EU Negotiations

In Brussels, I interviewed national delegates to the EU responsible for immigration cooperation, from 24 out of the (then) 25 member states. My questions focused on the EU's immigration agenda, and the progress that had been made towards developing a common policy. Though I did not directly ask about 9/11, many of the delegates spontaneously cited 9/11 and terrorism in general as causing a lack of progress on the issue. As we will see below, where cooperation had been achieved, it tended to be in favor of restrictive measures that allowed for a wide degree of national discretion. Cooperation among member countries also tended to sideline the EU institutions (Commission, Parliament, Court of Justice), preventing them from ensuring that such a policy met the Tampere goals of openness, human rights, etc. For instance, much of the post-9/11 discussion shifted from questions of legal immigration to questions of illegal immigration. In the words of the Finnish delegate on questions of illegal immigration, "we can agree on anything at the EU level—return, deportation—it's a sexy topic, especially after 9/11."[4]

What about legal migration? As mentioned above, the Commission in early 2001 proposed an EU system of labor migration, complete with an EU-wide standardized work permit and system of labor recruitment. However, after 9/11, Commission President Antonio Vittorino allowed this measure to die. According to an Estonian delegate, "Vittorino wanted the next Commission to have it. He wanted to collect a trophy, so he got some terrorism measures passed." In general, this Estonian delegate highlighted the "security perspective" that permeated the negotiations, arguing that 3/11 (the Madrid train bombings) also had a big effect, and that "politics is reactionary."[5]

My interview with a British delegate was revealing because this official admitted that the U.K. has a bad reputation on immigration cooperation. Britain (along with Denmark and Ireland) secured the right to "opt out" from the EU's immigration policy portfolio under the 1997 Amsterdam Treaty. This includes the Schengen free travel zone. The U.K. does opt in to certain EU immigration policy instruments, but generally only those that help on the security side (illegal immigration, asylum). The British delegate whom I interviewed admitted that "people accuse us of cherry picking, and I can see their point. We opted into illegal immigration because we thought it would be of assistance. The U.K. wasn't interested in EU visa policy before, because they were handled under Schengen. But 9/11 gave it impetus. So now, if the U.K. isn't involved, we'd be left out, because it's evolving."[6] On the issue of visas, we see that 9/11 pushed the EU to accelerate cooperation in a restrictive policy area—namely, the creation of identity databases for tracking immigrants who enter borders. While not in line with the more "open" side of the Tampere goals, this can be seen as a limited form of cooperation, albeit one that sidelines EU institutions in favor of national governments. The three highest-profile databases are the Visa Information System, which contains information on visa applicants, the Schengen Information System, which contains information on all persons entering the Schengen free travel zone, and the Eurodac System, which contains information on all asylum applicants in the EU (to prevent "asylum shopping," whereby refugee claimants lodge claims in multiple countries).

One key factor in pushing national governments to oppose EU cooperation, especially in the post-9/11 climate, is the national media (Givens and Luedtke 2005). Several of the interviewed delegates cited their national media as a block on their own margin of maneuver in support of immigration policy harmonization. The Danish delegate highlighted the media's strong support of the hard-line policy by the right-wing Danish government, arguing that the media links immigration with terrorism and a perception that immigrants don't want to integrate into Danish society.[7] Not coincidentally, Denmark (along with the U.K.) has been the strongest opponent of EU policy cooperation on immigration matters. The delegate from the Netherlands highlighted the media's role in both tightening asylum policy and pushing the "no" vote on the Constitution. "The Dutch media are saying 'be tougher' . . . most of the time they aren't hampered by knowledge! The media are more polemic in the last 10 years—they want to stir things up, they are not informed. There was one article on the Constitution. It was positive, they listed 25 positive things, but they talked about one negative thing, and that was the headline!"[8]

The delegate from Slovenia highlighted a debate in his national media over the question of whether Slovenia's small (mainly Bosnian) Muslim community should be allowed to build a mosque. He worried that Slovenia has "lots of Bosnians—some extremists were active in Bosnia, fighters in the war—Slovenes are afraid of the influence of Bosnia."[9] The Polish delegate openly expressed relief that Poland has few Muslim immigrants. Europe "has a problem with Muslim immigrants. They are not integrated; they cultivate some kind of ghettoes. This is dangerous for social cohesion. Fortunately, we are not confronted with this. The only proper way is to integrate these people."[10]

The delegate from Luxembourg highlighted another reason why 9/11 sidelined EU institutions in favor of a national bias: lack of trust in the European Parliament's ability to be "tough" enough on immigration. According to this official, if the Parliament wants "to be taken as a serious partner, they will have to show a sense of responsibility." However, "if they want to continue to be the voice of the NGOs [immigrant advocacy and human rights groups] . . . then it will be very, very difficult." This official admitted that the Council "would be willing to give in on certain points," but only if "the EP [European Parliament] shows that they're handling it responsibly, and accepts more restrictive measures." As an example, he cited the issue of biometric identity documents, complaining that the EP's emphasis on this issue has been only on privacy (the right of individuals to protect their personal data from government tracking) and arguing that this orientation on the EP's part "is not responsible."

This official did praise certain EP members, but made sure to point out that the "responsible" members had previously worked for national governments, and thus had a different outlook (such as the Belgian MEP, Antoine Duquesne, who had previously been Belgium's interior minister). In his words, "these guys understand the issues, the link between illegal immigration, terrorism and organized crime. They can't talk openly about it, but national guys get intelligence info. People who have been on the inside, they know more, and have a different view than those on the outside."[11]

For those in Brussels who supported a harmonized immigration policy, the tragedy was that 9/11 created a climate of national obstinacy that may not have otherwise existed. I interviewed one member of the European Commission who had been responsible for attempting to convince member states to agree on common immigration rules. She argued that her agenda was the victim of a poor context, shaped by 9/11:

> Migration policy [at the EU level] started almost at the same time as security and terrorism come to the surface. Many people linked our differences when starting the migration policies with the fact that it was 9/11, all these issues and security, etc., and so even when we discussed, believe it or not, migration of researchers, it was really all there: "but what if they are terrorists" . . . at every single meeting we heard this! Even the researchers, who are sort of the most welcomed people because they have a brain, they get integrated, they have money, even if [for] these people, you are focused so much on security, what for family reunification? The problem is that security got so important in the news and everywhere that it very much turned the migration policies toward security rather than "migrant as an opportunity."[12]

Another EU law whose negotiation was affected by the post-9/11 climate was the directive on free movement of EU citizens. I spoke with one of the civil servants from the Commission who wrote and negotiated this directive, and this official argued that "it would have been much better to do this directive earlier, because enlargement and the new prioritization of immigration and asylum created more fear in the member states, especially after 9/11, etc.; there's been a strong accent on security issues. So there are all these 'flanking measures' to make it more secure."[13]

As already mentioned, the after effects of 9/11 were certainly to blame in the failure to pass the proposed directive on labor migration. In the words of the Swedish delegate, the problem with the directive "was that it was created in an environment that wasn't conducive to that discussion at all. It was a little bit ambivalent time because you'd had very big growth, you'd had the U.S. and the E.U. on the back of that faring very well, but then 9/11 came and so there was a very ambivalent time during which this draft directive was being negotiated."[14] A delegate for the Green group in the European Parliament agreed. In our interview, she stated that the Green group is in favor of an EU legal migration system. "The Greens have proposed a system of something like green cards—legal migration as a solution to illegal immigration, but member states have tended to close their eyes—after 9/11, referring to terrorists, mixing things up."[15]

While five of the directives on legal migration passed, the post-9/11 climate, again, rendered their passage subject to more national discretion and less of a role for EU institutions. Three of the five successful directives allowed member states with generous legislation to lower their standards. These were the directives on family reunification, long-term residents, and the development of a fingerprint database for all immigrants entering the Schengen free travel zone. The other two successful directives did not allow member states to lower their standards of immigrant rights protection, but this is not surprising given that both directives were on low-salience topics: the admission of students, and the admission of researchers. Despite the fact that discussions of terrorism seeped into the negotiations over these directives, it must be admitted that students and researchers do not trigger public and media attention and opposition to the same degree as other types of immigrants, especially because they are seen as short-term stayers with potential long-term benefits and few costs to the host society.

In order to gain a more specific view of where EU immigration law currently stands in the post-9/11 world, I will now cover the two most important (successful) directives in detail: 1) the directive on long-term residents, and 2) the directive on family reunification. In these sections, it will be shown that between the (pre-9/11) draft proposals for the laws, and the (post-9/11) passage of the laws, the standard of human rights protection was whittled down in order to appease security fears, and to allow countries with generous legislation (most notably France and Belgium) to lower their standards.

The Long-Term Residents Directive

In March of 2001, the European Commission proposed a new EU law, known as the Directive Concerning the Status of Third-Country Nationals Who Are Long-Term Residents. In the preamble to this directive, the Commission reminded member states that they had informally committed to a program of EU policy harmonization regarding immigrants at the Tampere European Council in 1999 (European Commission 2001b). The Commission argued that "the proposal is part of a broader effort on immigration which the Commission has been making for several years now" and it reminded the Council (the body representing the member states) that several other pieces of legislation were "on their table" but seemed to be stalled (European Commission 2001b: 434).

In the Directive, the Commission laid out a proposed framework of law that would regulate the entry, stay, rights, and status of long-term immigrants. This legal framework would be binding on member states, obligating them to uphold certain minimum standards in terms of rights and freedoms accorded to immigrants. Thus, the directive was a "baseline" harmonization, and many immigrant advocacy non-governmental organizations (NGOs) criticized it as allowing for a "lowest common denominator" policy that would empower national governments to lower their standards of immigrant rights.

Just how generous or restrictive was the directive, vis-à-vis the already existing laws in the 15 member states? Among the most liberal countries, such as France and Belgium, the proposed Long-Term Residents Directive (LTRD) was less generous than national laws in all important respects (though it was more generous than the comparable laws in many other member states). A detailed comparative legal study of member state laws concerning long-term residents, conducted by Groenendijk, Guild, and Barzilay (2000), revealed the following:

- While one could obtain long-term resident status after three years in France or Belgium, the Directive mandated five.
- While Belgian and French law gave the automatic right to bring one's family members, the Directive did not give this right.
- While long-term residents had free access to the labor market in France and Belgium, the Directive offered national governments the chance to give priority to their own nationals. On the topics of social security and social assistance, Belgium and France gave equal treatment with nationals, but the Directive allowed discrimination.
- While Belgium granted voting rights to immigrants, the Directive did not offer this.
- While immigrants in Belgium and France could not lose their status if they became unemployed, the Directive allowed for this possibility.
- While Belgium and France mandated waiting periods before loss of status if an immigrant left the country, the Directive allowed for immediate loss of status.
- While Belgium and France gave the right to apply for citizenship after three and five years, respectively, the Directive did not give this right.

In short, although the LTRD was much harsher than Belgian and French law, it was much more generous than the laws in countries that had weaker institutional protection for immigrant rights (i.e., countries where governments had succeeded in cracking down on immigrant rights domestically). These ten countries included Austria, Denmark, Germany, Greece, Ireland, Italy, Luxembourg, Portugal, Spain, and the U.K. (though Denmark, Ireland, and the U.K. opted out of the negotiations).

Thus, the stage was set for a battle in the European Council, whereby the Commission tried to defend the text of its proposed directive, and the seven countries participating listed above (led by Germany) tried to whittle down the text, moving it in a more restrictive direction, and in a direction that would allow more national discretion over law (in other words, not binding countries to "hard" targets or standards). France and Belgium, along with Finland, the Netherlands and Sweden, were relatively supportive of the Commission's text, and were also relatively supportive of having the Directive be binding in all respects (minimizing national discretion), mainly because the Directive was already much less generous than their own national laws, and they wanted to be "forced" to implement these new restrictions (European Council 2002).

The seven skeptical member states pressed in the negotiations for a Directive that would contain weak legal language, and would allow them the utmost discretion. A Commission official told me that the Commission got some leverage by reminding member states of their grand promises (in the Tampere Conclusions), when it came time to draft legislation.[16] This shows that, despite an adverse climate, one cannot underestimate the agenda-setting and leadership role of the Commission (Pollack 1998). However, the resulting Directive, finally adopted in January of 2004, must be seen primarily as a German victory and a setback for pro-immigrant advocates. The same Commission official admitted to me that the resulting LTRD does not live up to the Tampere Conclusions in many areas. In fact, the final Directive allows so much national discretion that a British official told me that the U.K. is now seriously considering opting in![17]

Despite a few victories for the pro-immigrant camp, such as the duration of residence needed before gaining LTR status (Italy wanted it to be six years, but the Commission and its allies succeeded in keeping it to five years), on the whole the Directive does not offer much positive evidence for expanding immigrant rights in the short term. Member states gained the important rights to set numerical quotas on immigrants, and to require that immigrants comply with certain "integration" measures, including taking language classes. Importantly for assessing immigration policy harmonization's impact on European integration in general, these and other departures from the principle of equal treatment for long-term residents were allowed through multiple uses of the word "may" (instead of "shall") in the language of the Directive, so that member states are not faced with hard legal obligations. A key part of the EU's expanding power is the coherence of its legal framework, so that the European Court of Justice (ECJ) can later use legal language to raise the standard of rights protection. With this past history in mind, member states agreed to a Directive that contained weak legal language because they clearly wished to free themselves from further legal action by the ECJ. In the post-9/11 political climate, this gave states the margin of maneuver that they perceived as necessary to tighten their systems and avoid judicial scrutiny.

However, there are some signs that supranational influence may increase in the future, and thus that member states may eventually lose this margin of maneuver. One Council legal specialist with whom I spoke admitted that the Court may not be "impressed" with the text of the Directive, and particularly the removal of the word "right" (of residence) from the final draft. He wondered if the ECJ could in the future possibly infer a right, using the language of EU treaties as a broad legal base. This same official told me that, in view of the very minimal and restrictive harmonization contained in the LTRD, he sees this directive as an intermediate stage, and thinks that there will be a new one within 10 years.[18] In 10 years, the institutional balance may favor the EU's governing bodies, due to the creeping nature of European integration (once a policy area has been turned over to Brussels, the member states tend to lose control eventually). Thus, clearly the ECJ, the Commission, and the European Parliament still have some room to maneuver in promoting harmonization and raising immigrant rights even further, against (some) national preferences. And it should not be forgotten that the Directive did obligate many member states (though not France and Belgium) to raise their standards of immigrant rights. For instance, national law in some countries mandated as much as 15 years' residence before getting LTR status, but the Directive gave five as a baseline. And, despite strong resistance by Italy and other member states, the Commission (supported by a handful of member states) succeeded in defending this five-year rule.

The Family Reunification Directive

Family reunification is perhaps the most important category of immigration into the EU, given that other channels of legal migration (labor migration and, more recently, asylum seeking) are relatively closed. Therefore, family reunification has always occupied a primary place in the EU's efforts to create a common immigration and asylum policy. In response to the Tampere call to action in 1999, the Commission immediately proposed an EU law on the right to family reunification in December of that year. The proposed draft directive was praised by many NGOs as being a progressive step in the realization of the objectives agreed upon at Tampere (Unlu 2004).

The first proposal was directed towards creating a common policy in which national considerations would be subordinated to a common policy, with the aim of securing human rights. The EP raised the first obstacle to the development of a common European policy on the right to family reunification. In September of 2000, the Parliament called for amendments dealing with whether or not asylum seekers under "subsidiary protection"[19] would be entitled to the family reunification rights spelled out in the directive (European Parliament 2000).

The Commission responded with an amended proposal in October 2000. No conclusions emerged from the subsequent Council negotiations, however, given divergent member state positions on the desired degrees of both restrictiveness and harmonization. Discussions were unsuccessful, and some national governments (especially Germany) pressed for introducing further restrictions. While the Laeken European Council in December 2001 stated objectives similar to Tampere and acknowledged the need for harmonization of national legislation towards the creation of a common European immigration policy, the 9/11 context had changed things. This time, the prospects for a common policy came with some restrictions. The Laeken Council called for "a need for new impetus and guidelines to make up for delays in some areas" (European Council 2001).

Accordingly, in April 2002, the Council invited the Commission to present an amended proposal that would be more palatable for national governments (i.e., more restrictive towards immigrant rights in the post-9/11 context). The Commission prepared the proposal in May of 2002, and negotiations began in earnest. Ultimately, in September 2003, the Directive on the Right to Family Reunification was finally adopted, though it was a shadow of its former self (Unlu 2004).

The ultimate version of the Directive made the provisions of the initial proposal much stricter through many amendments. One of these provisions concerns the reunification of children with their families. The first proposal granted all underage children the right to reunification, but the final version contains a restriction of the right to family reunion for children above the age of 12 (Zimmerman 2002). The Directive gives national governments the option of giving an "integration test" to children over 12, failure of which would indicate a lack of potential to integrate into society (and which could be grounds for refusing admission to the country). Many felt that this restriction was specifically aimed at young Muslim men, who would be deemed a security threat and subjected to closer scrutiny. The European Parliament, arguing that this part of the Directive was in violation of international law, challenged the Directive before the European Court of Justice but lost.

In order to thoroughly analyze the politics of the Family Reunification Directive, we need to compare its level of immigrant rights protection with the national legislation of member states. Although many countries had very restrictive laws regulating the issue of family reunification, some countries were legally more liberal and inclusive in granting family reunion rights. The Directive stands somewhere between the more restrictive and the more liberal laws of the member states. Some countries (like Italy) did not have to make any changes to national legislation. But as with the Long-Term Residents Directive, Belgium and France generally had legislation that was more generous than the Directive—thus, the utility for these governments of supporting a binding strong directive: it would allow them to lower immigrant rights at home, and be able to look tough on security in a post-9/11 world.

More than France, Belgium had especially generous legislation on family reunification. The immigration laws of Belgium (and the Netherlands) include provisions about same-sex partners that give them similar rights under certain conditions to those of married heterosexual couples (Berlin Institute for Comparative Social Research 2003). On the contrary, there is not a word about same-sex partners in the Directive. There are also some clauses in national legislation that show more liberal attitudes than the EU stance on various issues, including waiting to obtain the initial residence permit, gaining an autonomous resident status, and retaining the residence permit after divorce or death of the husband. Under the Directive, member states have the right to extend the waiting-time limit to three years due to the complications born out of the "complexity of the examination of the application," although the length of procedure had been only one year in Belgium (BICSR 2003). The Directive also sets the limit of maximum five years of residence necessary to get an autonomous residence permit. The Belgian law, however, has a maximum of only 15 months (BICSR 2003).

French law was also more generous than the Directive in that it granted the right to retain a residence permit to women who are united with their families after divorce or the death of the spouse. In France, stay permits are at risk only during the first two years of marriage, which is more inclusive than the Directive (BICSR 2003).

In short, by supporting this directive, France and Belgium obtained the opportunity to weaken their own domestic legislation in the name of harmonization. One Belgian civil servant that I interviewed was sure that the Directive would allow his government to escape pressure by the extreme-right party, the Vlaams Belang.[20] Other countries also gained the same opportunity. For instance, one Commission employee pointed out to me that Spain, which previously had no integration test for minors, had used the Directive to quickly implement this provision, thus gaining the authority to block immigrant youth from entering the country. In the future, it would be easier for the Spanish government to restrict the "right" of family reunification for an immigrant youth who was considered a threat to societal security.

Conclusion

This brief review of EU immigration law as it evolved post-9/11 illustrates that a focus on security allowed the ambitious goals of Tampere and the Commission's pre-9/11 proposals to be whittled down considerably. Countries such as France and Belgium, which formerly had generous legislation, were able to use EU immigration law to gain the freedom to crack down on immigrant rights. Not only did 9/11's aftermath shift the nature of the immigration laws that did pass, but it also warped the entire EU immigration policy agenda by shifting resources and attention away from the topic and towards terrorism and police matters. Indeed, the millennium began brightly for those who favored an open immigration policy that could contribute to Europe's economic mobility and respect high standards of human rights. However, in the words of Carl Levy (2003: 7), "this trend towards liberalization seemed to be stopped dead in its tracks by the events of September 11." Given the continued strong showing of the far right in national elections, growing worries over integration of (primarily Muslim) immigrants, and the discovery of new plots, such as the 2006 conspiracy by Britons of Pakistani descent to blow up 10 airplanes, it remains to be seen whether Europe can ever live up to the Tampere goals so optimistically announced more than seven years ago.

In the most recent Conclusions of the European Council, eight years after Tampere, the Germany Presidency brokered the following language:

> The European Council welcomes the recent agreement on the Regulation on the Visa Information System and the exchange of data between Member States on short-stay visas as well as the Council Decision on access for consultation of the VIS by designated authorities of Member States and by Europol for the purposes of prevention, detection and investigation of terrorist offences. Particular efforts must continue to be made to strengthen police and judicial cooperation and the fight against terrorism. Europe's citizens expect the EU and its Member States to take decisive action to preserve their freedom and security, particularly in the fight against terrorism.
>
> (European Council 2007)

The fact that this text was inserted into a section on EU immigration policy was a telling sign of the priorities of the EU's Justice and Interior Ministers. Ironically, the threat of terrorism may enhance European cooperation to a degree that the Tampere goals (free movement, equality, liberalization) may never have achieved on their own. The only question is whether this cooperation will result in a truly "Europeanized" immigration policy, complete with substantial roles for the European Parliament, Commission, and Court of Justice, or whether national discretion and worries over sovereignty will continue to trump the advantages of allowing 500 million citizens to freely travel and seek work with relatively few obstacles.

Notes

1 The author thanks Arnaud Houdmont for translating the article.
2 Author Interview #43, Joanna Apap, Center for European Policy Studies, Brussels, Belgium, July 15, 2003.
3 Interview #43 (previously cited).
4 Author Interview #14, Finnish EU delegate (anonymous by request of subject), Brussels, Belgium, December 8, 2004.
5 Author Interview #15, Estonian EU delegate (anonymous by request of subject), Brussels, Belgium, November 22, 2004.
6 Author Interview #11, British EU delegate (anonymous by request of subject), Brussels, Belgium, July 15, 2003.
7 Author Interview #22, Danish EU delegate (anonymous by request of subject), Brussels, Belgium, November 12, 2004.
8 Author Interview #30, Dutch EU delegate (anonymous by request of subject), Brussels, Belgium, March 9, 2005.
9 Author Interview #13, Slovenian EU delegate (anonymous by request of subject), Brussels, Belgium, December 8, 2004.
10 Author Interview #12, Polish EU delegate (anonymous by request of subject), Brussels, Belgium, January 21, 2005.
11 Author Interview #31, Luxembourg EU delegate (anonymous by request of subject), Brussels, Belgium, November 26, 2004.

12 Author Interview #55, European Commission official (anonymous by request of subject), Brussels, Belgium, January 25, 2005.
13 Author Interview #56, European Commission official (anonymous by request of subject), Brussels, Belgium, July 30, 2003.
14 Author Interview #20, Swedish EU delegate (anonymous by request of subject), Brussels, Belgium, January 24, 2005.
15 Author Interview #28, official with European Parliament Green group (anonymous by request of subject), Brussels, Belgium, March 2, 2005.
16 Author Interview #57, European Commission official (anonymous by request of subject), Brussels, Belgium, July 22, 2003.
17 Author Interview #11.
18 Author Interview #58, official with Council Legal Services (anonymous by request of subject), Brussels, Belgium, July 18, 2003.
19 Subsidiary protection is a type of sanctuary given to a displaced person who does not technically meet the Geneva Convention's definition of a "refugee."
20 Author Interview #5, Philippe De Bruycker, Brussels, Belgium, April 26, 2005.

References

Apap, Joanna, and Sergio Carrera. 2004. "Progress and Obstacles in the Area of Justice and Home Affairs in an Enlarging Europe: An Overview," in Joanna Apap, ed., *Justice and Home Affairs in the EU: Liberty and Security Issues after Enlargement*, pp. 1–26. Northampton: Edward Elgar.

BICSR (Berlin Institute for Comparative Social Research). 2003. *Overviews of the Current National Legal Frameworks Guiding the Residence of Female Marriage Migrants*. Berlin: Berlin Institute for Comparative Social Research.

British Government. 2002. *Nationality, Immigration and Asylum Act 2002*. London: The Stationery Office.

European Commission. 2001a. *Communication from the Commission to the Council and the European Parliament: On an Open Method of Coordination for the Community Immigration Policy*. Brussels: Commission of the European Communities.

European Commission. 2001b. *Proposal for a Council Directive Concerning the Status of Third-Country Nationals Who Are Long-Term Residents*. Brussels: Commission of the European Communities.

European Council. 1999. *Presidency Conclusions: Tampere European Council, 15 and 16 October 1999*. Brussels: European Council.

European Council. 2001. *Laeken Declaration: Europe at a Crossroads*. Brussels: European Council.

European Council. 2002. "Interinstitutional File: 2001/0074 (CNS), Working Party on Migration and Expulsion, Subject: Draft Council Directive Concerning the Status of Third-Country Nationals Who Are Long-Term Residents." Brussels: European Council.

European Council. 2003. *Directive 2003/86/EC of 22 September 2003 on the Right to Family Reunification*. Brussels: European Council.

European Council. 2007. *Presidency Conclusions of the Brussels European Council, 21/22 June*. Brussels: European Council.

European Parliament. 2000. *Report on the Proposal for a Council Directive on the Right to Family Reunification*. Brussels: European Parliament.

Givens, Terri, and Adam Luedtke. 2004. "The Politics of European Union

Immigration Policy: Institutions, Salience and Harmonization." *Policy Studies Journal* 32(1): 145–165.

Givens, Terri, and Adam Luedtke. 2005. "European Immigration Policies in Comparative Perspective: Issue Salience, Partisanship and Immigrant Rights." *Comparative European Politics* 3(1): 1–22.

Groenendijk, Kees, Elspeth Guild, and Robin Barzilay. 2000. *The Legal Status of Third Country Nationals Who are Long Term Residents in a Member State of the European Union.* Nijmigen: Rapport voor Europese Commissie.

Huysmans, Jef. 2005. *The Politics of Insecurity: Fear, Migration and Asylum in the EU.* London: Routledge.

Levy, Carl. 2003. "The European Union After 9/11: The Demise of a Liberal Democratic Asylum Regime?" National Europe Centre Paper 109, Australian National University.

Macias, Juan Miguel Lian. 2002. "Counterterrorism: An Example of Cooperation." Speech at NATO seminar on the role of the EAPC in combating terrorism. Warsaw, Poland.

Monar, Jörg. 2002. "Justice and Home Affairs." *Journal of Common Market Studies* 40: 121–136.

Papademetriou, Demetrios. 1996. *Coming Together or Pulling Apart?: The European Union's Struggle with Immigration and Asylum.* Washington, DC: Carnegie Endowment for International Peace.

Pollack, Mark A. 1998. "The Engines of Integration? Supranational Autonomy and Influence in the European Union," in Wayne Sandholtz and Alec Stone Sweet, eds., *European Integration and Supranational Governance,* pp. 217–249. New York: Oxford University Press.

Rudolph, Christopher. 2003. "Security and the Political Economy of International Migration." *American Political Science Review* 97(4): 603–620.

Simon, Julian. 1989. *The Economic Consequences of Immigration.* Cambridge: Basil Blackwell.

Unlu, U.C. 2004. "The Directive on the Right to Family Reunification: Efforts of the European Union to Create a Common Policy on Immigration and Integration." Unpublished manuscript.

van der Klaauw, Johannes. 2004. "The Future Common Asylum System: Between a Closed-Circuit and an Open-Ended Scheme?" in Joanna Apap, ed., *Justice and Home Affairs in the EU: Liberty and Security Issues after Enlargement,* pp. 235–258. Northampton: Edward Elgar.

de Vreese, C.H., and H.G. Boomgarden. 2005. "Projecting EU Referendums: Fear of Immigration and Support for European Integration." *European Union Politics* 6: 59–82.

Weiner, Myron. 1995. *The Global Migration Crisis: Challenge to States and to Human Rights.* New York: Longman.

Wynia, Syp. 2005. "Een Zwart Scenario." *Elsevier,* March 5, pp. 1–6.

Zimmerman, Elizabeth. 2002. *European Union Plan to Restrict Immigration.* Oak Park: International Committee of the Fourth International.

8 Borders, Security, and Transatlantic Cooperation in the Twenty-First Century

Identity and Privacy in an Era of Globalized Surveillance

Valsamis Mitsilegas

Introduction

A dominant feature of the development of law and policy on immigration and border controls this decade in Europe and America has been the emphasis on security. Governments and legislators have increasingly justified the adoption of immigration and border control measures as necessary to fight terrorism, extending what has been described in the context of the EU of the 1990s as an (in)security continuum (transferring the "illegitimacy" of crime to immigrants) to the issue of terrorism.[1] In the 2000s, the main source of production of the new (in)security continuum—a process in which political discourse presents the issues of migration, borders, and terrorism and the subsequent legislative and policy responses to each of these phenomena as being inextricably linked—has been the United States. September 11, 2001 prompted the adoption of a series of enforcement measures aiming to protect U.S. territory from terrorism and prevent future terrorist attacks. In the light of how the 9/11 attacks occurred, it is perhaps unsurprising that major emphasis was placed on border controls, or, as the new securitized jargon would have it, "border security."

The plethora of domestic U.S. measures had a ripple effect on the development of similar legislation and policy outside the US, however, both by demanding third countries to comply with U.S. legal requirements and by providing inspiration/models for similar action elsewhere. A prime example of these developments has been the European Union. Not only were its Member States asked to comply in various contexts with U.S. standards, but at the same time some of these standards provided the model for EU institutions in their effort to develop a common EU border security approach; in particular, EU leaders wanted to react to subsequent attacks in Madrid and London. The interplay between European and American standards has not been straightforward and has raised a number of questions regarding: 1) the compatibility of standards in the EU and the U.S., in particular with regard to the collection and exchange of passenger data; 2) the challenges that the new approach poses to civil liberties, in particular from the perspective of the European Union; and

3) the possibility for convergence of EU and U.S. law and policy on "border security" and the impact it may have on the development of global standards in the field. This chapter will examine these questions and assess developments thus far by casting light on the impact they may have on reframing the relationship between the individual and the State.

The U.S. Approach: Borders and Homeland Security

The immediate reaction to 9/11 was the adoption of the USA Patriot Act, which was signed into law on October 26, 2001, less than six weeks after the attacks (McCarthy 2002). The Act significantly expanded State powers to fight terrorism, and a central element was the removal of barriers in the communication between law enforcement and intelligence agencies. At the same time, the concept of "Homeland Security" was firmly established in U.S. anti-terrorism law: by early October 2001, the President had established by Executive Order the Office of Homeland Security.[2] This would be the first step towards establishing a Department of Homeland Security. Following a contested debate regarding the balance of powers between the executive and the legislature in the new agency, the Homeland Security Act 2002 created the Department (Stanhouse 2003–04; Thessin 2003). That same year, the then U.S. Office of Homeland Security (2002) published the "National Strategy for Homeland Security," a report that firmly established "homeland security" as a legitimate U.S. law and policy objective and contained a comprehensive plan of legislative and operational action.

The Strategy focused extensively on the issues of border security and information sharing and systems. On borders, it stated that "the increasing mobility and destructive potential of modern terrorism has required the U.S. to rethink and rearrange fundamentally its systems for border and transportation security" and that border security must be conceived as "fully integrated requirements because our domestic transportation systems are intertwined inextricably with the global transport infrastructure" (p. 21). Reconceptualizing the border based on security considerations would lead, according to the Strategy, to an entity managing border crossings being located in the Department of Homeland Security (p. 22) and to a great emphasis on the widening and deepening of information collection and sharing (including of biometrics) from a variety of sources. It is indicative that the wording of both the chapters on border security and information sharing converges in this respect. The Strategy calls for the establishment of a "border of the future" (smart borders) and of a "system of systems" which will provide "the right information to the right people at all times" (p. 56).

This logic of maximum information collection and sharing[3] is inextricably linked with the (in)security continuum approach: According to the Strategy, the "border of the future . . . will provide greater security through better intelligence, coordinated national efforts, and unprecedented international cooperation against the threats posed by terrorists, the implements of terrorism, international organized crime, illegal drugs, illegal migrants, cyber crime, and the destruction or theft of natural resources" (p. 22). This will be achieved through collecting information, which "contributes to every aspect of homeland security"—databases used for law enforcement, immigration, intelligence, and public health surveillance will be connected and information will be shared "horizontally" across each level of government and "vertically" among federal, state, and local governments, private industry, and citizens (pp. 56–57). This approach was justified on the basis of existing information gaps in the system; it does justice to the view that the "homeland security" concept in fact presupposes the vulnerability of U.S. territory and calls for maximum interagency cooperation to prevent the entry of suspect individuals and even identify the potential "enemy within" (Ceyhan 2004).

In the field of aviation, the emphasis on information gathering was already reflected in the Aviation and Transportation Security Act passed by Congress in November 2001.[4] The Act required that a computer-assisted passenger pre-screening system be used to evaluate all passengers before they board an aircraft (U.S. GAO 2005a). To address this requirement, the Transportation Security Administration (TSA) began to develop the so-called Computer-Assisted Passenger Pre-Screening System II (CAPPS II) Program, which would follow the pre-existing CAPPS I Program. However, unlike its predecessor (which the airlines operated), the TSA would operate CAPPS II. Following concerns primarily regarding civil liberties,[5] the program was abandoned in August 2004.

A new program—Secure Flight—has since replaced CAPPS II. The purpose of this new program is "to compare information on domestic airline passengers against information on known or suspected terrorists to identify passengers who should undergo additional security scrutiny" (U.S. GAO 2005b). The new program only contains some of the elements of CAPPS II and, importantly, will pre-screen only passengers flying domestically within the U.S., rather than all passengers flying into and out of the U.S. (which may be linked to the fact that the latter flights are covered by U.S. law obliging air carriers to send Passenger Name Record [PNR] data to the Customs Bureau of the Homeland Security Department). The system was being tested at the time of this writing, and upon its operation pre-screening will pass to the TSA (U.S. GAO 2005a).[6]

Significant developments have also been taking place regarding border controls and surveillance of third country nationals wanting to enter the U.S. The Enhanced Border Security and Visa Entry Reform Act of 2002 called for substantial security upgrades in documents and set an October 2004 deadline for foreign nationals' travel documents to include machine-readable data, such as fingerprints, for identification purposes (Andreas 2003). This approach is also linked with the development of the so-called US-VISIT (Immigrant Status Indicator Technology) Program, officially launched in January 2004, whose purpose is to collect, maintain, and share information, including biometric identifiers, on foreign nationals who travel to the U.S. The system—which involves fingerprinting and photographing foreign nationals at the border—initially applied to select nationalities, but has now been rolled out for all foreign visitors (Salter 2004). As the Department of Homeland Security noted, it is "part of a continuum of security measures that begins overseas, when a person applies for a visa to travel to the U.S., and continues on through entry and exit at U.S. air and seaports and, eventually, at land border crossings" (Bennett 2005: 127). The emphasis on invasive controls and biometrics has had, as will be seen below, some influence on the development of similar EU standards. However, there are still privacy concerns regarding the operation of US-VISIT, even from U.S. government auditors (U.S. GAO 2005c). Nevertheless, the 2004 Intelligence Reform and Terrorism Prevention Act (IRTPA) states that "completing a biometric entry and exit data system as expeditiously as possible is an essential investment in efforts to protect the U.S. by preventing the entry of terrorists."[7]

The enhancement of databases, interagency cooperation, and interoperability has also been emphasized. Prime examples of this approach are Executive Order 13356 of August 27, 2004 and Executive Order 13388 of October 25, 2005, both on "the strengthening" and "further strengthening," respectively, of "the sharing of terrorism information to protect Americans."[8] Order 13356 calls on agencies *inter alia* to give the highest priority to the interchange of information among agencies as well as between agencies and state and local government authorities, and to share terrorism information free of originator controls. Order 13388 reiterates these provisions, but it also calls for the establishment of an "Information Sharing Council." Among the Council's missions, it will provide advice on the establishment of an "interoperable terrorism information sharing environment to facilitate automated sharing of terrorism information among appropriate agencies."[9] This call echoes the Department-level commitment in the 2004 Act to fully integrate all databases and data systems that process or contain information on aliens that certain immigration and border-related divisions maintain in the Department of Homeland Security, the Department of Justice, and the State Department.[10]

This widening and deepening of the collection and exchange of personal (and at times intimate) data causes serious privacy concerns (especially in the light of the broad meaning that "terrorism information" may take). It may lead to the collection of personal data on a wide range of everyday activity over a period of time and may also lead to the profiling of individuals and data mining, in particular if such data is shared between a number of government agencies. Notwithstanding privacy concerns (including the recent U.S. government reports on testing the new systems), the emphasis continues to be placed on maximum personal data collection and sharing. Earlier in 2006, the Department of Homeland Security announced further "border security" measures (DHS 2006).[11] Emphasis is placed on: 1) "travel documents for the 21st century," including the issuing of "e-passports" that contain a contactless chip to which biometric and biographic information is written; 2) "real time DHS–State information sharing, leading to real time comparison of electronic files of every traveler entering the U.S.";[12] and 3) "paperless" visa processing. Last, but not least, the new plan calls for the pooling of data "with like-minded foreign governments"—this task may be more challenging than expected, as discussion of the response to U.S. requirements in Europe will demonstrate.

The EU Response to U.S. Requirements: The Passenger Name Data (PNR) Saga [13]

Responding to the 9/11 attacks, the United States passed legislation in November 2001 that required air carriers operating flights to, from, or through the U.S. to provide U.S. Customs with electronic access to data contained in their automatic reservation and departure control systems.[14] This data, known as Passenger Name Records (PNR), constitutes a record of each passenger's travel requirements and contains all the information necessary to enable reservations to be processed and controlled by the booking and participating airlines. PNR data can include a wide range of details, from the passenger's name and physical address to their email address, credit card details, and on-flight dietary requirements. PNR is thus broader than the Advance Passenger Information (API) data, which mainly include basic categories of passport data.[15] Furthermore, U.S. law required airlines to give U.S. Customs authorities access to their databases (a "pull" system), instead of a "push" system whereby airlines transmitted data to the authorities.

The U.S. legislation is applicable to all flights to the U.S., including flights from the European Union. EU airlines would thus have to comply with the legislation if they did not want to be subject to various sanctions including heavy fines and even the possible cancellation of landing rights at U.S. airports. Concerns were voiced in the EU that U.S. legislation was too invasive of privacy and could be in conflict with Community and Member States' data protection standards, however. The Commission informed the U.S. authorities of these concerns, which led to a postponement of the entry into force of the U.S. legislation until March 5, 2003. At the same time, the Commission began negotiations with U.S. authorities in order to formulate standards governing the transfer of PNR data to the U.S. that would comply with EC data protection standards. In the course of negotiations, the European Parliament adopted a series of Resolutions urging the Commission to ensure that these standards are fully respected.[16] The "Article 29 Working Party" on data protection[17] also scrutinized the U.S. requirements and was highly critical of U.S. demands (Article 29 Working Party 2003).

Negotiations were protracted and lasted well beyond March 5, 2003, when U.S. law formally entered into force vis-à-vis EU airlines. The Commission and the U.S. authorities finally entered into an agreement on December 16, 2003. Following a series of undertakings by the U.S. authorities, the Commission accepted that U.S. data protection standards in the context of PNR transfers were adequate. In a Communication issued on December 16, the Commission justified its decision, stating:

The option of insisting on the enforcement of the law on the EU side would have been politically justified, but . . . would have undermined the influence of more moderate and co-operative counsels in Washington and substituted a trial of strength for the genuine leverage we have as co-operative partners.

(European Commission 2003: 5)

The Commission called for a global EU approach to the sharing of PNR data. On the issue of EU/U.S. transfers, the Commission noted that the way forward was to establish a legal framework for existing PNR transfers to the U.S. This would consist of an "adequacy" Decision by the Commission certifying that the U.S. data protection standards were adequate, followed by a "light" bilateral international agreement between the Community and the U.S. Although the American legislation was prompted by the 9/11 events and is viewed in the U.S. as a counterterrorism measure, the Commission approached it as a first pillar "internal market" measure and not as a third pillar "counterterrorism" measure. Making the most of its mandate, the Commission saw this as an opportunity to consolidate its position as the EU and Member States chief representative in negotiating standards in the field. It does not seem accidental that the Communication on PNR also calls for a "global" EU approach and discussions in international fora such as the International Civil Aviation Organization (ICAO),[18] where presumably it was hoped that the Commission, and not the Council or Member States, take the lead.

The "first pillar" choice is also legally significant, as it led to the assessment of the "adequacy" of U.S. data protection standards—and thus the legality of PNR transfers by EU airlines—being made under the 1995 E.C. Data Protection Directive.[19] Article 25 of the latter provides that the Council and the European Parliament would not make adequacy decisions under the ordinary EU legislative procedure, but under "comitology," i.e., a Committee consisting of representatives of Member States and chaired by the Commission. Not the most transparent method of decision-making, it leaves little, if any, space for parliamentary scrutiny. In the U.K., the government did not submit drafts of the Adequacy Decision for scrutiny to the EU Committees of the Houses of Parliament, notwithstanding the existence of specific requests to that effect.[20]

The Article 29 Working Party on Data Protection examined the draft adequacy Decision.[21] In an Opinion published in January 2004, the Working Party expressly stated that "the progress made does not allow a favourable adequacy finding to be achieved" (Article 29 Working Party 2004). Following similar considerations, and notwithstanding its limited role under the comitology process, on March 30, 2004, the European Parliament adopted a Resolution calling on the Commission to withdraw the draft adequacy Decision.[22] The European Parliament drew attention to many of the data protection points made above, and, on the issue of legality, noted that there was no legal basis in the EU permitting the use of PNR commercial data for public security purposes—there was a need, according to the Parliament, for a specific legal basis covering these cases. The draft Adequacy Decision might well be a lowering of the data protection standards in the 1995 Directive.

The European Parliament also took the step of requesting an Opinion from the European Court of Justice on the compatibility of the EC Treaty with the draft PNR international agreement, which would be concluded after the adoption of the Adequacy Decision. The European Parliament would wait for the Court's Opinion prior to submitting their opinion on the agreement to the Council under the consultation process of Article 300 TEC. The Council set a deadline for the Parliament's response of April 22, extending it eventually to May 5, 2004 (House of Lords European Union Committee 2004c: fn. 20). With the Court case pending, and the Parliament not having submitted its opinion, the Council decided to go ahead with the agreement without having received the Parliament's Opinion. In the Decision authorizing the Conclusion of the Agreement, the Council evoked the urgency that this uncertainty caused for carriers and passengers (Preamble, recital 2).

The Commission Adequacy Decision was finally adopted on May 14, 2004.[23] Three days later, a Council Decision authorized the President of the Council to sign the Agreement with the U.S. on PNR transfers on behalf of the Community.[24] The terms of the Agreement and the U.S. Undertakings have not changed from the draft that the Article 29 Working Party and the European Parliament so heavily criticized. According to these documents:

- U.S. Customs requires 34 categories of PNR data including name, address and billing address, email address, all forms of payment information, travel itinerary, frequent-flyer information, travel status of passenger, no-show information, one-way tickets, all historical changes to the PNR and "general remarks."
- U.S. Customs and Border Protection (CBP) will "pull" passenger information from air carrier reservation systems until such time as air carriers are able to implement a system to "push" the data to CBP.[25]
- CBP will use PNR data strictly for purposes of preventing and combating terrorism and related crimes and other serious crimes that are transnational in nature.[26]
- Storage of PNR data will take place for 3.5 years. Data that have not been manually accessed during this period will be destroyed. Data that have been accessed will be kept for a further eight years. These provisions will not apply to PNR data that are linked to a specific enforcement record.[27]
- CBP may provide data to other government authorities, including foreign government authorities, with counter-terrorism or law-enforcement functions on a case-by-case basis for the purposes of preventing and combating the above-mentioned offences.[28]
- In the event that a PNR requirement is imposed by the EU, CBP will,

strictly on the basis of reciprocity, encourage U.S.-based airlines to cooperate.[29]

- The Undertakings will apply for a term of 3.5 years and may be extended and/or reviewed.[30]
- The Undertakings do not create or confer any right or benefit on any person or party. Their provisions do not constitute a precedent for any future discussions with the Commission, the EU, or third states.[31]

   The European Parliament brought an action before the European Court of Justice asking for the annulment of the Decision authorizing the Conclusion of the EC/U.S. Agreement.[32] Parliament based its action on the grounds of the latter infringing the right to privacy and data protection and breaching the principle of proportionality as well as on legal grounds.[33] Advocate General (AG) Léger issued his Opinion on November 22, 2005.[34] On the procedural question, the central point was whether the aim of the Agreement would be a matter for the first or the third pillar. The Advocate General[35] rejected the Commission's argument that, while PNR exchange was a counterterrorism matter for the U.S., for the EC it was a matter related to the smooth functioning of the internal market, and concluded that Decision and Agreement must be annulled as it is the third—and not the first—pillar that provides the correct legal basis for a measure that is essentially a counterterrorism measure.[36] On the issue of fundamental rights, the AG took the view that the review of the margin of appreciation of the institutions in negotiating such standards should be limited to determining whether there was any manifest error of assessment on the part of the Council and the Commission—in this case he took the view that the institutions did not exceed their powers.[37]

   The Court issued its ruling in May 2006.[38] Unlike the AG, the Court avoided making a statement on the compatibility of the Agreement with fundamental rights; however, the Court agreed with the AG that the Adequacy Decision and the Decision authorizing the signature of the Agreement must be annulled on the grounds that Article 95 EC, read in conjunction with Article 25 of the Directive, cannot justify Community competence to conclude the Agreement.[39] The Court accepted that the transfer of PNR data to the Homeland Security Department "constitutes processing operations concerning public security and the activities of the State in areas of criminal law."[40] It would thus seem that the Agreement should have been concluded under the third, and not the first, pillar. However, the Court preserved the effects of the Agreement until September 30, 2006, for reasons of legal certainty until a follow-up solution is found.[41] This has led to the conclusion of two subsequent PNR agreements between the European Union (this time) and the United States (House of Lords European Union Committee 2007). The first one, which replaced the EC/U.S. Agreement, had a limited duration and was replaced in the summer of 2007 by a second Agreement which is largely along the spirit and the lines of the original, Commission-negotiated EC–U.S. Agreement. If anything, it appears that privacy and oversight safeguards have gradually been weakening and are arguably lower in the latest version of the Agreement (Mitsilegas 2007b).

The Community/Union negotiations with the U.S. highlight the dilemma of whether the EU should choose to cooperate with third countries if speaking with one voice would mean that its own standards and values would be compromised (Mitsilegas 2003). The Agreement has been heavily criticized, but it was swiftly agreed to (as it was framed as an urgent response to terrorism). Nevertheless, it faces opposition by both data protection watchdogs and the European Parliament. The first joint review of the operation of the Agreement is not encouraging on the grounds of access to data and passengers' rights (COM 2005b), concerns that also arose from the Privacy Office of the U.S. Department of Homeland Security as expressed in the relevant report (DHS 2005).[42]

The negative reactions to the Agreement, which were accompanied by the negative opinions by parliaments and data protection watchdogs, may betray a deep-seated mistrust towards the protection of civil liberties in the U.S., in particular in this era of the "war on terror." Even if it appears somewhat exaggerated to those advocating closer transatlantic cooperation, the lack of transparency and the absence of any meaningful scrutiny by the European Parliament or national parliaments has almost fatally undermined the legitimacy of what EU negotiators have proposed and/or accepted as a compromise. Ironically, renegotiation of the Agreements under a third pillar legal basis, while legally sounder, provides even fewer opportunities for scrutiny. From an EU privacy law perspective, it may provide even fewer data protection/privacy safeguards, in that there is no EU third pillar data protection instrument as such.

Biometrics, Databases, and Interoperability

The EU has also been moving towards the increased use of biometrics and the development of bigger, interoperable databases. U.S. influence in this context is evident; at times, U.S. domestic law requirements are evoked to justify swift EU action, and at other times, U.S. policy is used as an inspiration for EU policy. For example, EU legislators used U.S. requirements with regard to the adoption of biometric standards in passports and threats to discontinue the visa-waiver program (which includes the majority of EU Member States) if biometrics were not included in EU passports to pass such standards.[43] Political pressure towards inserting biometrics into identity documents led to the December 2004 adoption of a Regulation introducing biometric identifiers (in the form of facial images and fingerprints) in EU passports.[44] The legal basis of the Regulation is Article 62(2)(a) TEC, on border controls, but it was deemed to be a security measure.[45] The Regulation was finally adopted notwithstanding serious objections regarding the appropriateness of the legal basis and the existence of EC competence to adopt binding legislation on the content of identity documents—existing EU measures take the form of non-legally binding Resolutions. In addition, Article 62(2)(a), the basis for the Regulation, refers to controls of the external border of the EU and not to the content of EU travel documents, and Article 18(3) TEC explicitly states that Community action to facilitate the exercise of citizenship rights does not apply to provisions on passports, identity cards, residence permits, or any such document.

In spite of these legal concerns, and concerns on the proportionality of the measure,[46] negotiations on the measure went ahead and the second biometric identifier (fingerprints) was added. In spite of the adverse reaction of the Article 29 Working Party (House of Lords European Union Committee 2004d), the Regulation was adopted swiftly thereafter in December 2004—perhaps to pre-empt a greater say of the initially critical European Parliament, which would become a co-legislator with a right to veto the biometrics proposal after January 1, 2005.[47]

Notwithstanding a series of technical problems that have occurred, work on biometrics in visas and residence permits of third country nationals continues. The Justice and Home Affairs (JHA) Council adopted detailed conclusions on the development of the Visa Information System in February 2004, stating clearly that one of the purposes of the system would be to "contribute towards improving the administration of the common visa policy and towards internal security and combating terrorism." The Council called for the inclusion of biometric data on visa applicants in Visa Information System (VIS) for verification and identification purposes, "including background checks."[48] Biometrics are also included in the second generation of the Schengen Information System (SIS II) (Mitsilegas forthcoming).[49] Moreover, in a recent Communication, the Commission—in a manner reminiscent of U.S. initiatives—discusses the role of biometrics in "secure borders" and the development of an "integrated technological approach—e-borders" extending the obligations of carriers to transmit passenger data and the creation of a generalized and automated entry and exit system to the EU (COM 2006: 6). The development of such a system echoes the extensive reference to biometrics and information systems in the Hague Program, which provides a clear example of the new (in)security continuum:

> the management of migration flows, including the fight against illegal immigration should be strengthened by establishing a continuum of security measures that effectively links visa application procedures and entry and exit procedures at external border crossings. Such measures are also of importance for the prevention and control of crime, in particular terrorism. In order to achieve this, a coherent approach and harmonized solutions in the EU on biometric identifiers and data are necessary.[50]

It is a commonly argued point that biometric data will be of value to enforcement agencies if they form part of easily accessible databases.[51] It is thus no coincidence that in the EU, as in the U.S., calls for the introduction of biometrics went hand in hand with calls for facilitating their inclusion in databases and enhancing the "interoperability" of these databases so that data could be exchanged easily. For some years, the Commission has been developing the so-called second generation Schengen Information System (SIS II) with the aim of including increasingly detailed data (including biometrics), enabling the interlinking of alerts, widening of access by authorities for counterterrorism purposes,[52] and enabling possible synergies with other systems like the VIS.[53] An example of how central this project is for the Commission is that a new unit on "large-scale information systems" was created within the directorate general for Justice and Home Affairs (JHA DG) on December 16, 2002.[54]

In a similar manner to the U.S., under the banner of "interoperability," we are moving thus towards a system where EU databases containing a significant amount of sensitive personal data can be interconnected and accessed by a number of different agencies (COM 2005a).[55] Indeed, in its recent Commission Communication on interoperability (COM 2005a), the Commission's stated purpose is to highlight how, beyond their present purposes, databases "can more effectively support the policies linked to the free movement of persons and serve the objective of combating terrorism and serious crime" (COM 2005a: 2). This is notwithstanding the fact that the various EU databases contain quite diverse categories of data and were constructed to serve very diverse purposes, ranging from facilitating the assessment of visa and asylum applications (VIS and EURODAC, respectively) to police cooperation and counterterrorism (aspects of SIS, Europol). Interoperability—especially if it is justified under the blanket need for a "war on terror"—renders any safeguards that limit access and use of these databases for specific purposes meaningless (Mitsilegas 2007a).

This complexity is further compounded by the fact that EU databases, because of their diversity, are created under different legal bases (first/third pillar), and are governed by different data protection regimes. Database management is very fragmented in the third pillar, where specific rules and specific supervision arrangements apply to the specific bodies maintaining the databases (such as Europol and Eurojust), with no general, across-the-board standards or supervision. These piecemeal arrangements appear rather limited and ineffective in a climate where 1) the extension of current databases and the creation of new ones is advocated,[56] and 2) the facilitation and operational cooperation of maximum access to personal data between the various agencies at the EU level (such as Europol, Eurojust, the European Borders Agency, the Police Chief's Task Force, and SitCen) as well as at national levels (including cooperation between police and intelligence agencies) is the centerpiece of EU action in JHA for the next five years.[57]

Conclusion: Identity and Privacy in an Era of Globalized Surveillance

The above analysis demonstrates that in recent years there has been a marked convergence in the approach of the EU and the U.S. with regard to "border security," based on the "securitization" of migration/mobility and justified by the need to fight terrorism. This approach is centered on prevention, aiming at collecting a wide range of personal data—in particular by passengers—before they travel. In this manner, the movement of individuals can be tracked around the world and, by piecing together the various information over time, authorities can create profiles of individuals in order to assess their perceived terrorism risk. This preventive strategy has led to a shift from border controls to the maximum surveillance of populations. As I have noted elsewhere (Mitsilegas 2005: 178):

> The net of State surveillance is widening and thickening in a variety of ways. Personal data is now gathered on all the population, and not merely on specific categories of suspect individuals—so surveillance shifts from specific to generalised. More data is collected from various sources, aiming to create a profile of individuals and to track their movements across the globe—their entry and exit in national (and Schengen) territories is monitored and recorded. Information is gathered before, during and after entry in these territories. The quality of information gathered has changed as well, with the State invading further the private sphere by collecting information on the very essence of one's humanity and identity, i.e. biometrics. Data transmission has shifted from reactive (with private companies responding to law enforcement requests on specific suspects) to proactive—for instance, data on all passengers must be transmitted by airlines to the authorities.

All this leads to what Haggerty and Ericson (2000: 619)[58] have named "the disappearance of disappearance," a process whereby "it is increasingly difficult for individuals to maintain their anonymity or to escape the monitoring of social institutions"—in this case, the State abetted by the private sector.[59]

As far as the European Union is concerned, this shift has presented a number of constitutional challenges. In the PNR saga, a central question has been to what extent it is acceptable for the EU to cooperate with third countries (such as the U.S.) and comply with their standards, if it is perceived that these standards violate fundamental rights and fundamental principles of EU law and national Constitutions of Member States. Agreeing on standards that may compromise EU constitutional principles and values causes great concerns, in particular in view of the fact that standards agreed between the EU and the U.S. are very likely to form the model for the development of global standards in the field, and the basis under which EU external relations with candidate countries, neighbors, and the rest of the world are based.

These concerns also apply on the level of internal EU law and policy, where EU institutions—in particular, the Commission—are moving towards emulating the U.S. model as regards the development of biometric technology, e-border controls, and interoperable databases—and, following recent Commission proposals, as regards the development of an EU PNR system based on the U.S. model. But increased surveillance in this context not only challenges civil liberties in the EU, but also sits uneasily with the very objective of abolishing internal border controls in an "area of freedom, security and justice." New "border security" developments mean that surveillance of individuals is actually maximized, albeit not necessarily on the internal border. The level of scrutiny of these developments in the EU is currently not ideal, with fragmentation and secrecy exacerbated by the current pillar structure and the increased emphasis on "operational" and not legal measures that may be less amenable to scrutiny.

Convergence of EU and U.S. law and policy on "border security" may have a significant impact worldwide, especially if both powers push towards the adoption of their standards in international fora (such as ICAO as regards the identification of passengers). In the global context, but also in domestic discussions of attempts to maximize "border security" via the surveillance of populations, both the EU and the U.S. public and legislators face the central issue of how best to achieve the protection of the private life of the citizen and to resist transforming the relationship between the individual and the State into one where State surveillance and control is maximized. Along with the discussion of the protection currently offered by Constitutional and human rights provisions (in the EU these would include mainly national constitutional provisions, the ECHR, and to some extent the Charter of Fundamental Rights), a central issue is whether current privacy frameworks—especially those at the national level—are adequate to address the challenges posed by new technologies and globalized surveillance schemes.[60] This is particularly the case with "data mining" (Gandy 2003: 26–41) and the inclusion of unique intimate personal data, such as biometrics, in databases. It has been demonstrated that "the electronic trace" reverses the logic between information and identity—as in the case of biometric identification, identity is no longer confirmed by providing information (such as a passport), but is presumed on the basis of information already existing in a database (Leterre 2006). This change, along with the invasive character of biometric data and the endless possibilities of profile-building on the basis of numerous everyday personal data, must be taken into account in the development of new standards of privacy protection, articulating the protection of one's very Self against the State.

Notes

1 On a seminal analysis of the (in)security continuum in Europe, see Bigo (1996).
2 Executive Order No. 13,288, 66 Fed. Reg. 51812 (October 8, 2001). See Cmar (2002).
3 Another example of this has been the launch in 2002 by the U.S. Defense Department of the Total Information Awareness Project, its rather Orwellian title leading it to be later renamed as the Terrorist Information Awareness Project. The project would use biometric data and transactional data from a number of everyday activities, such as communication, financial transactions, medical, and education sources, and so on. Intense criticism of the project led to its termination, but the strategy for data collection is clear. For details see Galison and Minow (2005).

4 Aviation and Transportation Security Act, Pub. L., No. 107–71, 115 Stat. 595 (2001).
5 It was argued that CAPPS II was to be used for purposes extending beyond the "war on terror"—see transcript of Testimony of Marc Rothenberg, President, Electronic Privacy Information Center (EPIC) (Rothenberg 2005).
6 On the implementation of the system, see U.S. GAO (2004). A more recent report demonstrated that, in testing the system, TSA's disclosure of its use of personal information was not consistent with U.S. Privacy Act (U.S. GAO 2005b).
7 IRTPA Section 7208(a). (Congressional Reports: H. Rpt. 108–796. http://www.gpoaccess.go/serialset/creports/intel_reform.html (accessed July 19, 2006)). The Act defines a biometric identifier as "a technology that enables the automated identification, or verification of the identity, of an individual based on biometric information," which in turn is defined as "the distinct physical or behavioural characteristics of an individual that are used for unique identification, or verification of the identity, of an individual"; Section 4011 amending Section 44903(h) of title 49, S Code.
8 Executive Order 13356 of August 27, 2004. Strengthening the Sharing of Terrorism Information to Protect Americans. http://www.fas.org/irp/offdocs/eo/eo-13356.htm (accessed July 19, 2006). Executive Order 13388 of October 25, 2005. Further Strengthening the Sharing of Terrorism Information to Protect Americans. http://www.fas.org/irp/offdocs/eo/eo-13388.htm (accessed July 19, 2006).
9 EO 133 Section 5.
10 IRTPA Section 7208(e).
11 See http://www.dhs.gov/dhspublic/display?theme=43&content=5347&print=true: DHS Factsheet: Secure Borders and Open Doors in the Information Age. See also the speeches by Condoleezza Rice (http://www.state.gov/secretary/rm/2006/59239.htm) and Homeland Security Secretary Michael Chertoff (http://www.dhs.gov/dhspublic/display?theme=44&content=5409&print=true) (accessed July 17, 2006).
12 The factsheet states that, under the US-VISIT program, 45 million passengers were checked between January 2004 and December 2005.
13 For a detailed analysis, see Mitsilegas (2005). The part of this section examining the background and conclusion of the Agreements is based on this article. See also Mitsilegas (forthcoming).
14 Title 49, U.S. Code, Section 44909(c)(3) and title 19, Code of Federal Regulations, Section 122.49b.
15 The EC has adopted in 2004 a Directive requiring airlines to transmit a series of API data to border control authorities. See Mitsilegas (2005).
16 See Resolutions P5_TA(2003)0097 and P5_TA(2003)0429. www.europarl.europa.eu (accessed July 17, 2006).
17 The Working Party was established under the 1995 EC data protection Directive (Article 29) and consists of Member States' Information Commissioners. Its role is advisory.
18 On the work of ICAO on PNR, see ICAO Facilitation Division—12th session, Cairo 2004, *Airline Reservation System and Passenger Name Record (PNR) Access by States*, doc. FAL/12-WP/74, March 15, 2004.
19 OJ L 281, 11.23.1995, p. 31.
20 See correspondence between Lord Grenfell, Chairman of the House of Lords EU Committee, and Lord Filkin, Minister at the Department for Constitutional Affairs, on scrutiny arrangements. Lord Filkin noted that the U.K. government had not identified this proposed decision "as being of such importance as to trigger the exceptional arrangements for the deposit for scrutiny of Commission

comitology legislation." Letter to Lord Grenfell of February 26, 2004. Both published in House of Lords European Union Committee (2004b, 2004c).

21 The Working Party has a mandate to do so under Article 30(1)(b) of the data protection Directive.

22 P5_TA-PROV (2004) 0245.

23 Commission Decision of May 14, 2004 on the adequate protection of personal data contained in the Passenger Name Record of air passengers transferred to the United States' Bureau of Customs and Border Protection, OJ L 235, 6.7.2004, p. 11. The Undertakings of the U.S. Homeland Security Department are annexed in pp. 15–21. The list of PNR data is annexed in p. 22.

24 OJ L 183, 20.5.2004, p. 83. The text of the Agreement is annexed in pp. 84–85. The Agreement was signed on May 28, 2004.

25 Undertakings of the Department of Homeland Security Bureau of Customs and Border Protection (CBP), OJ L235, 6.7.2004, p. 15, point 13. It is not clear how the legality of pulling data from carriers' systems will be monitored or how it will be ensured that extracting data from airlines' databases is limited to data on passengers on flights to or via the U.S.

26 Ibid. point 3.

27 Ibid. point 15.

28 Ibid. point 29.

29 Ibid. point 45.

30 Ibid. point 46.

31 Ibid. points 47 and 48.

32 The Court of Justice, based in Luxembourg, has a key role in interpreting and applying EC law. The main forms of action to the Court are infringement proceedings for breach of EC law; proceedings establishing the validity of EC action; and preliminary rulings on questions on interpretation of Community law sent to the ECJ from national courts. In annulment proceedings (where the Court rules on the validity of EC law and of which the PNR action is an example), the Court can annul EC law on legality grounds. For details, see Arnull (2006).

33 The European Parliament argues that Article 95 TEC (on the internal market) is not the right legal basis for the contested Decision. It also argues that its assent should be required for the adoption of the Decision authorizing the conclusion of the international agreement, and not its mere consultation, as has happened. This is because, according to the Parliament, the agreement constitutes an amendment of the 1995 data protection Directive. See Council doc. 11876/04, Brussels, August 6, 2004.

34 See www.curia.europa.eu (accessed July 17, 2006).

35 There are eight Advocates General at the Court of Justice. An Advocate General is assigned to each case. His/her role is to prepare an impartial Opinion on the case in question. The Opinion normally contains an analysis of the factual and legal issues concerned and provides a Recommendation to the Court on how the case should be decided. The AG's Opinion is not binding, although usually the Court follows its main thrust. See Arnull (2006).

36 See, in particular, paragraphs 138–150 and 161 of the Opinion. Under similar reasoning, the AG rejected the Parliament's argument that the adequacy Decision amended the 1995 EC data protection Directive (and therefore the first pillar Agreement negotiations should give Parliament a greater say)—paragraph 184.

37 In particular, paragraphs 231 and 256.

38 Joint cases C-317/04 and C-318/04, *European Parliament* v *Council*. The European Data Protection Supervisor supported the Parliament, while the Commission and the U.K. supported the Council.

39 Judgment ECR [2006] I–4721, paragraph 67.
40 Ibid. paragraph 56.
41 Ibid. paragraphs 71–74.
42 The Report highlights that questions are still open regarding, for instance, data retention periods and access to data.
43 See, *inter alia*, "Commission proposes to put biometrics in EU citizens' passports," *European Report*, vol. 2845, February 21, 2004.
44 Council Regulation (EC) No. 2252/2004 of December 13, 2004 on standards for security features and biometrics in passports and travel documents issued by member states, OJ L 385, 29.12.2004, p. 1.
45 See letter of May 11, 2004 by Home Office Minister Caroline Flint to Lord Grenfell, Chairman of the House of Lords EU Committee, stating that "our view is that the current proposal is first and foremost a security measure." (House of Lords European Union Committee 2004a).
46 On both concerns, see the detailed analysis by Statewatch, prepared by Steve Peers (2004).
47 The need for the swift adoption of the proposal has also been justified on the grounds that the U.S. would abandon its visa-waiver program with its members in the EU which had not introduced biometrics in their passports by a certain date. Like in the PNR case, the EU has managed to obtain an extension to the U.S. deadline for the insertion of biometrics, but this new U.S. deadline will not be met and it is unlikely to be extended by the U.S. (see letter of March 31, 2005 from the Chairman of the U.S. House Judiciary Committee to the Commission and the Council, reproduced in www.statewatch.org).
48 See also the Opinion of the Article 29 Working Party on the inclusion of biometrics in residence permits and visas taking into account the establishment of VIS—Opinion No. 7/2004, doc. 11224/04/EN, WP 96.
49 For background information, see docs. 5709/6/06 Rev. 6, Brussels, June 6, 2006. Along with the eastward enlargement of the EU in 2004, one of the main justifications for the development of the Second Generation SIS has been the need to fight terrorism (see, in particular, the EU Counter-terrorism Action Plan of September 21, 2001). In 2004, the Council adopted a first pillar Regulation and a third pillar Framework Decision introducing some new functions for SIS, "including in the fight against terrorism" (OJ L162 of 30.4.2004 and OJ L68 of 15.3.2005 respectively). These measures introduced changes to the use of Schengen data and enabled access to the Schengen database by Europol and Eurojust.
50 The Hague Program: Strengthening Freedom, Security and Justice in the European Union. Point 1.7,2, OJ C53, March 3, 2005, p. 7.
51 For analyses on biometric policy, see Liberatore (2005) and Thomas (2006).
52 In 2004, the Council adopted a first pillar Regulation and a third pillar Decision concerning the introduction "of some new functions for the Schengen Information System, including in the fight against terrorism." The Regulation extends access to SIS data to national judicial authorities and access to immigration data to authorities responsible for issuing visas and residence permits and examining visa applications. The Decision extends access to "criminal law" SIS data to Europol and Eurojust.
53 Widening of access to VIS is also being envisaged. The JHA Council conclusions on the development of VIS in February 2004 called for access to VIS to be granted *inter alia* to border guards and "other national authorities to be authorized by each Member State such as police departments, immigration departments and services responsible for internal security." For details, see Mitsilegas (forthcoming).

54 See the Commission Communication on the development of SIS II—777 final, COM (2003).
55 The Communication provides a definition of "interoperability," which is the "ability of IT systems and of the business processes they support to exchange data and to enable the sharing of information and knowledge." According to the Commission, this is a technical rather than a legal/political concept (p. 3). In his Opinion on the Communication, the European Data Protection Supervisor has criticized this emphasis on the technical (March 10, 2006).
56 The Commission Communication on interoperability (COM 2005a) makes reference to European registers for travel documents and identity cards (p. 9) and perceived shortcomings arising from the absence of registration of EU citizens at European level (p. 6).
57 See, in particular, the Hague Program (2005), Sections 2.1–2.5.
58 See also, especially on the shift of monitoring from reactive to proactive, Levi and Wall (2004).
59 David Lyon (2003) has pointed out that, despite the focus on developments in the private sector when analyzing surveillance, the State remains relevant and can use the information gathered by "private" surveillance.
60 On a discussion of the limits of U.S. privacy law in this context, see Galison and Minow (2005).

References

Andreas, Peter. 2003. "Redrawing the Line: Borders and Security in the Twenty-First Century." *International Security* 28(2): 78–111.
Arnull, Anthony. 2006. *The European Union and its Court of Justice*. 2nd ed. Oxford: Oxford University Press.
Article 29 Working Party. 2003. *Opinion 4/2003 on the Level of Protection ensured in the U.S. for the Transfer of Passengers' Data*, 11070/03/EN, WP 78.
Article 29 Working Party. 2004. *Opinion 2/2004 on the Adequate Protection of Personal Data contained in the PNR of Air Passengers to be transferred to the United States' Bureau of Customs and Border Protection (U.S. CBP)*, adopted on January 29, 2004, doc. 10019/04/EN, WP 87.
Aviation and Transportation Security Act. 2001. Pub. L., No. 107–71, 115 Stat. 595.
Bennett, Colin J. 2005. "What Happens When You Book an Airline Ticket? The Collection and Processing of Passenger Data Post-9/11," in Elia Zureik and Mark B. Salter, eds., *Global Surveillance and Policing*, pp. 113–138. Devon, UK: Willan.
Bigo, Didier. 1996. *Polices en réseaux: l'expérience européenne*. Paris: Presses Science Po.
Ceyhan, Ayse. 2004. "Securité, frontières et surveillance aux Etats Unis après le 11 Septembre 2001." *Cultures et Conflits* 53: 113–145.
Cmar, Thomas. 2002. "Recent Developments—Office of Homeland Security." *Harvard Journal on Legislation* 39(2): 455–474.
COM (Commission Communication). 2003. *On the Development of SIS II—771 Final*.
COM (Commission Communication). 2005a. *597 Final*. Brussels, November 24.
COM (Commission Communication). 2005b. *Staff Working Paper on the Joint Review, Final*. Brussels, December 12.
COM (Commission Communication). 2006. *402 Final*. Brussels, July 19.

DHS (Department of Homeland Security). 2005. *A Report Concerning Passenger Name Record Information Derived from Flights between the U.S. and the European Union.* September 19. http://www.dhs.gov/xlibrary/assets/privacy/privacy_pnr_rpt_09-2005.pdf.

DHS (Department of Homeland Security). 2006. *Factsheet: Secure Borders and Open Doors in the Information Age.* http://www.dhs.gov/dhspublic/display?theme=43&content=5347&print=true (accessed July 17, 2006).

European Commission. 2003. Communication from the Commission to the Council and the Parliament, *Transfer of Air Passenger Name Record (PNR) Data: A Global EU Approach*, COM (2003) 826 final, Brussels, December 16.

Galison, Peter and Martha Minow. 2005. "Our Privacy, Ourselves in the Age of Technological Intrusions," in Richard Ashby Wilson, ed., *Human Rights in the "War on Terror,"* pp. 261–266. Cambridge: Cambridge University Press.

Gandy, Oscar H. 2003. "Data Mining and Surveillance in the Post-9/11 Environment," in Kristie Ball and Frank Webster, eds., *The Intensification Of Surveillance: Crime, Terrorism and Warfare in the Information Age*, pp. 26–41. Ann Arbor: University of Michigan Press.

Haggerty, Kevin D., and Richard V. Ericson. 2000. "The Surveillant Assemblage." *British Journal of Sociology* 51(4): 605–622.

House of Lords European Union Committee. 2004a. Letter by Caroline Flint, Home Office Minister, of May 11, 2004 to Lord Grenfell, Chairman of the House of Lords EU Committee. Correspondence with Ministers, 25th Report, 2003–04, HL Paper 140.

House of Lords European Union Committee. 2004b. Letter by Lord Filkin of February 26, 2004 to Lord Grenfell in House of Lords EU Committee. Correspondence with Ministers, 25th Report, 2003–04, HL Paper 140.

House of Lords European Union Committee. 2004c. Letter by Lord Filkin of April 27, 2004 to Lord Grenfell in House of Lords EU Committee. Correspondence with Ministers, 25th Report, 2003–04, HL Paper 140.

House of Lords European Union Committee. 2004d. Letter by Peter Schaar, Chairman of the Working Party, of November 30, 2004, to Josep Borrell Fontelles, Chairman of the European Parliament. Correspondence with Ministers, 25th Report, 2003–04, HL Paper 140.

House of Lords European Union Committee. 2007. *The EU/US Passenger Name Record (PNR) Agreement.* 21st report, session 2006–07, HL Paper 108.

Leterre, Thierry. 2006. "Le Repérage par la trace électronique," in Xavier Crettiez and Pierre Piazza, eds., *Du Papier à la biométrie*, pp. 290–291. Paris: Presses des Sciences Po.

Levi, Michael, and David S. Wall. 2004. "Technologies, Security and Privacy in the post-9/11 European Information Society." *Journal of Law and Society* 31(2): 194–220.

Liberatore, Angela. 2005. "Balancing Security and Democracy: The Politics of Biometric Identification in the EU." *European University Institute Working Paper 30.* Robert Schuman Centre of Advanced Studies.

Lyon, David. 2003. "Surveillance after September 11, 2001," in Kristie Ball and Frank Webster, eds., *The Intensification of Surveillance: Crime, Terrorism and Warfare in the Information Age.* London: Pluto Press.

McCarthy, Michael T. 2002. "Recent Developments—USA Patriot Act." *Harvard Journal on Legislation* 39(Summer): 435–453.

Mitsilegas, Valsamis. 2003. "The New EU/US Co-operation on Extradition, Mutual Legal Assistance and the Exchange of Police Data." *European Foreign Affairs Review* 8(4): 515–536.

Mitsilegas, Valsamis. 2005. "Contrôle des étrangers, des passagers, des citoyens: surveillance et anti-terrorisme." *Cultures et Conflits* 58: 155–182.

Mitsilegas, Valsamis. 2007a. "Border Security in the European Union: Towards Centralised Controls and Maximum Surveillance," in Annaliese Badaccini, Elspeth Guild, and Helen Toner, eds., *Whose Freedom, Security and Justice? EU Immigration and Asylum Law and Policy*, pp. 359–394. Oxford: Hart Publishing.

Mitsilegas, Valsamis. 2007b. "The External Dimension of EU Action in Criminal Matters." *European Foreign Affairs Review* 12: 457–497.

Mitsilegas, Valsamis. Forthcoming. "Databases in the Area of Freedom, Security and Justice," in Helen Xanthaki, ed., *Towards a European Criminal Record*. Cambridge: Cambridge University Press.

Peers, Steve. 2004. "The Legality of the Regulation on EU Citizens Passports." November 26, 2004. www.statewatch.org.

Rothenberg, Marc. 2005. "Testimony to the Sub-Committee on Economic Security, Infrastructure Protection, and Cybersecurity, Committee on Homeland Security, U.S. House of Representatives." November 3.

Salter, Mark B. 2004. "Passports, Mobility and Security: How Smart Can the Border Be?" *International Studies Perspectives* 5(1): 71–91.

Stanhouse, Darren W. 2003–4. "Ambition and Abdication: Congress, the Presidency and the Evolution of the Department of Homeland Security." *North Carolina Journal of International Law and Commercial Regulation* 29: 691–711.

Thessin, Jonathan. 2003. "Recent Developments—Department of Homeland Security." *Harvard Journal on Legislation* 40: 513–535.

Thomas, Rebekah. 2006. "Biometrics, International Migrants and Human Rights." *European Journal of Migration and Law* 7: 377–411.

U.S. GAO (Government Accountability Office). 2004. *Aviation Security: Computer-Assisted Passenger Prescreening System Faces Significant Implementation Challenges*, February 13. http://www.gao.gov/new.items/d04385.pdf.

U.S. GAO (Government Accountability Office). 2005a. *Aviation Security: Secure Flight Development and Testing under Way, but Risks Should Be Managed as System Is further Developed*, March. http://www.gao.gov/new.items/d05356.pdf.

U.S. GAO (Government Accountability Office). 2005b. *Aviation Security: Transportation Security Administration Did Not Fully Disclose Uses of Personal Information during Secure Flight Program Testing in Initial Privacy Notes, but Has Recently Taken Steps to More Fully Inform the Public*, July 22. http://www.gao.gov/new.items/d05864r.pdf.

U.S. GAO (Government Accountability Office). 2005c. *Homeland Security. Some Progress Made but Many Challenges Remain on US Visitor and Immigrant Status Indicator Technology Program*, February. http://www.gao.gov/new.items/d05202.pdf.

U.S. Office of Homeland Security. 2002. *National Strategy for Homeland Security*, July.

9 Towards a Common European Asylum Policy

Forced Migration, Collective Security, and Burden Sharing

Eiko R. Thielemann

Introduction

Forced migration to Europe differs significantly from that to the U.S. Most persons arriving in the U.S. for humanitarian reasons do so as resettled refugees, which allows for considerable control over numbers and for the pre-screening of those admitted. In Europe, in contrast, individuals claiming persecution arrive almost exclusively as (spontaneous) asylum seekers at the border and the decision as to whether or not they qualify for protection is therefore taken while the claimants are already on a state's territory. The security challenges resulting from spontaneous asylum seekers are therefore potentially greater than those of resettled refugees.

Asylum seekers have long been regarded as constituting a variety of security challenges for European states. They constitute a large category of foreign arrivals—the largest in some countries (such as in Germany in 1992). These challenges are often closely related to the massive fluctuations in asylum seekers and the limited effectiveness of receiving states to control such flows. As such, the events surrounding September 11 reinforced a pre-existing European security agenda vis-à-vis asylum seekers in Europe (Bigo 1994; Guild 2003; Huysman 2000) and strengthened a belief in the necessity for closer cooperation among the EU Member States on border-control issues more generally. Although the Members devoted the first EU Justice and Home Affairs (JHA) Council meeting following the U.S. 9/11 attacks exclusively to the EU response on security and other measures to combat terrorism, the specific measures adopted focused on wider security issues (judicial cooperation, cooperation between policy and intelligence services, cooperation with the U.S. and joint measures at the EU's external borders) but did not make an explicit link between terrorist attacks and the inflow of asylum seekers into Europe (JHA Council 2001).

Hence, unlike in the U.S. where September 11 had quite a wide-ranging impact on U.S. immigration law, the terrorist attacks in New York, Madrid, and London were seen in Europe as again highlighting the need to consolidate efforts to achieve more effective border controls through enhanced EU cooperation in the wider JHA area. The major driving force behind developments in EU–JHA matters in general, and moves towards a common European asylum policy in particular, were therefore not a response to particular terrorist incidences such as those of September 11 but the result of broader security implications (perceived and real) of the European integration process itself (Byrne, Noll, and Vedsted-Hansen 2002; Guiraudon 2000; Lavenex and Uçarer 2002; Stetter 2000).

Two developments are particularly important here. First, the removal of internal borders as part of the single market program and the Schengen process meant that once inside one Member State, foreigners could move quite easily onto other Member States. Second, the process of enlargement meant that over time the external borders of the EU have faced poorer and more volatile neighbors while the capacity of the new Member States to effectively control their (and hence the EU's) borders is considerably lower than that of the old Member States.

The security concerns related to these developments have been heightened by the highly varied attractiveness among the EU Member States as destination countries for asylum seekers, leading to the fear that asylum inflows may overburden some states and that unilateral restrictive efforts to gain control over such flows might result in highly undesirable consequences for the other Member States, asylum seekers, and the wider integration process itself. Recent developments towards a common asylum policy in Europe have therefore been closely linked with the perceived need for "burden-" or "responsibility-sharing" in this area (Noll 2000; Suhrke 1998; Thielemann 2003). The Member States' commitment in this regard was perhaps most clearly stated at the Brussels European Council meeting in November 2004. In their final declaration, EU leaders stressed that the development of a common policy in the field of asylum, migration, and borders "should be based on solidarity and fair sharing of responsibility including its financial implications and closer practical co-operation between member states" (European Council 2004). The United Nations High Commissioner for Refugees (UNHCR) echoes this concern because "burden-sharing is a key to the protection of refugees and the resolution of the refugee problem" (UNHCR 2001). In 2005, the then UN High Commissioner Lubbers stated:

> There is a need for responsibility and burden-sharing within the EU . . . I fear that high protection standards will be difficult to maintain in a system which shifts responsibility to states located on the external border of the EU, many of which have limited asylum capacity.
>
> (Lubbers 2005)

However, despite of a lot of legislative activity, the EU's refugee burden-sharing initiatives have not been fully effective. Some of the recent measures introduced even appear to have reinforced the observable imbalances in responsibilities. As such, the EU has arguably undermined its own burden-sharing objectives with security implications for individuals inside and outside the Member States.

To substantiate this argument, this chapter will first discuss the extent and causes of unequal asylum and refugee burdens. An analysis of the various types of burden-sharing initiatives available in this area will follow. Finally, there will be an analysis of the specific refugee burden-sharing instruments developed within the EU's emerging asylum system and a discussion of why their effectiveness has been limited and sometimes counterproductive.

How (Un)Equal is the Distribution of Refugee Burdens?

When comparing their relative contributions to refugee protection, states are likely to disagree about how such contributions should be assessed. However, by looking at some of the most directly linked responsibilities associated with international refugee flows, it is possible to arrive at some approximations of relative responsibilities that countries face or are prepared to accept. Table 9.1 overleaf tries to do just that. It presents UNHCR data on asylum and resettlement for a selection of 15 member countries of the Organization for Economic Co-operation and Development (OECD) for the period 1994–2002.

Column 1 shows the average number of asylum applications received in each country over the time period and column 2 indicates what percentage of these arrivals were given permanent or temporary protection status by the state in question. Column 3 lists the number of refugees who arrived via resettlement programs (i.e., not as "spontaneous" asylum seekers). The final column combines the numbers of "recognised" asylum seekers (i.e., those who have been granted some form of protection status) with the average number of resettled refugees and puts the combined total in relation to a country's population size (as a measure of absorption capacity). This provides the average accepted asylum/refugee burden for each state, relative to a country's size. This "relative" figure is arguably a more appropriate measure of "burdens" or "responsibilities" than comparing absolute numbers of asylum seekers/refugees that do not take account of vast differences in countries' size and hence absorption capacity. One finds strong variation not just among OECD states but also among EU countries—states such as the Netherlands, Denmark, and Sweden face significantly higher asylum and refugee related responsibilities than do other Member States.

Why are Refugee Burdens Unequally Distributed?

When trying to account for the current distribution of refugee burdens among countries, three principal explanations have been suggested. These relate to free-riding opportunities, state interests, and variation in pull factors.

Table 9.1 Average accepted protection burden (1994–2002)

Country	1 Average annual number of asylum applications*	2 Average recognition rate (%)**	3 Average resettlement arrivals	4 Average accepted protection burden***
Netherlands	35,345	62.7	308	1.399
Switzerland	25,208	39.3	0	1.376
Denmark	8,312	61.6	1,034	1.181
Sweden	15,556	45.1	1,945	1.031
Norway	7,836	35	1,494	0.967
Canada	29,755	59.8	10,898	0.959
Belgium	21,532	32.3	0	0.678
Australia	9,086	18.1	10,222	0.636
United States	75,484	29.7	76,243	0.369
United Kingdom	61,077	36.1	39	0.362
Germany	100,844	15.7	0	0.188
France	30,595	18.4	0	0.092
Italy	9,223	24.6	0	0.049
Spain	7,352	24	0	0.048
Japan	187	13.5	162	0.001

Notes
* Figures generally refer to the number of persons who applied for asylum. The figures used here are generally first instance ("new") applications only. Source: Governments, UNHCR. Compiled by UNHCR (Population Data Unit). See also: http://www.unhcr.ch (Statistics).
** Total recognition rates in industrialized countries (first instance). Includes persons recognized (under Geneva Convention) and those "allowed to remain" (on the basis of subsidiary protection) divided by the total of recognized, allowed to remain and rejected. Source: UNHCR Statistical Yearbooks.
*** Number of asylum seekers given permanent or temporary protection status combined with number of resettlement arrivals per 1,000 of population per year.

Free-Riding Opportunities in the Provision of Collective Security

Similar to the NATO burden-sharing debate, there have been protests and free-riding accusations from the main receiving countries of asylum seekers as well as threats by some states to opt out of the Geneva Convention for the Protection of Refugees to which all OECD countries are signatories. A number of scholars, most prominently Suhrke (1998), have suggested that refugee protection has (at least in part) important "public good" characteristics. Suhrke argues that the reception of displaced persons can be regarded as an international public good from which all states benefit. In her view, increased security is the principal (non-excludable and non-rival) benefit, as the accommodation of displaced persons may reduce the risk of their fueling and spreading the conflict from which they are fleeing.

As with the provision of other international public goods, such as collective defense, one might therefore expect substantial free-riding opportunities with regard to refugee protection. While empirical evidence suggests that small countries exploit larger countries with regard to the NATO burden-sharing debate (Olson and Zeckhauser 1966), analysis of the refugee reception burden suggests the opposite. Figure 9.1 suggests that, in the case of the reception of refugees by OECD countries, smaller states appear to shoulder disproportionate burdens.

States' Security Interests and Normative Preferences

Another way to try to explain the unequal distribution of refugee burdens is to analyze specific state interests and countries' normative preferences in this area. Some economists have developed a refined version of Olson's public goods approach, one that is based on the so-called "joint product" model (Sandler 1992).[1] This model suggests that what might appear as a pure public good in fact often brings excludable (private) benefits to a country. Based on this "joint product model," we would expect that a country's contributions to the provision of a particular collective good (which has both public and private characteristics) will be positively related to the proportion of excludable benefits accruing to that country. It seems reasonable to assume that one country's efforts in the area of refugee protection will have some positive spillover effects on other countries in the region. However, refugee protection arguably provides a spectrum of outputs ranging from purely public to private or country-specific outputs. This means that refugee protection provides more than the single output of "security" implied by the pure public goods model: it also provides country-specific benefits such as status enhancement or the achievement of ideological goals (such as when the West was keen to accept political refugees from behind the Iron Curtain during the Cold War). Moreover, we can also expect relatively more benefits from refugee protection measures accruing to countries closer to a refugee-generating conflict.[2] In other words, what is often regarded as a public good has in fact excludable (private) benefits to a country. The "joint product model" therefore suggests that a country's contributions to the provision of refugee protection (with its public and private characteristics) will be positively related to the proportion of excludable benefits accruing to that country.

From a norm-based perspective, patterns of burden-sharing can be explained with reference to the observed variation in states' commitment to norms that are related to the particular burden in question. From this perspective, the burden that a state is prepared to accept will be linked to the strengths of a state's preferences on safeguarding certain norms (such as general human rights standards or norms of distributive justice). It has been shown that states' willingness to shoulder protection burdens are positively correlated with their relative commitment to the norm of solidarity with people in need; countries that accept a disproportionate number of protection seekers are also the ones with a strong commitment to domestic redistribution (extensive welfare states) and above average foreign aid contributions (Thielemann 2003). A state's greater willingness to accept burdens (for whatever of the above

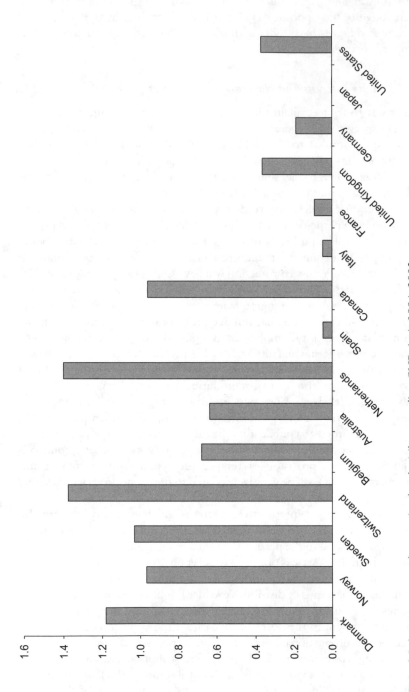

Figure 9.1 Average accepted protection burden[a] (by ascending GNP size), 1994–2002.

Note
a Number of asylum seekers given permanent or temporary protection status combined with number of resettlement arrivals per 1,000 of population per year.

reasons) often means that it will adopt a relatively lenient policy regime (more access, more attractive reception/integration package, etc.). Overall, however, there are reasons to expect that structural determinants are more important than policy-related factors for attempts to explain the relative distribution of asylum burdens among OECD countries.

Structural Pull Factors

As shown above, "spontaneous" asylum seekers constitute the majority of those arriving in Europe stating humanitarian reasons. Under the current international refugee protection regime, states of first asylum are obliged to determine the status of asylum seekers (i.e., assess whether they qualify as refugees under the 1951 Geneva Convention). Differences in structural pull factors (i.e., non-policy-related factors that make some host countries more attractive than others) have a very strong effect on the relative distribution of asylum seekers.[3] Table 9.2 (column 1) ranks Western European countries according to the average number of asylum applications per thousand of population. Table 9.2 also ranks those countries with regard to six indicators (columns 2–7) that stand for potential determinants or "pull factors" for an asylum seeker's choice of preferred host country. The correlation coefficient in the bottom row of the table indicates how closely each of the six indicators (explanatory variables) listed correlates with countries' relative asylum burden (in column 1).[4]

In this table, we find that the relative number of asylum applications is very highly and positively correlated with countries' prosperity ranking and one finds a negative and still quite strong correlation with unemployment rates. In other words, this suggests that countries that are relatively rich and possess relatively favorable labor market opportunities tend to receive relatively high numbers of asylum applications.

The third indicator relates to historical ties (colonial links, language ties, cultural networks, etc.) between countries of origin and destination that often have led to transport, trade, and communication links between such countries; these links tend to facilitate the movement of people from one country to the other (Massey et al. 1993: 445–447). One possible way to study the strength of such ties is to estimate the number of current or former citizens of a particular country of origin who reside in different destination countries. Drawing on this, Table 9.2 shows that high asylum burdens correlate strongly (and positively) with historical links between countries of origin and countries of destination. Host countries in which immigrant communities have become well established are likely to be countries confronted with relatively high asylum burdens.

The fourth indicator is more political in nature and seeks to capture the reputation that a particular country of destination enjoys abroad, especially in the developing world from which a large majority of asylum seekers originate. It is natural for asylum seekers to be concerned about personal security and the difficulties they might face regarding their acceptance into a new host society.

Table 9.2 Determinants of relative asylum burdens (averages 1985–2000)

	Relative asylum burden		Structural determinants								Geographic		Policy-related determinants	
			Economic				Historical		Political				Deterrence-policy	
			GDP per capita		Unemployment rate		Foreign (born) population		ODA		Distance (km)		Deterrence index	
1	CHE	3.3	LUX	0.033	ESP	19.5	AUT	60.9	NOR	1.02	PRT	4,886	DEU	4.5	1
2	SWE	2.6	CHE	0.032	IRE	14.4	DEU	41.6	SWE	0.92	ESP	4,461	CHE	4.0	2
3	DEU	2.0	NOR	0.028	BEL	12.1	DNK	29.6	DNK	0.86	IRE	4,355	AUT	3.0	3
4	DNK	1.8	DNK	0.026	ITA	11.2	NLD	26.3	CHE	0.68	NOR	4,224	PRT	2.9	4
5	AUT	1.7	SWE	0.025	FRA	10.6	CHE	21.8	DEU	0.51	GBR	4,043	GRC	2.8	5
6	NLD	1.7	DEU	0.023	FIN	9.4	SWE	16.4	FIN	0.41	FRA	3,918	FRA	2.5	6
7	BEL	1.6	FIN	0.022	DNK	9.0	NOR	9.7	AUT	0.40	BEL	3,805	ITA	2.5	7
8	NOR	1.3	AUT	0.021	GRC	8.1	BEL	9.6	FRA	0.36	NLD	3,783	ESP	2.2	8
9	LUX	0.9	FRA	0.021	GBR	7.9	FRA	7.4	LUX	0.36	LUX	3,718	NLD	1.8	9
10	FRA	0.6	NLD	0.020	DEU	7.9	ITA	5.3	NLD	0.36	CHE	3,642	LUX	1.6	10
11	GBR	0.5	BEL	0.020	NLD	7.0	FIN	3.9	BEL	0.34	FIN	3,612	DNK	1.5	11
12	IRE	0.5	GBR	0.018	AUT	6.0	GBR	1.3	IRE	0.27	DNK	3,502	IRE	1.5	12
13	GRC	0.3	ITA	0.018	PRT	5.9	GRC	–	ITA	0.26	SWE	3,473	BEL	0.9	13
14	FIN	0.3	IRE	0.016	SWE	4.5	IRE	–	ESP	0.22	ITA	3,409	NOR	0.9	14
15	ESP	0.2	ESP	0.012	NOR	4.1	LUX	–	GBR	0.21	DEU	3,380	SWE	0.8	15
16	ITA	0.2	GRC	0.009	CHE	2.5	PRT	–	PRT	0.18	AUT	3,166	GBR	0.8	16
17	PRT	0.0	PRT	0.008	LUX	2.2	ESP	–	GRC	0.14	GRC	2,929	FIN	0.8	17
Correlation coefficient		1.00		0.70		−0.52		0.63		0.43		−0.37		0.21	

Notes
AUT: Austria; BEL: Belgium; CHE: Switzerland; DEU: Germany; DNK: Denmark; ESP: Spain; FIN: Finland; FRA: France; GBR: Great Britain; GRC: Greece; IRE: Ireland; ITA: Italy; LUX: Luxembourg; NLD: Netherlands; NOR: Norway; PRT: Portugal; SWE: Sweden.
ODA: Overseas Development Aid

Here, we try to capture the reputation of a country in terms of its "liberal credentials" and concern for foreigners by analyzing countries' track records in the area of overseas development aid. The assumption is that countries that spend relatively more of their Gross Domestic Product (GDP) on aid to the Third World will tend to have a more caring reputation. Table 9.2 finds quite a strong and positive correlation between relative asylum burdens and host countries' reputation measured in this way. Host countries that spend a relatively high proportion of their GDP on overseas development aid tend to attract a relatively high share of asylum applications.

Fifth, although perhaps less important than in previous years due to techno-logical advancements, geographic distance between countries of origin and des-tination can still be regarded as an important proxy for the cost of movement between countries. With regard to the role of geographical factors, we find a negative, albeit weaker, correlation between relative asylum burdens and the average distance between countries of destination and the five most important countries of origin in any particular year. In other words, those countries that are more closely situated in geographic terms to important countries of origin are more likely to encounter a disproportionate share of asylum applications.

Finally, the data show a weak (and positive!) correlation between relative asylum burdens and policy-related deterrence measures. Despite quite sub-stantial variation in countries' average deterrence index[5] for the time period under investigation, we find little evidence for the claim that countries with stricter asylum regimes are the ones that find themselves with relatively smaller burdens in comparison to those that (on average) have operated more lenient regimes.[6] On the contrary, we find that some of the countries (such as Germany, Switzerland, and Austria), despite having put in place some of the most restrictive asylum policy regimes, nonetheless are among the most popular destinations for asylum applicants. Structural, not policy-related, pull factors therefore appear to constitute the most critical factors in explaining the unequal distribution of refugee burdens.

The Relationship between Security and Burden-Sharing

There are two security-related motivations for refugee burden-sharing. One derives from a traditional state perspective; the other looks at the issue from the perspective of an individual protection seeker. With regard to the first, states can be assumed to have an interest to contribute to regional or global refugee protection efforts, as the uncontrolled mass movement of displaced persons across international borders undermines the security objectives of countries in the region of destination. Moreover, a number of scholars, most prominently Suhrke (1998: 399–400), have suggested that refugee protection has impor-tant "international public good" characteristics which means that receiving countries are faced with significant collective action problems. Suhrke (1998) argues that, by granting refuge to displaced persons, host countries provide a public good from which all states benefit. She underlines the positive externalities (spill-ins) resulting from one country's refugee protection effort to another and writes: "If one state admits refugees, others will benefit from the greater international order that ensues regardless of their own admissions" (1998: 400). From this perspective, enhanced security and stability can be regarded as the principal collective benefit that is accruing to countries in the region of destination, as an accommodation of displaced persons (in particular, in the case of mass influx) can be expected to reduce the risk of them fueling and spreading the conflict refugees are fleeing from. However, countries have an incentive to hope for positive spill-ins and try to conceal their true preferences as to the extent to which they would like to see refugee issues be addressed. This is because they hope to be able to free-ride on the efforts of others, and hence refugee protection contributions can be expected to be provided at suboptimal levels. There are powerful incentives for individual states to avoid contributing resources to international collective goods. As they fear that the expression of willingness to contribute might mean that they will also be the ones who end up footing the bill, collective goods such as refugee protection are undersupplied and security goals of destination states regarding the effective management of the international movement of displaced persons will be compromised.

Arguably even more compromised as a result of collective action problems, however, are the security interests of individual protection seekers. Attempts by states to escape disproportionate burdens in this area have frequently led to burden-shifting dynamics in the wake of which established protection standards have been undermined. There is a widespread belief among host countries that states with relatively more lenient asylum and refugee policies will come to be regarded as a "soft touch" and will consequently have to cope with a disproportionately high number of refugees. To counter this, destination countries which have been concerned about their reception capacities, have engaged in attempts to outperform each other when it comes to the introduction of new restrictive policy measures. The aim of these efforts has been to make a country's asylum rules more restrictive relative to other potential host countries and ultimately to deter displaced persons from applying in a particular country. As countries have sought to copy deterrence measures introduced by other states, the result has been a "race to the bottom" in protection standards that has fundamentally challenged and in some cases undermined the security interests of forced migrants. Institutionalized EU burden-sharing initiatives have thus been developed to help overcome collective action problems, curtail free-riding opportunities and halt the decline in protection standards. In doing so, Member States hoped to address the security concerns of both states and individual protection seekers.

Types of International Burden-Sharing Regimes

What instruments are available to states seeking to equalize burdens or responsibilities? One can distinguish two substantively different types of

Table 9.3 Types of international burden-sharing mechanisms

		Dimensionality	
		One-dimensional	*Multi-dimensional*
Distribution rule	**Hard**	Binding rules	Explicit compensation
	Soft	Voluntary pledging	Implicit trade

international burden-sharing regimes and four principal burden-sharing mechanisms (Table 9.3). First, there are *one-dimensional* burden-sharing regimes that aim to equalize states' efforts on one particular contribution dimension, usually by seeking to equalize the number of asylum seekers and refugees that states have to deal with. This tends to be done in two ways—through binding rules or through voluntary pledging mechanisms. Policy harmonization would be an example of the former method, as it is based on the assumption that agreeing on a common set of rules will overcome burden inequalities. By obliging states to harmonize their policies or to comply with a set of common international rules, we may expect that individual countries will face converging burdens. The core idea of such a mechanism is that common rules will reduce the need for corrective action. Redistributive quotas are also classic examples of such "binding rules" mechanisms, as they try to equalize observed imbalances/inequities in burdens through some agreed distribution key (which is usually based on one or several fairness principles such as responsibility, capacity, benefit, or cost).[7] Germany, for example, operates such a quota regime for asylum seekers on its territory. Individuals who seek refugee status in Germany are initially processed in centralized reception centers, before they get distributed across the 16 Länder of the Federal Republic according to the Länder's population size (a capacity-based distribution key).

A second type of "one-dimensional burden-sharing mechanisms" are those which are based on non-binding "pledging" mechanisms. If states cannot agree on a binding distribution key, they can make appeals which ask states with smaller responsibilities to alleviate some of the high burdens that other states are being faced with. During the Kosovo crisis in 1999, the UNHCR operated such a system through which it encouraged countries to alleviate the burdens of bordering countries, such as Macedonia, by agreeing to resettle refugees in their territory.

Multi-dimensional burden-sharing regimes are those that do not seek to equalize burdens/responsibilities on one particular contribution dimension alone, but instead operate across several contribution dimensions. On the one hand, some multi-dimensional regimes are based on an explicit compensation logic. In these cases, a country's disproportionate efforts in one contribution dimension are recognized and that country gets compensated (through benefits or cost reductions) on other dimensions. An example of this is Schuck's proposal for a market-based refugee sharing system (1997) which is similar to the Kyoto emission trading scheme. According to this model, an international agency would assign a refugee protection quota to each participating state, on the basis of which states would then be allowed to trade their quota by paying others (with money or in kind) to take over their protection obligations.

A second type of a multi-dimensional burden-sharing mechanism is based on an implicit trading logic which recognizes that states contribute to international collective goods such as refugee protection in different ways (see Thielemann and Torun 2006). In the refugee context, these include what might be called *pro-active* measures, which attempt to halt the escalation of potential refugee problems by, for instance, sending peacekeeping troops to a region in order to prevent or contain forced migration. Another set of contributions are those which can be called *reactive* measures. The latter measures deal with the consequences of refugee problems once they have occurred, in particular by admitting protection seekers to a host country's territory. During the negotiations of recent EU refugee burden-sharing initiatives, the British and French governments expressed their wishes that their participation in peacekeeping operations should be taken into account when assessing the burdens borne by individual Member States.[8] This suggestion, however, has not been followed up in the more recent EU discussions.

Refugee Burden-Sharing Regimes in the EU

It has been argued that the unequal distribution of asylum and refugee burdens can threaten the collective security interests of Member States, by imposing disproportionate responsibilities on some of those Member States which are least equipped to effectively deal with the challenges posed by situations of "mass influx." What types of burden-sharing initiatives has the EU then pursued in an attempt to equalize Member States' responsibilities in this area? When reviewing European legislative initiatives in this area, one finds that Member States have developed initiatives that are based on the first three of the four burden-sharing mechanisms discussed above.

Since the mid-1980s, the EU has worked towards the convergence of Member States' laws on forced migration. What started with initially non-binding intergovernmental instruments has since been followed by developments in Community law. Most noteworthy here are several directives that have aimed to level the asylum playing field and to lay the foundations for a Common European Asylum System.[9] The 2003 *Reception Conditions Directive* guarantees minimum standards for the reception of asylum seekers, including housing, education, and health. The 2004 *Qualification Directive* contains a clear set of criteria for qualifying either for refugee or subsidiary protection status and sets out what rights are attached to each status. The 2005 *Asylum Procedures Directive* seeks to ensure that, throughout the EU, all procedures at first instance are subject to the same minimum standards.

The significance of these initiatives notwithstanding, policy harmonization can of course only address imbalances due to differences in domestic legislation in the first place. As discussed above, policy differences are only one of several determinants for a protection seeker's choice of host country, with structural factors such as historic networks, employment opportunities, geography, or a host country's reputation being at least equally, if not more, important. If structural pull factors are indeed so crucial, then policy harmonization might actually do more harm than good to the EU's efforts to achieve a more equitable distribution of asylum seekers across the Member States. EU policy harmonization curtails Member States' ability to use national asylum policy to counterbalance their country's unique structural pull factors (language, colonial ties, etc.). This is why policy harmonization might undermine efforts to achieve more equitable responsibility-sharing (Thielemann 2004).

The most prominent EU burden-sharing regime that relies on a "voluntary pledging" mechanism is the 2001 Council Directive on Temporary Protection in the Case of Mass Influx.[10] The directive develops a range of non-binding mechanisms based on the principle of "double voluntarism": the agreement of both the recipient state and the individual protection seeker is required before protection seekers can be moved from one country to another. Under this instrument, Member States are expected, in spirit of "European solidarity," to indicate their reception capacity and to justify their offers for resettlement. These pledges are to be made in public, allowing for mechanisms of peer pressure or "naming and shaming." The Directive has not yet been used and therefore the effectiveness of this new instrument of "soft" coordination still remains to be tested in practice.

In the EU, the most developed multi-dimensional refugee burden-sharing regime based on the idea of "explicit compensation" is the European Refugee Fund (ERF), which aims "to promote a 'balance of efforts' in receiving and bearing the consequences of displaced persons" in order "to demonstrate solidarity between the Member States" in their efforts to promote the social and economic integration of displaced persons.[11] To do this, the ERF allocates common European funds based on the comparative numbers of asylum seekers and refugees in each Member State. In operation since 2000, the ERF aims to financially compensate those Member States faced with disproportionate responsibilities by supporting States' actions that promote the social and economic integration of asylum seekers as well as their return to their countries of origin.

The most obvious problem with the ERF has to do with the Fund's limited size (initially €216 million over five years), which pales into insignificance compared to national expenditures in the area of reception, integration, and return of asylum seekers and refugees. Including administrative costs, legal bills, accommodation, and subsistence, Britain spent just under €30,000 per asylum seeker in 2002 according to U.K. Home Office estimates. According to figures from the ERF's mid-term review, the U.K. was the second largest recipient of the Fund in 2002, receiving approximately €100 per asylum application. One can therefore conclude that the overall effect of the ERF up to now has been more important in symbolic terms than it has been in terms of its substantive effect in promoting a balance of efforts between the Member States. Even with the recently agreed tripling of the Fund for the 2005–10 funding period, revenues from the ERF are highly unlikely to alleviate Member States' concerns about the economic (and social) costs associated with refugees and enhance their willingness to provide refuge to displaced persons. In addition, the analysis of ERF allocation shows that the Fund's principal beneficiaries have been destination countries with the largest absolute number of asylum seekers and refugees, even though theses countries arguably were not facing the largest burdens in this area (Table 9.4).

The Fund, hence, does not take relative absorption capacity into account. This means that for any given number of displaced persons a country like Luxembourg receives the same financial help as Germany, irrespective of the two countries' fundamental differences in terms of population or geographic size, etc. The underlying assumption appears to be that a particular number of protection seekers require the same amount of effort, no matter whether the receiving State is small or large, rich or poor, etc. This is clearly not the case, as a small country receiving the same number of protection seekers will require greater efforts than a large one. In other words, the Fund's redistributive element currently compensates Member States according to the absolute

Table 9.4 The redistributive impact of the European Refugee Fund

Rank	Country	Number of asylum applications per 1,000 of population	Country	Percentage of ERF contributions to Member States
1	**Belgium**	4.2	Germany	20.05
2	**Ireland**	2.9	United Kingdom	19.11
3	**Netherlands**	2.8	France	11.50
4	Denmark	2.3	**Netherlands**	9.46
5	Austria	2.2	Sweden	8.37
6	Sweden	1.8	Italy	8.06
7	United Kingdom	1.7	**Belgium**	5.73
8	Luxembourg	1.4	Austria	5.06
9	Germany	0.9	**Ireland**	2.69
10	Finland	0.6	Spain	2.59
11	France	0.6	Finland	2.35
12	Greece	0.3	Greece	2.35
13	Italy	0.3	Portugal	1.77
14	Spain	0.2	Luxembourg	1.12
15	Portugal	0.02	Denmark*	
	Correlation coefficient	1		**0.06**

* Denmark has an opt-out of EU asylum policy and is therefore not a beneficiary of the ERF.

numbers of protection seekers received, rather than according to the relative responsibilities or burdens that Member States face. The Fund's redistributive impact consequently remains very limited, and therefore, from a solidarity or burden-sharing perspective, the ERF's current arrangements appear sub-optimal.[12] Ultimately, neither the ERF, nor the other instruments described above, can be said to effectively contribute to the goal of responsibility sharing among Member States.

Given the limitations of the existing EU refugee-sharing initiatives, it might be time to further explore the fourth burden-sharing mechanism discussed above: trade. The Member States have not yet used this mechanism in their burden-sharing efforts. Several objections can be made against a Kyoto-style refugee burden-sharing regime based on the idea of "explicit trading," therefore raising legitimate unease about treating refugees as commodities in inter-state transactions (Anker, Fitzpatrick, and Schacknove 1998; Schuck 1997: 289–297).

An alternative "implicit trade" model suggests that countries can be expected to specialize according to their comparative advantage as to the type and level of contribution they make to international collective goods. Applied to the area of forced migration, Thielemann and Dewan (2006) have suggested that countries can contribute to refugee protection in two principal ways: proactively through peacekeeping/making, and reactively through providing protection for displaced persons. With some countries making disproportionate contributions to "pro-active" refugee protection contributions (such as through peacekeeping efforts) and other countries contributing disproportionately with "reactive" measures related to refugee reception, it appears that some implicit trading in refugee protection contributions is already taking place.

Moreover, such apparent specialization in countries' contributions has potentially important implications for attempts to develop multilateral burden-sharing initiatives that are perceived to advance States' interests in providing more equitable, efficient, and effective refugee protection. First, evidence of inter-country specialization suggests that overall refugee protection contributions are perhaps not as inequitable as often assumed. Second, it is possible that burden-sharing initiatives that attempt to force all nations to increase contributions in any one category of provision are likely to be counter-productive to the efficient provision of collective goods such as refugee protection. It can then be argued that the provision of this collective good is closer to optimum when countries are able to specialize with regard to their contributions.

The existence of country-specific benefits from refugee protection combined with tendencies for specialization in States' contributions helps to raise the efficiency of refugee protection efforts. When looking only at reactive protection contributions (as most burden-sharing models do), it is tempting to suggest that some (larger) countries should contribute more in this area. Similarly, equalizing reactive contributions also appears to be the general thrust of recent European policy initiatives. However, any attempt to impose quotas or other similar methods should be considered a hindrance towards greater specialization and trade with adverse overall effects. Burden-sharing initiatives, if they are to strengthen refugee protection, need to be aware of variations in States' preferences and need to recognize the comparative advantages individual States possess in this area. If they do not, they risk undermining the search for more effective refugee protection solutions.

Conclusion: Providing Security—Towards a Comprehensive Burden-Sharing Approach

This chapter has argued that border security in the EU's single market is one of the major driving forces behind recent steps to develop a common European asylum policy. Unlike in the U.S., where terrorist attacks have had a direct impact on developments in U.S. immigration law, developments in EU asylum and refugee policy have continued to be dominated by the security implications of the processes related to the EU's ongoing "deepening" and "widening." This chapter shows that the distribution of refugee burdens in Europe is highly unequal and that efforts to achieve a more "equitable balance of efforts" in this area have dominated legislative developments on asylum in the EU over recent years. It has been argued here that the shortcomings of existing EU burden-sharing initiatives have undermined refugee protection contributions and have done little to address Member States' security concerns in situations of mass influx. To address these concerns more effectively, the chapter has made the case for the development of more comprehensive refugee burden-sharing regimes. Against the background of continuing concerns about how to secure the EU's external borders while providing effective safeguards for refugees that overcome prevalent collection actions problems, the need to explore new options for a more equitable, efficient, and effective refugee burden-sharing regime in Europe is more urgent now than ever.

Notes

1 For an attempt to apply the join-product model to refugee protection, see Betts (2003).
2 However, empirical tests on this in the area of refugee protection have produced mixed results. During the Kosovo conflict, Greek sensibilities concerning its minority in the north of Greece meant that Greece accepted a lot fewer Kosovo refugees than one would have expected on the basis of geographic proximity (Thielemann 2003a).
3 This section draws on Thielemann (2004).
4 A correlation describes the strength of an association between variables. For a set of variable pairs, the correlation coefficient gives the strength of the association. The correlation coefficient is a number between 0 and 1. If there is no relationship between the predicted values and the actual values, the correlation coefficient is 0 or very low (the predicted values are no better than random numbers). As the strength of the relationship between the predicted

values and actual values increases, so does the correlation coefficient. A perfect fit gives a coefficient of 1.0. A negative coefficient signifies an inverse relationship.

5 This index seeks to capture the relative restrictiveness of a country's asylum policy regime. Due to limitations in the available data, it is impossible to include all restrictive measures in the calculation of such an index. However, by focusing on five key deterrence measures that capture all three principal deterrence dimensions (access, determination, and integration), it is possible to arrive at a reasonable approximation of such a ranking. The five indicators are: 1) existence of "safe third country" provisions; 2) below average recognition rate; 3) residence restrictions; 4) restrictions on access to cash welfare payments; and 5) work restrictions. For each measure I created a dummy variable that takes the value 1 for each year that a particular measure was in operation in a particular country and the value 0 for all other years. This leaves me with an index ranging from between 0 (lowest deterrent effect) to 5 (highest deterrent effect) for each country in each year. For a more detailed discussion of this index, see Thielemann (2004, 2006).

6 With the use of more advanced statistical techniques and the use of lagged independent variables, it can be shown that, while newly introduced deterrence measures can have a significant effect on the relative distribution of asylum burden, this effect tends to be short-lived due to copy-cat strategies by other countries which swiftly cancel out the desired effect of such measures (Thielemann 2006).

7 The "responsibility" principle is commonly used in environmental regimes and also known as the "polluter pays" principle. The "capacity" principle refers to a state's "ability to pay" (and is often linked to relative GDP). The "benefit" principle proposes that states should contribute to a particular regime in relation to the benefit they gain from it and the "cost" principle suggests that states' relative costs in making certain contributions should be taken into account when establishing burden-sharing regimes.

8 JHA (Justice and Home Affairs) Council resolution of 25 September 1995 "on burden-sharing with regard to the admission and residence of displaced persons on a temporary basis" (OJ No. C 262/1, October 7, 1995).

9 JHA Council Directive 2003/9/EC of January 27, 2003; JHA Council Directive 2004/83/EC of April 29, 2004; and JHA Council Directive 2005/85/EC of December 1, 2005.

10 JHA Council Directive 2001/55/EC of July 20, 2001, OJ L 212, August 7, 2001.

11 JHA Council Decision of September 28, 2000 (2000/596/EC), L252/12 of October 6, 2000.

12 For a more extended discussion of the ERF, see Thielemann (2005).

References

Anker, Deborah, Joan Fitzpatrick, and Andrew Shacknove. 1998. "Crisis and Cure. A Reply to Hathaway/Neve and Schuck." *Harvard Human Rights Journal* 11: 295–310.

Betts, Alexander. 2003. "Public Goods Theory and the Provision of Refugee Protection: The Role of the Joint-Product Model in Burden-Sharing Theory." *Journal of Refugee Studies* 16(3): 274–296.

Bigo, Didier. 1994. "The European Internal Security Field: Stakes and Rivalries in a Newly Developing Area of Police Intervention," in Malcolm Anderson and

Monica den Boer, eds., *Policing Across National Boundaries*, pp. 161–173. London: Pinter.

Byrne, Rosemary, Gregor Noll, and Jens Vedsted-Hansen, eds. 2002. *New Asylum Countries: Migration Control and Refugee Protection in an Enlarged European Union*. The Hague: Kluwer.

European Council. 2004. *The Hague Programme—Strengthening Freedom, Security and Justice in the European Union (Presidency Conclusions)*, Brussels, November 4/5. http:www.europol.europa.eu/jit/hague_programme_en.pdf (accessed April 4, 2008).

Guild, Elspeth. 2003. "International Terrorism and EU Immigration, Asylum and Border Policy: The Unexpected Victims of 11 September 2001." *European Foreign Affairs Review* 8: 331–346.

Guiraudon, Virginie. 2000. "European Integration and Migration Policy: Vertical Policy-Making as Venue Shopping." *Journal of Common Market Studies* 38(2): 251–271.

Huysmans, Jef. 2000. "The European Union and the Securitization of Migration." *Journal of Common Market Studies* 38: 751–777.

JHA Council. 2001. *Conclusions Adopted by the Council* (Justice and Home Affairs), Brussels, September 20. http://ec.europa.eu/justice_home/news/terrorism/documents/concl_council_20sep_en.pdf (accessed April 4, 2008).

Lavenex, Sandra and Emek Uçarer, eds. 2002. *Migration and the Externalities of European Integration*. Lanham, MD: Lexington Books.

Lubbers, Ruud. 2005. *Talking Points for the Informal Justice and Home Affairs Council*, Luxembourg, January 29. http://www.unhcr.org/admin/ADMIN/41fb91342.html (accessed April 4, 2008).

Massey, Douglas S., Joaquin Arango, Graeme Hugo, Ali Kouaouci, Adela Pellegrino, and J. Edward Taylor. 1993. "Theories of International Migration: A Review and Appraisal." *Population and Development Review* 19(3): 431–466.

Noll, Gregor. 2000. *Negotiating Asylum, the EU Acquis, Extraterritorial Asylum and the Common Market of Deflection*. The Hague: Kluwer Law International.

Olson, Mancur, and Richard Zeckhauser. 1966. "An Economic Theory of Alliances." *Review of Economics and Statistics* 48: 266–279.

Sandler, Todd. 1992. *Collective Action: Theory and Applications*. New York: Harvester Wheatsheaf.

Schuck, Peter. 1997. "Refugee Burden-Sharing: A Modest Proposal." *Yale Journal of International Law* 22: 243–297.

Stetter, Stephan. 2000. "Regulating Migration: Authority Delegation in Justice and Home Affairs." *Journal of European Public Policy* 7(1): 80–102.

Suhrke, Astri. 1998. "Burden-Sharing during Refugee Emergencies: The Logic of Collective Action versus National Action." *Journal of Refugee Studies* 11(4): 396–415.

Thielemann, Eiko Ralph. 2003a. "Between Interests and Norms: Explaining Patterns of Burden-Sharing in Europe." *Journal of Refugee Studies* 16(3): 253–273.

Thielemann, Eiko Ralph, ed. 2003b. "European Burden-Sharing and Forced Migration." Special issue of the *Journal of Refugee Studies* 16(3): 225–358.

Thielemann, Eiko Ralph. 2004. "Why European Policy Harmonization Undermines Refugee Burden-Sharing." *European Journal of Migration and Law* 6(1): 43–61.

Thielemann, Eiko Ralph. 2005. "Symbolic Politics or Effective Burden-Sharing? Redistribution, Side-Payments and the European Refugee Fund." *Journal of Common Market Studies* 43(4): 807–824.

Thielemann, Eiko Ralph. 2006. "The Effectiveness of Governments' Attempts to Control Unwanted Migration," in Craig A. Parsons and Timothy M. Smeeding, eds., *Immigration and the Transformation of Europe*, pp. 442–472. Cambridge: Cambridge University Press.

Thielemann, Eiko Ralph, and Torun Dewan. 2006. "The Myth of Free-Riding: Refugee Protection and Implicit Burden-Sharing." *West European Politics* 29(2): 351–369.

UNHCR (United Nations High Commissioner for Refugees). 2001. *Official Documents Burden-Sharing—Discussion Paper Submitted by UNHCR 5th Annual Plenary Meeting of the APC*; ISIL Year Book of International Humanitarian and Refugee Law, vol. 17 (2001). http://www.worldlii.org/int/journals/ISILYBIHRL/2001/17.html (accessed April 4, 2008).

Part III

The Commonwealth Perspective

10 Immigration, the War on Terror, and the British Commonwealth

James Jupp

Introduction

The United Kingdom and the three states of the "old Commonwealth" (Canada, Australia, and New Zealand) share many traditions and a common heritage based on their colonial history and ensuing mass migrations from the British Isles over the past three centuries. These four states—as well as the United States—also share the more recent parallel movements toward increased acceptance of ethnic minorities with commensurate decreased official discriminatory practices, devolution of colonial-based power to local authorities, and decreasing immigration restrictions. As new migrants from a much wider array of nations bring along language, laws, attitudes, beliefs, fears, and prejudices, these countries are becoming much less homogeneous than in the past or in the idealized picture local nationalists tend to paint. The search for uncontested traditions and ethnic and religious homogeneity is increasingly irrelevant and even futile.

Britain still sits at the center of the Commonwealth through the role of the monarchy, which Canada, Australia, and New Zealand all continue to recognize. However, through linguistic, economic, and cultural ties, ancestral origins, and mutual wartime alliances, the influence of the United States often seems more important than that of the United Kingdom. At the core of the "old Commonwealth," a significant redefinition of what binds the "British" together has been taking place. The "special relationship" of the five English-speaking states has often been strained and exaggerated, but it is not irrelevant. Thus, when the United States was attacked on September 11, 2001, the impact on the four "British" societies was immediate.

It made little difference whether Conservative governments were in office, as in Australia, or Labor and Liberal as in Britain, Canada, and New Zealand. The events of 9/11 and the global impact of immigration have changed the way homeland security is perceived and how it can be implemented. This chapter will describe the similarities and differences between the four "old Commonwealth" states in terms of immigration and diversity, previous experiences with threats to homeland security, governmental responses in terms of immigration and security policy changes, and the impact 9/11 has had on these countries and their efforts to provide "peace, order, and good government" to their people. Beginning with a description of how each parliamentary democracy works in each of the Commonwealth countries to provide the context within which laws are produced, this chapter will discuss major legislative changes and the rapid expansion of security organizations and their budgets.

Peace, Order, and Good Government

"Peace, order, and good government," the slogan used around the Empire for a century, was based on the rule of law, an incorruptible expatriate civil service, and the support of locally elected leaders. In Canada, Australia, and New Zealand, electorates validated authority through participatory democracy even more visibly than in the United Kingdom itself, where an aristocratic element continued in politics into the early twentieth century. As in most democracies, these nations have expanded the franchise to members of population subgroups, including "manhood suffrage" in Australia in the 1850s, female suffrage in Australia and New Zealand by 1900, and so forth.

Parliamentary democracy implies the peaceful resolution of conflict within a universally valid system of laws and administration. In Canada and Australia, it also implies federalism. New Zealand alone abolished the second chamber of its parliament and recently crowned its democracy with a complex system of proportional representation. Australia experimented with various systems but, unlike Canada and New Zealand, did not create many effective minor parties. With variations, the party systems remain divided between conservatives (Conservative, Liberal, National) and reformists (Labour, Liberal), with bases in business and labor respectively. Party governments have enjoyed relatively long and stable tenures since 1997 in Britain, 1996 to 2007 in Australia, 1999 in New Zealand, and from 1993 to 2006 in Canada.

The states of the British Commonwealth have been reluctant to change their basic institutions, especially as their core populations derive their legacy from the British Isles (Jupp 2004). These institutions include:

- a strictly limited monarch as head of state, represented outside Britain by governors-general nominally appointed by the Queen
- dual chambers of parliament, with effective power resting with the party holding a majority of elected lower house seats
- basically a two-party system with very tight party discipline from which alternative governments are elected
- a cabinet composed of professional politicians
- a long tradition of common and statute law that protects individual rights and property
- a strong central government controlling most financial resources
- a national government that can be confident of achieving its legislative program between general elections.

Modifications to this general pattern include the following: New Zealand, Queensland, and the Canadian provinces do not have upper houses; power is devolved in the Australian and Canadian federations and to Scotland, Wales, and Northern Ireland; lesser parties can be represented, especially in New Zealand and some Canadian provinces; Canada and New Zealand have bills of rights but Australia does not; and Britain is governed by European Union legislation. It is widely accepted that the principle of responsible government—that ministers are answerable to Parliament for their department—has lost its force. In this context, homeland security measures have been introduced and court action has frustrated or delayed some of these measures, especially as all but Australia are bound by human rights legislation.

In respect to the new "war on terrorism," democratic governments face the following basic problems: to track down potential terrorists with maximum efficiency and minimum impact on the innocent; to alleviate community tensions; to restrain the enthusiasm of newly empowered security agencies; to maintain a reasonable level of civil and human rights; to operate a humane and liberal immigration program (Gibney 2004); and to retain sufficient resources to deal with organized crime and the drug trade.

That first element, finding terrorists with a minimal impact on the innocent, is often at the crux of the question of immigration. Changes to immigration policy have reflected societal trends of openness as multiculturalism has become more widely accepted, tempered more recently with restrictiveness as "the other" is increasingly considered threatening.

Changes in Immigration Policy, Immigrant Composition, and Multiculturalism

Immigration has had a major impact on all of these countries, as a good-sized minority of their populations is born overseas: 24 percent in Australia, 20 percent in New Zealand, 18 percent in Canada, and 9 percent in Britain (comparable to other West European states). In addition, these intakes are no longer drawn from predominantly "Euro-Christian" sources; until the 1960s, Australia, Canada, and New Zealand maintained "whites only" immigration policies that favored the British (Adelman et al. 1994; Hawkins 1989), and Britain had an open-door policy for all Commonwealth citizens in contrast to the restrictions it placed on "aliens" (Spencer 1997), although it has never publicly acknowledged a racial exclusion policy. The United States ended its national origins quota system in 1965; within a decade, all four states had significantly abandoned their immigration traditions and preferences. As these states expanded their immigration policies, however, most migrants tended to have some familiar characteristics (many immigrants were British subjects from South Asia, many Arabs in Britain, Canada, and Australia were Christians, and Middle Eastern immigration scarcely touched New Zealand). Canada, Australia, and New Zealand all abolished racial policies. Britain, in contrast, ended the open-door policy towards Commonwealth citizens in 1962 and

1968, moving towards equalizing the status of all immigrants (other than the Irish).

These changes in immigration policy had important impacts on the ethnic composition of society and especially of the major cities. By the early 1980s, British subjects lost the right to enter and leave freely without visas, even requiring immigration clearance to Australia on the same basis as everyone else. Australia constructed a more rigid control system than most other developed societies (Jupp 2007). Only New Zealanders remained exempt from the need for a visa issued overseas. Britain, while steadily equalizing the status of Commonwealth and alien immigrants, remained more generous in allowing visa-free admission and in extending civil rights to Commonwealth citizens once they had entered the country. A major consequence of this has been that large ethnic minorities from South Asia, Africa, and the West Indies living in Britain enjoy the right to vote and to take part in public life. Until the development of European Union common citizenship under the Schengen agreement, this meant that non-European immigrants in Britain often had greater civil rights than Europeans. In fact, the British, Canadian, and New Zealand parliaments include Muslim members (Fetzer and Soper 2004; Vertovec 1997); the Australian Parliament does not, and in fact restrictive civil rights policies limit the enfranchisement of all but naturalized Australian citizens.

Successful multicultural societies are able to accept a large number of immigrants of various backgrounds with a minimum amount of public anxiety. For example, Canada accepts about 200,000 new settlers each year and Australia accepts about 100,000. Parties opposed to the level and sources of immigration, such as Reform in Canada, One Nation in Australia, and New Zealand First, are either absorbed into the existing partisan framework or wiped out at the polls. In fact, these societies tend to support relatively radical political groups and refugees from other nations. The British liberal tradition of giving support to opponents of oppressive regimes (including British colonial ones) was fully represented in London. A variety of organizations based their headquarters there, including many radical and separatist groups like the Tamil Tigers, opponents of South African apartheid, and, of course, anti-Communist organizations from the Soviet bloc, as befits the city in which Lenin formed the Bolshevik faction in 1903. Canada and Australia followed in this tradition of hosting radical groups; Canada, for example, gave refuge to American draft resisters and opponents of the Vietnam War. Canada also hosted various organizations with secessionist claims on India and Sri Lanka, while Australia did the same for others aiming to "liberate" East Timor, Croatia, Eritrea, and Bougainville. New Zealand provided refuge for Fiji Indians dislodged by the coups of 1987 and 2000, who were thoroughly democratic victims; although it felt pressure from the United States and France, its geographic isolation protected it from the outside world. Australia in particular acquired an unfortunate reputation for granting settlement to suspected war criminals and for failing to find them or prosecute them. Some Australian Croats engaged in local violence in the 1970s as well as planning an abortive "invasion" of Yugoslavia.

By 2001, all four states were more ethnically, politically, and culturally diverse than at any time in the modern era. Assimilation to a British Protestant model was less probable than ever before, despite the urging of politicians and journalists from the majority culture. Canada was the first to embrace official multiculturalism in 1970 as an extension of the longstanding Anglo-French biculturalism. The Whitlam Labor government in Australia declared its commitment to multiculturalism in 1973. New Zealand, often considered very "English," spent more effort on developing policies towards the large Maori and Samoan populations, which numbered 20 percent of the total in 2001. By 2001, there were substantial non-European origin minority populations: 8 percent in Britain (mainly South Asians, West Indians, and Africans), a similar percentage in Australia (mainly Chinese, Arab, Vietnamese, Indian, and Aboriginal), 25 percent of New Zealanders (mainly Maori, Samoan, Indian, and Chinese) and 13 percent of Canadians (mainly Chinese, Indian, West Indian, and Native Canadians).

Until the 1970s, very few Muslims resided in these nations, and even today Muslims represent small enclaves—2.7 percent in Britain, 2.0 percent in Canada, 1.5 percent in Australia, and 0.6 percent in New Zealand. Islamic immigrant communities in the four nations are drawn from a variety of backgrounds. In Britain, these include Pakistanis, Bangladeshis, Gujaratis from India and East Africa, Somalis, Cyprus Turks, and Arabs from most Middle Eastern countries (Anwar 1979; Ballard 1994; Lewis 1994). Many are British subjects. Recently, a surge of refugees has added Iranians, Bosnians, Kosovars, Afghans, and North Africans, who are much less likely to be British subjects. The Muslim population has grown steadily and the last major intake of Muslim legal refugees in Australia was from Somalia and Bosnia in the late 1990s. In Australia, Muslim settlers come from Lebanon, Turkey, Egypt, Afghanistan, Bosnia, Pakistan, Indonesia, and Iraq for the most part (Saeed 2003; Saeed and Akbarzadeh 2001). At least one third of Muslims are locally born in Australia and the U.K. Canadian Muslim immigrants are largely South Asians, Arabs, and West Indians, with refugee numbers added from Lebanon and Somalia (Janhevich and Ibrahim 2004). As in Australia and New Zealand, the great majority are recent immigrants. Two-thirds are Canadian citizens. In New Zealand, Muslims come mainly from states within the British Commonwealth, such as Pakistan, India, Bangladesh, and Fiji (Prasad and van der Welt 2002).

Language and tradition, historical enmities, and differing schools of Islam divide this diverse population. The Deobandi tradition from India and Pakistan is very influential in Britain but much less so in Australia. Shias from Iraq, Iran, and Lebanon have become significant because of the large refugee outflows since the 1970s, but have made less of an impact in Britain than in Canada and Australia. In Britain and Canada, significant numbers come from the Indian communities of East Africa. Kashmiri influence is important in Britain. This variegated "community" is only slowly coalescing, a process hastened by events in the Middle East.

It is important to note that immigration restrictions in these countries may not affect Islamic terrorist attacks because many are locally born Muslims or converts. Unlike in the U.S., where most of the 9/11 hijackers were Saudi immigrants, immigration control is irrelevant for many accused or convicted in the "British" countries. The future potential of immigration restrictions may be important, however, especially as "jihadis" are reputedly organized from Southeast Asia to attack Jewish targets in Western states (*Australian*, August 4, 2006). The main influence on immigration policy has been to make it almost impossible for asylum seekers to enter Australia and to finally move Britain towards a more rational, points-tested skilled migration program. Neither policy will necessarily have any impact on the entry of terrorists.

Previous Experience with Violence and Terrorism

With democratic institutions and effective bureaucratic structures firmly in place, as well as a broad national consensus on the rule of law and peaceful politics, the "old" Commonwealth states were able to resist most serious internal threats for over a century, although Britain has had its infamous "Troubles" with the Irish Republican Army (IRA). This relative stability and internal peace is especially notable in contrast to the histories of most societies in Europe and Latin America and even the United States. With the exception of the IRA in Britain, terrorism or armed secession did not occur during that time. As I shall discuss in a later section, how Britain dealt with the IRA informed their reactions to current threats from Islamic terrorists.

While many immigrants are peaceful and law-abiding individuals who are seeking a better life for themselves and their families, they are often reviled as untrustworthy and threatening to longstanding citizens of any given nation. These states shared a traditional, only recently questioned, perspective that immigrants and ethnic minorities raise issues of civil order and crime, and that the introduction of inassimilable aliens would provoke civil disorder. New Zealand and Canada held this view against the Chinese and East Indians respectively. The arrival of large numbers of Jews into London's East End following the Russian pogroms of 1881 provoked the 1905 Aliens Act in the United Kingdom. Serious and deadly rioting occurred in Belfast in the early 1920s, and an undercurrent of prejudice against the Irish was transferred to Australia, Canada, and New Zealand.

Before 2001, the four Commonwealth states had only a limited direct experience of Islamist terrorism, mainly focused on the threat of airplane hijacking. London, with its large Arabic population and longstanding relations with the Arab world, was centrally concerned with IRA attacks, which killed one Conservative parliamentarian and almost killed then Prime Minister Margaret Thatcher in 1984. Railway stations and public places were routinely searched for bombs. Irishmen were arrested, trials conducted, and at least one major miscarriage of justice committed. Despite all this, movement control between the Irish Republic and the United Kingdom remained minimal and the right of Irish citizens to reside, work, and vote in the U.K. was not affected.

Immigration for permanent settlement from the Commonwealth was controlled, but millions of temporary visitors, students, and tourists passed through London Heathrow—the biggest international airport in the world. With the extension of immigration rights to citizens of the European Union, numbers coming from the continent also rose. Once Communism ceased to be of concern after 1990, the embassies of Islamic states such as Iran or Libya were watched and occasional violence erupted around them. Fears of a general terrorist attack on the scale of 9/11 were not a significant influence on policy or security administration. Police were normally unarmed and citizens did not carry identity cards; the situation in Canada, Australia, and New Zealand was even more relaxed. In fact, terrorism was virtually unknown in Australia and New Zealand, despite some feeble attempts to create Black Power movements in the early 1970s among Aborigines and Maoris. Activist minorities gave moral support to foreign organizations that might have been termed "terrorist." These included ultimately quite respectable bodies like the African National Congress of South Africa.

The Islamist terrorist movements pose quite new problems. They are not inspired by national liberation or proletarian revolution, but by millenarian and universal objectives (Klausen 2005). They use very modern methods of communication that reach across national boundaries. They travel through international networks that owe little or nothing to governments. Despite the emphasis on Al-Qaeda after 2001, they are not centrally organized or led, nor are they controlled by distant states or staffed predominantly by "foreign agitators." Unlike the Irish and Communist cells, they are not recognizably part of the national culture, although many of their activists are locally born or religious converts from the majority population. The networks of informers on which the police and security organizations had relied are ineffective. Much of the activists' work is conducted in Arabic or Urdu; while 200,000 people speak Arabic in Australia and an even larger number speak Urdu in Britain, the security organizations are reluctant to recruit them. In Britain, the vetting process suggested that mass recruitment to MI5 attracted Al-Qaeda infiltrators (*Guardian*, July 4, 2006).

With a limited experience with Islamist terrorism and few security officers in Australia, Canada, or New Zealand with Middle Eastern or Indian subcontinent backgrounds, tracking and controlling the small minority of militant radicals in the large Islamic populations presents many problems. Arrests made in Britain, Canada, and Australia suggest some common links. Many have traveled to or have associations with Pakistan. A very small number have trained with the Taliban in Afghanistan, including Australia's only Guantanamo internee, David Hicks. Many have connections with a handful of mosques, such as the Finsbury Park mosque in London or the small mosque of Benbrika in Melbourne. This at least makes it easier to track them. British police failed to do so for the three men from Leeds who attacked the London transport system on July 7, 2005, one of whom they had previously questioned.

Attempts to create a "moderate" Muslim movement against terrorism, which would theoretically have a great impact on reducing the terrorist threat, have been largely thwarted due to several unfortunate events. Within an atmosphere of fear, several miscarriages of justice have occurred, especially in Britain, including wrongful arrests, the death of an innocent bystander, an unjustified raid on a private home, deteriorating community relations, and media hysteria; the Israeli attack on Hezbollah in July 2006 only served to make matters worse. Large demonstrations were held in Britain and Australia, where previously "moderate" Muslim leaders denounced Israel, Zionism, and the United States.

Responses to the threat of terrorism varied among these countries, but not necessarily because they faced a "real and present danger." That this exists for the United States and Britain can hardly be denied after the events of 9/11 and 7/7. Whether the same is true for Canada, Australia, and New Zealand is more problematic. Canada and New Zealand have not joined in the Iraq War and have a less intimate involvement with the United States than Britain or Australia. Canada and Australia have both recently uncovered evidence of plots to attack national infrastructures and Britain has already suffered a major attack and uncovered others before they developed. To date, New Zealand has not experienced or uncovered a terrorist attack. If terrorist attacks are part of a global attack on Western democracy and culture—as leaders of the United States, Britain, and Australia regularly claim—then these states need to consider protective measures if only as a precaution (Huntington 1996).

Theoretic and Real Governmental Responses to Terrorism

Terrorism was not high on the public agenda in any of the four states (the Blair Labour government had calmed the Irish situation at that time) when the Twin Towers were destroyed in September 2001. It then moved up the agenda rapidly, with major legislative changes and the rapid expansion of security organizations and their budgets. It made little difference whether Conservative governments were in office, as in Australia, or Labor and Liberal as in Britain, Canada, and New Zealand. Many commentators argue that "Westminster" governments are in a strong position to push through whatever legislation they think fit, which is clearly very convenient in times of crisis. This is particularly relevant to defense, security, and immigration legislation. All four governments have ample capacity to effect emergency measures. Party loyalty normally ensures that a majority vote will quickly resolve even contentious issues.

All states moved to prohibit "moral and financial support for terrorist organizations" in their post-9/11 legislation, which aroused fear of persecution of longstanding connections. For example, the leaders of the government-sponsored Muslim reference group in Australia asked that Hezbollah be removed from the list of terrorist groups during the Lebanese crisis (*Australian*, August 4, 2006), but the Prime Minister responded with a strong refusal. Immigration systems have been tightened, even in Britain, where they were remarkably liberal in some respects. This has caused major reforms of the appropriate agencies, especially the Home Office in Britain and the Department of Immigration in Australia. Both were officially criticized for their "organizational culture." In response, the agencies improved how they process asylum seekers, with Australia even developing an expensive information technology system designed to supervise all international movements.

In addition, new pressure from the U.S. has encouraged many changes in security procedures. All have changed the format of their passports to satisfy U.S. requirements. All have extended electronic tagging, immigrant alert systems, and new forms of identification. As in Britain, Australians and New Zealanders did not have identity cards. An attempt to introduce one in Australia was abandoned in the face of public opposition 20 years ago but is now being revived. Consequently, due to 9/11, both Britain and Australia are planning to introduce identity cards with microchips to all passport applicants.

Theoretically, governments in the British tradition should be able to take decisive action quickly, especially when compared with the uncertainty and bargaining of American politics. The role of lawyers and the courts has also been less significant in the public policy area than in the United States. In practice, however, the executive powers of U.S. governments have expanded rapidly since 1941 when "continuing warfare" began. The new Department of Homeland Security was rapidly formed in the U.S., but no comparable restructuring happened in the Commonwealth systems. In both Britain and Australia, party revolts and judicial obstruction have frustrated the governments' efforts to do so. In some ways, the "British" states have more appropriate mechanisms of control than pluralist America. The separation of powers has never worked against the executive as effectively as in the U.S. and is usually considered a "polite myth." Leadership of the legal and justice systems rests with a government member (the Lord Chancellor or the Attorney General). Governments normally control their parliaments through a disciplined party. The constitutionality of laws cannot be challenged in Britain, which has no written constitution. Britain has always resisted having a Bill of Rights, being obliged only recently to accept the European Union model. Australia still resists having any such legislation, although it does accept United Nations conventions with some reluctance. In contrast, Canada and New Zealand have legislated to protect human rights and consequently have had less draconian security and immigration practices.

Proliferation and competition between agencies, often a serious problem in the U.S., has to some extent been overcome in these four nations. In Australia, the Minister for Immigration became the Attorney General, ensuring continuity and coordinated policies. In Britain, the many functions of the Home Office became too burdensome, and it was severely criticized in consequence. The Home Secretary promised a "complete overhaul." The Canadians and New Zealanders seemed reasonably confident that they had overcome some of these problems. Arrests and trials resulted from detective work prior to incidents.

Historically, these states have generously exchanged intelligence and defense information, and, despite variations between these Commonwealth states, obviously they participate in a high degree of exchange of information with the United States. Before the rapid increase of Islamist terrorism at the turn of the century, intelligence work in the four states was concentrated on Soviet espionage, producing several major successes in Britain and Canada but a more limited effect in Australia and virtually none in New Zealand. Intelligence agencies such as the British MI5 or the Australian Security Intelligence Organization were trained and equipped to deal with foreign intelligence and to deal with East European expatriate communities. British police and military intelligence was most useful in coping with the IRA. The London Metropolitan Police and the Royal Canadian Mounted Police had the most experience dealing with immigration issues, but, while all permanent immigration applications were theoretically vetted, the likelihood of foreign infiltration for terror was very limited.

There are only nine police forces in Australia and 52 in the United Kingdom. In Canada the Royal Canadian Mounted Police have provided services across provincial boundaries for many years. New Zealand has had a single police force for 120 years. Until the Second World War it was assumed that police "special branches" could deal with security and intelligence. Since 1945, however, security organizations have proliferated; growing rapidly in size since 9/11, they come directly under government control and are protected from inquiry even when appearing in court cases.

Differences and Details in Security, Previous Experience, and Response

The United Kingdom

Of the four states, Britain undoubtedly has the longest experience of violent attacks for political ends. The army has been deployed consistently against the IRA and its offshoots in Ulster, unlike the situation in the other three states, where terrorism has been seen as a police and security service concern. Britain became victim of Irish militancy, especially in the IRA bombings of 1939 and the much longer campaign after the civil rights movement in Ulster of 1969. This tension was the impetus for most measures against terrorism in Britain. As movement between Ireland and Britain is normally free of controls in peacetime, immigration policy was not considered a protection against terrorism.

The U.K. was an obvious target for retribution from Islamic terrorists over the government's close relationship with the Bush administration. But the only successful terrorist action—the London Transport suicide bombing of July 7, 2005—was organized on an amateur basis by locally born youths, using nothing more sophisticated than readily available chemicals and a free Underground map. This changed the official perception of terrorism away from immigration control and towards infiltrating local communities and checking on extremist mosques and individuals. Massive movements of asylum seekers from Africa and the Middle East, many of them Muslims, placed Britain's immigration controls under severe strain, especially the seriously overstretched Home Office, which assumed the responsibility for both immigration and law and order.

Britain had a range of security organizations, the best known of which were MI5 for domestic intelligence and counter-espionage work and MI6 for overseas operations. Each police force developed a special branch that had domestic intelligence responsibilities. These were most active within Irish and Communist organizations, relying on informers and normal detective work. Overall supervision and assistance rested with the Metropolitan Police ("Scotland Yard"). Telephonic and electronic signals were controlled from a once highly secret center in Cheltenham. All these activities were protected under the Official Secrets Act, which prevented them from being publicly scrutinized. Their budgets and personnel were also secret. Not even their locations were public knowledge until a change of policy 20 years ago. Recruitment was often based on "old boy" networks as immortalized in the fiction of John Le Carré and other authors. Some expertise was available from former colonial officers in the Palestine or Indian services or from the Ulster Constabulary. The Foreign Office and the defense forces could also command considerable expertise. While these services prided themselves on their record during the Second World War, the exposure of Soviet penetration through Burgess, Maclean, and Philby in the 1960s tarnished their reputations. This led to reforms including a more open basis for recruitment, which was extended still further after 2001 with public advertising and interviews.

Despite these changes, the pressures of poorly controlled immigration and the threats and realities of terrorism became increasingly difficult for the Home Office and the police. Serious errors followed the London bombing, including the failure of West Yorkshire police to identify a problem among the young Leeds bombers before it was too late. With more security cameras per head than any other European country, Britain had pictures of the bombers arriving with their backpacks, but by then they were already dead along with 50 others. Another death followed quickly when police shot an innocent Brazilian at an Underground station in the belief that he was a terrorist. More trouble followed in June 2006, when 250 police raided a suburban London home on false information about its Muslim residents, one of whom was wounded. Blame quickly shifted from Scotland Yard to MI5, which had ordered the raid despite police reservations. At the same time, the Police Complaints Board report showed that higher-level officers knew the Brazilian victim was innocent soon after his death, but failed to reveal this information in a timely fashion. Completing this chapter of accidents, officials publicly admitted that a thousand released prisoners awaiting deportation had somehow become lost.

Taken together with the increasing knowledge that authorities were losing control of the asylum-seeker intake process, the entire Home Office structure was questioned. Eventually Home Secretary John Reid promised to clear the backlog of about 500,000 asylum seekers "within five years or less." The Immigration and Nationality Directorate would be turned into an executive agency, and the prison and probation system reformed. All this would be achieved with a dramatic reduction in staffing and a "challenge to unaccept-able behaviour and a change to the culture of the department" (*Guardian*, June 19, 2006).

These reforms were greeted with some skepticism and did little to address the problems surrounding terrorism, where an atmosphere of panic had damaged reputations after the London bombings.

Canada

Canadian experience of violent politics in the past has centered on French Canadian secessionism in Québec. The "quiet revolution" of the 1960s was not always peaceful; bomb attacks and kidnappings disturbed the peace during this period. Eventually the Parti Québecois at the provincial level and the Bloc Québécois nationally were formed to accommodate separatist demands within the party structure. Major concessions, especially on language use, were granted under Pierre Trudeau's Liberal Party government. Adopting multi-culturalism as national policy accomplished this reversion to democratic conflict resolution. Terrorism then became directed outward towards disputes in India and Sri Lanka (Bell 2004), including armed battles in Toronto by supporters of the Sri Lanka Tamil Tigers and the destruction in flight of an Air India plane by Sikh militants in 1985, killing 329 people, most of whom were Canadian citizens.

In 2001, Canadian Prime Minister Jean Chrétien claimed: "there are no terrorists in Canada." Despite his assurances, his government budgeted for an additional C$8 million for enhanced security. In part due to continuing criticism from the United States over the porous nature of the Canadian bor-der, changes were largely concentrated on immigration control and border supervision, including enhanced security clearance of immigrants and refugees and use of armed marshals on selected flights. Canada also agreed to send a military contingent to Afghanistan. It did not, however, participate in the war in Iraq.

The legislative response was the Anti-Terrorism Act C-36 of 2001, which ratified the UN Conventions on terrorist financing and terrorist bombing and defined terrorist activity, distinguishing between a violent act and the advocacy of political or religious beliefs. Although the Act contains sunset clauses and requires the approval of the Attorney General in many instances in order to meet objections based on civil rights, it provided for the following measures:

- Knowingly collecting funds for or taking part in a terrorist organization would carry prison terms of 10 to 14 years.
- Electronic tagging and preventive detention would be extended.

- Money laundering on behalf of terrorist groups would be illegalized.
- Penalties for hate propaganda and terrorist Internet use and telephonic communication were extended.

By April 2004 a more detailed national security policy had been worked out under a new Conservative prime minister (Canada 2004). It claimed to be the "first ever comprehensive statement of national security policy which provides an integrated strategy for addressing current and future threats to our country." Contrary to Chrétien's optimism, the new administration admitted that Canada was not immune to the threat of terrorism. The new Anti-Terrorism Act conformed to the Charter of Rights and Freedoms and, because Canada has had much experience in fostering democracy, pluralism, and the rule of law, most of the emphasis was put on border and immigration control (mainly in response to American criticism) rather than internal security.

Canadian security rested largely with the Royal Canadian Mounted Police (RCMP) and the Canadian Security Intelligence Service. In June 2006, the RCMP claimed to have broken up at least a dozen terrorist groups during the previous two years (*Toronto Globe and Mail*, June 7, 2006). This, too, had a border protection aspect through the Integrated Border Re-enforcement Teams with the United States. Major arrests, the first in recent years, included 17 people described as "inspired by Al-Qaeda" who were held in Toronto in June 2006. As in Britain, all were local residents. They had allegedly purchased three tons of ammonium nitrate and had attended a training camp in Ontario. Later claims were made that they intended to attack the Ottawa parliament and that one had threatened to behead the new prime minister. Reactions ranged from attacking multiculturalism as conflicting "with our need to thwart global terrorism" (*Toronto Star*, June 2006) to defending "our tolerance and openness" the (*Globe and Mail*, June 2006). Official reaction remained calm; the Director of the CSIS argued that Canada was well coordinated and could avert an attack (*Globe and Mail*, June 20, 2006).

Australia

Although Australia has a closer relationship with the United States, it was not until after 1945 that the issue of internal security came alive. At the urging of Britain and the United States, the Australian Labor Party government established the Australian Security and Intelligence Organisation (ASIO) in 1945. It remains the major instrument of domestic counter-intelligence to the present (Hocking 2003). It was, however, primarily established to detect subversive rather than terrorist activity and, if necessary, frustrate local and international Communist activity. Although a referendum to outlaw the Australian Communist Party was defeated in 1951, it remained legal in all four states, though under supervision. The Communist influence on Australia declined rapidly after 1956 and the party was eventually dissolved. While ASIO might have claimed its intelligence work inhibited spying and industrial sabotage, its influence was not very noticeable.

Terrorism made its greatest impact on Australia in Bali in October 2002. Outside the control of the Australian government, it expedited closer cooperation between the Australian and Indonesian security forces. The attack killed 88 Australians, mostly young holiday-makers; it was directed not against Australian foreign policy, but rather against the perceived "immorality" of all foreign tourists to Bali. Australian intelligence services seemed unaware of the threat Jemaah Islamiya posed, although its leading member, Abubakr Bashir, had been tracked through 11 visits to Australia. Indonesians in Australia were not involved in subsequent anti-terrorism controls and the attempt to recruit them seems to have failed completely.

The legislation that was immediately introduced in 2001 and that several laws subsequently supplemented (Australia 2004a, 2004b) built on policies introduced over the preceding 10 years to cope with asylum seekers, which greatly restricted their access to the country. Those without visas had been subject to mandatory detention since 1991. Giving this policy more force, just before 9/11, the Australian military seized the Norwegian tanker *Tampa*, which had rescued over 400 individuals, mainly Muslims from Afghanistan and Iraq, from a sinking boat. The *Tampa* had intended to take them to the Australian territory of Christmas Island (Jupp 2007), but the Navy diverted most of the asylum seekers to the remote island of Nauru under the "Pacific solution." Others were detained at a desert camp and subsequently moved to a custom-built detention center in Woomera, South Australia. As in Britain and elsewhere, those detained periodically rioted and attracted some public sympathy. None of this had anything to do with terrorism, but this was obscured by 9/11 and the immediate calling of an Australian election, which the government won with a large majority.

These coincidental events confused terrorism and asylum seeking in the public mind. In 2006, the government sought to exclude the whole of Australia from its own "migration zone" and to send all undocumented asylum seekers off to Nauru, where they would be inaccessible. They would not be able to engage Australia's legal obligations, as Nauru is a sovereign state, if a very small one.

Eventually, Australia adopted measures specifically to deal with terrorism that were similar to those adopted in the United States and Britain. Each year, new legislation intensified controls and gave greater powers to ASIO and the Federal Police. State police forces were to implement many of the new laws. State governments agreed to this arrangement at a conference with the national government on September 27, 2005, despite the control of the Opposition Labor Party. The national government also created a Muslim reference group on a model adopted in Britain. This was not a great success and was in disarray within a year, largely because of the effect of the Israeli attack on Hezbollah in Lebanon, motherland to the largest number of Muslim immigrants.

New powers introduced since 2001 include the following: control orders and electronic tracking; preventive detention; stop and search powers; incitement of violence and support for Australia's enemies; controls over terrorist funds; definition of terrorist organizations; and the extension of the waiting period for naturalization from two to three years. Subsequent arrests and trials under these powers have focused on the Lebanese Muslim minority, which is heavily concentrated in Sydney. These measures have led so far to only two prison sentences, both for preparing, rather than committing, terrorist acts. Those arrested were nearly all permanent residents and citizens of Arabic origins, with a few converts to Islam. Evidence included collecting maps and taking photographs, possessing jihadist literature and purchasing chemicals capable of bomb manufacture. At the time of this writing, no terrorist actions have occurred.

New Zealand

New Zealand has very little experience with terrorism. Indeed, the only major instance occurred in 1985 when agents of the French government sank the Greenpeace boat *Rainbow Warrior* in Auckland harbor in defense of French nuclear testing in the Pacific. New Zealand remains firmly opposed to nuclear weapons and will not allow United States warships into local harbors. This led to the reduction of intelligence exchanges between the U.S. and New Zealand and significant U.S. hostility in military and trade relationships, despite the joint ANZUS Treaty with Australia and the United States.

Only a remote state like New Zealand can feel relatively relaxed with regard to terrorism. In addition, it has an incentive to remain free of entanglements with other larger states. Consequently, New Zealand has not engaged its forces in Iraq and has not permitted American or French interests to dominate its independent foreign policy. So far, it has experienced no terrorist incidents traceable to Islamist groups, but it is an immigrant society and is obliged to maintain security systems that focus on its small 30,000-member Islamic community.

Security in New Zealand rests with the New Zealand Police, the New Zealand Security Intelligence Service (NZ SIS), and the Government Communications Security Bureau. The police handle all normal police functions, including traffic offenses, for the whole country. The NZ SIS was created in 1956, well after its counterparts in Britain, Canada, and Australia. It has close relations with the British and Australian services, but links with the United States are limited. Its main function is information collection and analysis and it acknowledges that the police are "the lead agency responsible for terrorism in New Zealand." Its most controversial case was the attempted deportation of an Algerian asylum seeker, Ahmed Zaoui, who was detained under the Immigration Act in 2002.

Like its counterparts, New Zealand created new legislation in reaction to the attack on New York. The Terrorism Suppression Act of 2002, which came into effect in 2005, allowed for the listing of terrorist organizations and the prohibition of membership or financial support, following the pattern of control established elsewhere. The Act defines terrorism while protecting peaceful political activity; permits the designation of terrorist and associated entities on the basis of UN advice; protects classified security information; and outlines the conditions for appeal. In designating seven Islamic organizations in January 2006, Prime Minister Helen Clark said that none were known to have any New Zealand links.

The 2002 Act was followed by the Border Security Act of 2003 and the Counter Terrorism Bill. The latter would allow New Zealand to ratify two UN Conventions on terrorism; to criminalize improper possession of nuclear material or other similar materials; to increase penalties for terrorist acts; to permit electronic tracking; and to detain suspect property or cash at the border. These measures were already in place in the other Commonwealth states. As with previous legislation, the Bill was submitted to public representation through a parliamentary committee. As elsewhere, human rights groups criticized all New Zealand legislation, although it was generally milder.

Conclusions

A prime concern of every nation state is the defense of its territory and the protection of its citizens. Thus the mechanisms by which protective policies are made and implemented are of considerable importance. Protection and defense in an age of terrorism and weapons of mass destruction are both extremely complicated and excessively expensive.

The four "British" societies responded differently to the terrorist attacks on the United States, London, and Bali and to the counterattacks launched against the Taliban government of Afghanistan and the Ba'athist regime in Iraq. They took measures for their own protection, which also varied, despite much interchange of information and the original model of the U.S. Patriot Act. They took advantage of the crisis mentality terrorism unleashed to legislate for radical changes that would have been less acceptable in calmer situations. These included: de facto restrictions on the rights of their Muslim communities, while seeking also to co-opt and reorganize them; further restrictions on the rights of asylum seekers under the UN Convention and Protocol of 1951 and 1967; a reversion from multiculturalism towards assimilation; greatly expanded roles and budgets for security organizations; extended control over communications and personal identification; increased penalties for previously legal activities; tightened border controls; attempts to define national values; and increased international cooperation.

Court action frustrated or delayed some of these measures, especially as all but Australia were bound by human rights legislation. The legal profession contested actions such as detention without trial, secret trial sessions, and limitations on legal representatives. Preventive detention, which had been widely used in Northern Ireland, was particularly controversial. The U.S. Patriot Act inspired legal action regarding the offense of "preparing" a terrorist act, which led to several instances of long-term detention on remand for those who were eventually found not guilty. Stop and search laws had been an important source of resentment in Britain, as they were often directed against ethnic minorities suspected of drug dealing. Their extension to young Muslims will not improve community relations. The government watchdog on the Terrorism Act warned that "the misuse of stop and search powers under section 44 of the Act could fuel demands for its repeal" (*Guardian*, June 20, 2006).

Without an effective degree of cooperation, the legal developments since 2001 will be perceived as directed solely against an identified minority of the population. This will rapidly undo the multicultural pretensions of the four states, which the former Australian government and the newly elected government of Canada only grudgingly accepted (Cardozo and Musto 1997).

The experience of the four Commonwealth democracies suggests that it is no easy task to provide adequate physical protection and empower security agencies while simultaneously protecting civil and human rights, alleviating community tensions and treating immigrants and asylum seekers fairly. Restructuring the British Home Office and the Australian Immigration Department and the rapid expansion of MI5 and ASIO were urgently necessary to avoid serious errors and weaknesses. At the same time many personal rights and liberties were limited and community relations damaged. This was, perhaps, the ultimate terrorist victory (Keeble 2005). "Peace, order, and good government," the mandate shouldered by elected officials and administrators throughout the "old Commonwealth," is an unsuitable challenge for the faint of heart.

References

Adelman, Howard, Lois Foster, Allan Borowski, and Meyer Burstein, eds. 1994. *Immigration and Refugee Policy: Australia and Canada Compared*. Melbourne: Melbourne University Press.

Anwar, Mohamed. 1979. *The Myth of Return: Pakistanis in Britain*. London: Heinemann.

Australia. Joint Standing Committee on ASIO, ASIS and DSD. 2004a. *Report of the Inquiry into Australian Intelligence Agencies*. Canberra: Parliament of Australia.

Australia. Joint Standing Committee on Foreign Affairs, Defence and Trade. 2004b. *Watching Brief on the War on Terrorism*. Canberra: Parliament of Australia.

Ballard, Roger, ed. 1994. *Desh Pardesh: The South Asian Presence in Britain*. London: Hurst.

Bell, Stewart. 2004. *Cold Terror*. Mississauga, Ontario: Wiley Canada.

Canada. Privy Council Office. 2004. *Securing an Open Society: Canada's National Security Policy*. Ottawa: Privy Council Office.

Cardozo, Andrew, and Lewis Musto, eds. 1997. *The Battle over Multiculturalism*. Ottawa: Pearson-Shoyama Institute.

Fetzer, Joel, and Christopher Soper. 2004. *Muslims and the State in Britain, France and Germany*. Cambridge: Cambridge University Press.

Gibney, Matthew. 2004. *The Ethics and Politics of Asylum*. Cambridge: Cambridge University Press.

Hawkins, Freda. 1989. *Critical Years in Immigration: Canada and Australia Compared*. Sydney: University of New South Wales Press.

Hocking, Jenny. 2003. *Terror Laws: ASIO, Counter-Terrorism and the Threat to Democracy*. Sydney: University of New South Wales Press.

Huntington, Samuel. 1996. *The Clash of Civilizations and the Making of the New World Order*. New York: Simon and Schuster.

Janhevich, Derek, and Humera Ibrahim. 2004. "Muslims in Canada: an Illustrative and Demographic Profile." *Our Diverse Cities* 1(Spring): 49–56.

Jupp, James. 2004. *The English in Australia*. Melbourne: Cambridge University Press.

Jupp, James. 2007. *From White Australia to Woomera*. Melbourne: Cambridge University Press.

Keeble, Edna. 2005. "Immigration, Civil Liberties and National/Homeland Security." *International Journal* LX(2): 369–372.

Klausen, Jytte. 2005. *The Islamic Challenge*. Oxford: Oxford University Press.

Lewis, Philip. 1994. *Islamic Britain*. London: I. B. Tauris.

Prasad, Rajen, and Nick van der Welt. 2002. *Vibrant Voices and Visions for Ethnic New Zealand*. Wellington: New Zealand Federation of Ethnic Councils.

Saeed, Abdullah. 2003. *Islam in Australia*. Sydney: Allen & Unwin.

Saeed, Abdullah, and Shahram Akbarzadeh. 2001. *Muslim Communities in Australia*. Sydney: University of New South Wales Press.

Spencer, Ian. 1997. *British Immigration Policy Since 1939*. London: Routledge.

Vertovec, Steven. 1997. "Muslims, the State and the Public Sphere in Britain," in Gerd Nonneman, Tim Niblock, and Bogdan Szajkowski, eds., *Muslim Communities in the New Europe*, pp. 167–186. Reading, UK: Ithaca Press.

Notes on Contributors

Frank D. Bean is Chancellor's Professor and Director of the Center for Research on Immigration, Population, and Public Policy at the University of California, Irvine. Prior to joining the UCI Faculty, he served as Ashbel Smith Professor of Sociology and Public Affairs, Director of the Population Research Center, and Chair of the Department of Sociology at the University of Texas at Austin. He was also the founding Director of both the Program for Research on Immigration Policy and the Population Studies Center at The Urban Institute in Washington, DC. He is a member of Phi Beta Kappa, Phi Kappa Phi, and the Council on Foreign Relations, as well as a past recipient of a Guggenheim Fellowship. He has been a Visiting Scholar at the Research School for Advanced Social Sciences at the Australian National University, the American Academy in Berlin, and the Russell Sage Foundation, as well as Distinguished Senior Visiting Fellow at CCIS and the Center for U.S.–Mexico Relations at the University of California, San Diego. His current research focuses on the implications of U.S. immigration policies, Mexican immigrant incorporation, the implications of immigration for changing race/ethnicity in the United States, the determinants and health consequences of immigrant naturalization, and the development of new estimates of unauthorized immigration and emigration. In addition to many journal articles, his books and edited volumes include *America's Newcomers and the Dynamics of Diversity* (with Gillian Stevens; Russell Sage Foundation, 2003); *Immigration and Opportunity: Race, Ethnicity, and Employment in the United States* (with Stephanie Bell-Rose; Russell Sage Foundation, 1999); *Help or Hindrance? The Economic Implications of Immigration for African Americans* (with Dan Hamermesh; Russell Sage Foundation, 1998); *At the Crossroads: Mexico and U.S. Immigration Policy* (with Rodolfo de la Garza, Bryan Roberts, and Sidney Weintraub; Rowman & Littlefield, 1997); *The Hispanic Population of the United States* (with Marta Tienda; Russell Sage Foundation, 1990), and *Mexican American Fertility Patterns* (with Gray Swicegood; University of Texas Press, 1985).

Christina Boswell is Senior Lecturer in Politics at the University of Edinburgh. She has degrees from Oxford (B.A.) and the London School of

Economics (Ph.D.). Christina's research focuses on European migration policy, theories of the state, and the sociology of knowledge utilization in policymaking. She is author of *European Migration Policies in Flux* (Blackwell, 2003), *The Ethics of Refugee Policy* (Ashgate, 2005), as well as articles in *International Affairs, International Migration Review, Journal of Ethnic and Migration Studies, Journal of Common Market Studies, West European Politics, Journal of European Public Policy* and *Political Studies*. She is currently completing a project on the political functions of research in migration policy-making, forthcoming as *The Political Uses of Expert Knowledge: Social Research and the Politics of Migration* (Cambridge University Press, 2008).

Susan K. Brown is Associate Professor of Sociology at the University of California at Irvine. She received her Ph.D. from the University of Washington in 2001. Her research interests include international migration, educational inequality, and urban sociology. She is currently examining the spatial and socioeconomic mobility of those of Mexican origin in greater Los Angeles. She also looks at inequalities of access to higher education. Her publications include "Delayed Spatial Assimilation: Multi-Generational Incorporation of the Mexican-Origin Population in Los Angeles" (*City & Community*, 2007); "Structural Assimilation Revisited: Mexican-Origin Nativity and Cross-Ethnic Primary Ties" (*Social Forces*, 2006); "The End of Affirmative Action in Washington State and Its Effect on the Transition from High School to College" (with Charles Hirschman; *Sociology of Education*, 2006); and *Beyond the Immigrant Enclave: Network Change and Assimilation* (LFB Scholarly Publishing, 2004). She was also co-PI for a grant from the Russell Sage Foundation to study "Immigration and Intergenerational Mobility in Metropolitan Los Angeles."

Gary P. Freeman is Professor and Chair of the Department of Government at the University of Texas at Austin. He specializes in the politics of immigration, comparative social policy, and politics in Western democracies. His most recent writing has been directed at understanding the form of immigration politics in different countries and explaining the integration strategies employed by countries as they grapple with immigrant populations. He is currently working on the question of the linkage between immigration and the welfare state, especially the impact of ethnic and other forms of diversity on the solidaristic foundations of social policies. In addition to two books, *Immigrant Labor and Racial Conflict in Industrial Societies* (Princeton University Press, 1979) and *Nations of Immigrants: Australia, the United States, and International Migration* (Oxford University Press, edited with James Jupp, 1992), he is the author or co-author of "National Models, Policy Types and the Politics of Immigration in Liberal Democracies," *West European Politics* (2006); "Disaggregating Immigration Policy: The Politics of Skilled Labor Recruitment in the U.S." (with David Hill), in Smith and Favell (eds.), *The Human Face of Global Mobility* (Transaction,

2006); "Politics and Mass Immigration," in Goodin and Tilly (eds.), *The Oxford Handbook of Contextual Political Analysis* (Oxford University Press, 2006); "Does Politics Trump the Market in Contemporary Immigration?" in Guigni and Passy (eds.), *Dialogues on Migration Policy* (Lexington Books, 2006); and "Immigrant Incorporation in Western Democracies," *International Migration Review* (2004).

Terri E. Givens is Vice Provost and Associate Professor in the Department of Government at the University of Texas at Austin. She was formerly the Director of the Center for European Studies and Director of the France-UT Institute for Interdisciplinary Studies. She received her Ph.D. from the University of California, Los Angeles, and her B.A. from Stanford University. Her academic interests include radical right parties, immigration politics, and the politics of race in Europe. She has conducted extensive research in Europe, particularly in France, Germany, Austria, and Denmark. She has received a Ford Foundation Fellowship, the University of California, Berkeley, Chancellor's Postdoctoral Fellowship, and various other grants and fellowships to support her research in Europe. Her book, *Voting Radical Right in Western Europe*, was published in fall 2005 with Cambridge University Press. Her articles have appeared in *Comparative Political Studies*, the *Policy Studies Journal*, and *Comparative European Politics*. She is an active member of the American Political Science Association, the European Union Studies Association, and the Council for European Studies.

James Hampshire is a Lecturer in Politics in the Department of Politics and Contemporary European Studies at the University of Sussex, U.K. He is the author of *Citizenship and Belonging: Immigration and the Politics of Demographic Governance in Postwar Britain* (Palgrave, 2005). He is currently working on a book about the politics of immigration in liberal democratic states, due for publication with Polity in 2008.

James Jupp is Director of the Centre for Immigration and Multicultural Studies in the Research School of Social Sciences at the Australian National University. Dr. Jupp has published widely on immigration and multicultural affairs and has acted as a consultant for the Office of Multicultural Affairs, the Department of Immigration, and other public agencies. His publications include *Arrivals and Departures* (1966), *Ethnic Politics in Australia* (1984), *The Challenge of Diversity* (1989), *Immigration* (1991), *Nations of Immigrants* (1992), *The Politics of Australian Immigration* (1993), *Exile or Refuge?* (1994), and *Understanding Australian Multiculturalism* (1996). The second edition of *Immigration* was published by Oxford University Press in 1998. His study of recent immigration policy, *From White Australia to Woomera* (second ed. 2007), and *The English in Australia* (2004), were both published by Cambridge University Press. He was General Editor of the *Bicentennial Encyclopedia of the Australian People* from 1984 until its publication as *The Australian People* in September of 1988 and of the second edition published for the Centenary of Federation in

2001. He was educated at the London School of Economics between 1951 and 1956. His Doctorate of Philosophy, on the political development of Sri Lanka, was granted by the University of London in 1975 and published as *Sri Lanka: Third World Democracy* in 1978. He has held teaching posts in Political Science at the University of Melbourne, the University of York (England), the University of Waterloo (Canada), and the University of Canberra. In 1989, he was elected a Fellow of the Academy of the Social Sciences in Australia and served as its Executive Director from 1992 until 1995. He is an Adjunct Professor of the RMIT University in Melbourne. He was awarded membership of the Order of Australia (AM) on Australia Day 2004 for services to immigration and multicultural studies. Dr. Jupp was a member of the Advisory Council on Multicultural Affairs. He was Chairman of the Review of Migrant and Multicultural Programs and Services, which presented its report "Don't Settle for Less" to the Minister for Immigration in August 1986. He was formerly Chairman of the ACT Multicultural Advisory Council and of the ACT Reference Group of the Bureau of Immigration, Multicultural and Population Research. He was a member of the Planning and Steering Committees for the Global Cultural Diversity conference held in Sydney in April 1995.

David L. Leal is Associate Professor of Government and Director of the Public Policy Institute at the University of Texas at Austin. His primary academic interest is Latino politics, and his work explores a variety of questions involving public opinion, political behavior, and public policy. He has published over two dozen articles in journals such as *Journal of Politics, British Journal of Political Science, Political Research Quarterly, American Politics Research, Political Behavior, Armed Forces and Society, Polity, Social Science Quarterly, Policy Studies Journal, Urban Affairs Review*, and *Educational Policy*. He is also the co-editor of the *Latino Politics: Identity, Mobilization, and Representation* (University of Virginia Press, 2007) and author of *Electing America's Governors* (Palgrave-Macmillan, 2006). His current projects include a study of the binational civic engagement of Mexican immigrants, a project supported by the Carnegie Corporation, and Latino public opinion about public policy issues. He was an American Political Science Association Congressional Fellow from 1998 to 1999 and a Spencer/National Academy of Education Post-Doctoral Fellow from 2002 to 2004. He received his Ph.D. in Political Science from Harvard University.

Adam Luedtke is an Assistant Professor in Political Science at the University of Utah in Salt Lake City. He received his Ph.D. from the University of Washington, where his dissertation on the subject of European integration and immigration policy won honorable mention for the best dissertation prize from the European Union Studies Association. His research focuses on immigration policy, international organizations, and globalization. He has published chapters in three edited volumes, as well as articles in the following journals: *European Union Politics, Governance, Policy Studies*

Journal, Comparative European Politics, and the *Journal of Comparative Policy Analysis.* He is currently writing a book on the European Union's attempts to develop a common immigration policy.

Valsamis Mitsilegas is Senior Lecturer in Law at Queen Mary, University of London. From 2001 to 2005, he was legal adviser to the House of Lords European Union Committee. His interests and expertise lie primarily in the area of EU law, particularly EU Justice and Home Affairs (including immigration, asylum and border controls, criminal law, police and judicial cooperation in criminal matters, and the external dimension of EU action in these fields). Dr. Mitsilegas is also an expert in the field of national and international legal responses to transnational organized crime, money laundering, and terrorism. His work explores the impact of national, EU, and international measures justified as necessary to protect internal security on civil liberties and fundamental legal principles. In addition to a number of journal articles and book chapters, he is the author of the forthcoming *EU Criminal Law* (Hart Publishing) and co-author of *The EU and Internal Security* (Palgrave 2003). He is a regular consultant to parliaments, international organizations, and NGOs. He was recently appointed to act as Specialist Adviser to the House of Commons Home Affairs Committee for their inquiry on European Union Justice and Home Affairs issues. He is a member of a Working Party on EU Justice and Home Affairs convened by the Federal Trust and a member of an experts team drafting the annual Commission-funded report on the implementation of EU legislation on free movement of workers in the UK. He is also acting as expert adviser to the European Parliament Committee on Civil Liberties, Justice and Home Affairs (LIBE). He received his Ph.D. from the University of Edinburgh and LL.M. from the University of Kent.

Marc R. Rosenblum is Associate Professor of Political Science and the Robert Dupuy Professor of Pan-American Studies at the University of New Orleans and a Fellow at the Migration Policy Institute. Dr. Rosenblum is the author of *The Transnational Politics of U.S. Immigration Policy* (University of California, San Diego Center for Comparative Immigration Studies, 2004) and has also published over 20 journal articles, book chapters, and policy briefs on immigration, immigration policy, and U.S.–Latin American relations. He is currently completing a book on the timing and direction of U.S. immigration reform, *Defining Migration: America's Great Debate and the History of U.S. Immigration Policy* (Brookings Institution, forthcoming), and is the co-editor (with Daniel Tichenor) of *The Oxford Handbook of International Migration* (Oxford University Press, forthcoming). Dr. Rosenblum has held fellowships at the Columbia University New American Assembly (2006–07), the Council on Foreign Relations (2005–06), and the University of California's Institute on Global Conflict and Cooperation (1998–2000). He was the recipient of a University of New Orleans campuswide Early Career Achievement Award in 2005. Dr. Rosenblum earned his B.A. from Columbia University and his Ph.D. from the University of California, San Diego.

Idean Salehyan is an Assistant Professor of Political Science at the University of North Texas. He received his Ph.D. from the University of California, San Diego, in 2006. He has been a visiting scholar at the International Peace Research Institute of Oslo and was a British Academy Fellow at the University of Essex. His research interests include international migration, refugee and asylum policies, human rights, and armed conflict. His recent publications have appeared, or are forthcoming, in *International Organization, World Politics, Journal of Peace Research, Regulation and Governance, Political Research Quarterly, International Studies Quarterly,* and *Civil Wars.* He is also co-editor of *The International Migration of the Highly Skilled: Demand, Supply, and Development Consequences in Sending and Receiving Countries* (La Jolla, CA: Center for Comparative Immigration Studies).

Eiko R. Thielemann is a Senior Lecturer in European Politics and Policy in the Department of Government and the European Institute of the London School of Economics. He also is a visiting professor at New York University (NYU). Since completing his Ph.D. at the University of Cambridge in 2000, he has held academic positions at the University of Cambridge and the University of Southampton, as well as visiting posts at the Australian National University (ANU), the University of California San Diego (UCSD), and the University of Victoria. He has also worked as a consultant for the European Commission. His research focuses on EU and comparative policymaking on issues such as international cooperation (burden-sharing); asylum and immigration; multi-level governance, federalism, regionalism, and devolution; redistribution, regional and state aid policy. He has been a guest editor for the *Journal of Common Market Studies* and the *Journal of Refugee Studies* and is currently completing a research monograph on "Burden-Sharing: The International Politics of Unwanted Migration."

Michele Waslin, Ph.D., is the Director of Immigration Policy Research at the National Council of La Raza (NCLR), the largest national Hispanic civil rights and advocacy organization in the United States. In this capacity, Ms. Waslin tracks and analyzes immigration-related legislation at the national and state levels, advocates on behalf of the Latino community, conducts public education and media outreach, and provides technical assistance and training to community-based organizations. She has authored several publications on immigration policy and post-9/11 immigration issues. Ms. Waslin appears regularly in English- and Spanish-language media. Previously she worked as Policy Coordinator at the Illinois Coalition for Immigrant and Refugee Rights. She received her Ph.D. in 2002 in Government and International Studies from the University of Notre Dame and holds an M.A. in International Relations from the University of Chicago and a B.A. in Political Science from Creighton University.

Index

Diagrams are given in italics.